Understanding the Internet

A Socio-Cultural Perspective

Bridgette Wessels

Lecturer in Sociology,
Department of Sociological Studies,
University of Sheffield, UK

palgrave
macmillan

First published 2010 by
PALGRAVE MACMILLAN

Palgrave Macmillan in the UK is an imprint of Macmillan Publishers Limited, registered in England, company number 785998, of Houndmills, Basingstoke, Hampshire RG21 6XS.

Palgrave Macmillan in the US is a division of St Martin's Press LLC, 175 Fifth Avenue, New York, NY 10010.

Palgrave Macmillan is the global academic imprint of the above companies and has companies and representatives throughout the world.

Palgrave® and Macmillan® are registered trademarks in the United States, the United Kingdom, Europe and other countries.

ISBN-13: 978-0-230-51733-2 hardback
ISBN-13: 978-0-230-51734-9 paperback

This book is printed on paper suitable for recycling and made from fully managed and sustained forest sources. Logging, pulping and manufacturing processes are expected to conform to the environmental regulations of the country of origin.

A catalogue record for this book is available from the British Library.

A catalog record for this book is available from the Library of Congress.

10 9 8 7 6 5 4 3 2 1
19 18 17 16 15 14 13 12 11 10

Printed in China

For Jonjo

Contents

Acknowledgements

In the first instance I would like to thank Catherine Gray of Palgrave for the conversation in which the idea for this book was first aired. I would like to thank Emily Saltz equally, for commissioning the book and for her support in the process of writing the book. I would like to thank the Department of Sociological Studies, Sheffield University for providing the intellectual space to develop ideas for this book and Allison James for her encouragement to develop the project. I extend my thanks to Maurice Roche for his continued support, intellectual engagement and friendship whilst writing the book. Thanks to Helen Rana for proof reading and commenting on the manuscript. I am grateful for the support of friends especially Val and Chris Hall, Elaine Adam, Robin Smith, Sarah Counter, Amanda Wade and Fiona Shanks. Many of the scholars I have cited in this book have helped me in understanding the Internet and Society, there is not enough space to mention everyone but thanks go to Heinz Steinert, Roger Silverstone, Ian McLoughlin, James Cornford, Robin Mansell, David Chaney, Leslie Haddon and members of the Sussex Technology Group. Thanks also to students on my third Year Undergraduate course *Internet and Society* at the University of Sheffield, whose engagement in the topic motivated me to write the book. Finally, thanks to the reviewers whose comments helped to put the finishing touches to the book.

The author and the publisher would like to thank the following for permission to use copyright material: SAGE Ltd for permission to use Table 10.1, first printed in *New Media and Society*; Ashgate Publishing for permission to reproduce material from *Inside the Digital Revolution*.

1

Addressing the Internet as Socio-Cultural Forms

Introduction

The book explores the Internet within various dimensions of society and situates it within sets of social relations and various cultural contexts. The Internet is conceptualized in its different contexts of production and use as social and cultural forms. The argument is that the Internet is embedded in contemporary socio-cultural forms and by understanding the relations of production, the narratives and participation in these forms one can analyse the Internet's characteristics, meaning and significance to contemporary society. This approach produces an analysis of the Internet that is neither technologically nor socially determined.

To this end, the book discusses core aspects of contemporary social life such as work, citizenship, welfare and inequality as well as culture and everyday life in which the characteristics of the Internet are embedded, shaped and given meaning. Its characteristics such as interactive networked communication, virtual worlds and cyber cultures are understood as they materialize through social and cultural processes into specific social and cultural forms such as mobile work, e-citizenship, diasporic hubs and social networking sites. Through these explorations, the book examines whether society is undergoing transformations in which the Internet plays a part and, if there is change, what the significance of that change is to our understandings of social life. It concludes by arguing society is reconfiguring its forms of communication through its informational and intermediation processes. This communicative turn is resulting in an informational and intermediated society rather than an information society.

Outline and Context of the Argument

The Internet, as part of a whole range of Information and Communication Technologies (ICT),[1] is being used in a number of ways within late modernity.

1

In general terms, ICT are electronic systems that are used in telecommunications, computer-mediated communication and digital media. Examples of ICT, apart from the Internet, include personal computers, video games, interactive digital television, mobile phones and electronic payments systems. The Internet is a global system of interconnected computer networks that interchange data by packet switching using the standardized Internet Protocol (IP) Suite. It is a 'network of networks' that consists of private and public networks, academic, business and government networks, which are local and global in scope. Copper wires, fibre optic cables, wireless connections and other technologies link these networks. The Internet carries various information resources and services, such as electronic mail, online chat, file transfer and file sharing, online gaming, and the interlinked hypertext documents and other resources of the World Wide Web (WWW). The WWW is a system of interlinked hypertext documents accessed via the Internet. With a Web browser, a user views Web pages that may contain text, images, videos and other multimedia and navigates between them using hyperlinks. The ongoing developments of the WWW include the concept of Web 2.0, which is sometimes referred to as 'social computing' that describes intelligent web services in which users are more active on the Internet. Most Web 2.0 services involve a cluster of dynamic social networks, which the OECD calls the 'participative web' to stress the active roles of users (Frissen, 2008).

The way in which the Internet is produced, used and talked about interacts with, and is embedded in, the dimensions and dynamics of social life. It is, however, difficult to understand the ways in which these technologies are being shaped within the processes of contemporary social change on the one hand and how, on the other hand, they become institutionalized into social and cultural order. To understand the ways in which the Internet interacts with society involves considering the ways in which its characteristics are materializing into social and cultural forms. The use of the concepts of social and cultural forms is well established within the social sciences and is particularly used in sociology and cultural studies. Although these concepts have been adapted in different ways, they nonetheless provide ways in which social scientists can identify the organization of social and cultural life.

Social and cultural forms represent the articulation of economic, political and social dimensions of society. These forms are enacted out in action and interaction; they are performed and reflected back to social actors as material objects and culture. The use of social forms is often focused on social action and social institutions such as, for example, the organization of work, the family, and education and welfare. Cultural forms focus more on action that seeks to express subjective and inter-subjective meaning through specific performances: it thus covers the expression and performance of popular culture and high culture seen in, for example, film, theatre, visual arts, music and sport. However, aspects of the social and the cultural are interdependent, producing the interlinking of social and cultural forms. For instance, shopping is both a social and cultural activity and, in the context of consumer society, shopping malls can be viewed as cultural forms.[2] This extends into all domains of social life because the characteristics of social forms are culturally informed, shaped and experienced. Thus, patterns of parenting are given meaning through culture, work related social forms gain their distinctiveness through organizational cultures and entertainment genres foster engagement with audiences culturally in a number of ways such as, for example, fandom. Culture is therefore 'ordinary' as Raymond Williams argues, and communication is culturally shaped, and it makes and remakes culture. The focus on the meaningfulness of communication in all aspects of social life including socio-technical change is embedded in the cultural dynamics of communication and requires an understanding of the relationship between social, economic and cultural dimensions of technological change.

Therefore, although in analytical terms social scientists have made distinctions between social and cultural forms, this is questioned in anthropological terms. Clifford Geertz in particular addresses the interlacing of the social and the cultural. He argues that cultural and social phenomena are symbiotic and that culture is deeply embedded in the realities of social and economic structures (Geertz, 1973). This understanding of the interweaving of the economic, social and cultural aspects of the social world reaches into the richness of communication systems and socio-cultural life, as these systems are at once shaped by economic, social and political imperatives and made meaningful through culture. In this book, the term 'cultural forms' is used to address both the cultural meaningfulness of social forms as well as cultural forms within the genres of entertainment and other culturally defined activities. In effect the book addresses socio-cultural forms, communication and the Internet.

This perspective provides the provenance to address the meaning of communication and ICT in social life, which requires seeing the way people[3] communicate as cultural. In this book, the development of cultural forms in which communication is embedded is understood through the following framework. The cultural form has three interdependent dimensions which interact to produce distinctive phenomenon, such as the Internet as a communicative medium in society. One dimension is the 'relations of production', which involves the social organization of production and distribution of the form, including the specific features of the technology. Another dimension is the characteristic mode of narration, which embraces the themes and styles of the form. The third dimension is the type of interaction between producer, narrators and participants that characterizes participation in the form (Chaney, 1990; Wessels, 2000a). The interaction of these three dimensions and interdependencies generate particular social and cultural forms – socio-cultural forms. The Internet and WWW as a distinctive information and communication form is a cultural form in itself. However, its flexibility and adaptability means that it is also embedded within a range of socio-cultural forms, making it pervasive across society with its presence and absence felt by many people.

The variety of adaptations of the Internet in social and cultural life is shaping experiences of society. The context of these experiences emerges from distinctive modes of production and ways of life. These vary, but these contexts and people's actions within them are how the Internet gains its shape, meaning and use in society. This does not, however, mean that society has transformed into an information society, rather this book shows how society has developed new forms of communication, creating society that is intermediated and informational in new ways. This means that there is an ongoing and embedded interaction of mediated, disintermediated and reintermediated communication weaving through social life that crisscross between and across people and institutions. These combine in different constellations that are made up from different provinces and flows of information and knowledge between institutions and people that occur across time and place in all dimensions of social activity. This book explores the characteristics of this dynamic in the following contexts.

Outline of Chapters

Chapter 2 explores the history of the Internet and the World Wide Web (WWW) and shows how technology is socially shaped and culturally informed. The history of the Internet and the WWW shows how it rapidly developed from its conception in 1962 in military research to its commercialized use in 1995. Its 'relations of production' involve military and academic researchers, graduate students, hackers and various counter cultural groups who work with a narrative of networked computer communication. A key characteristic of participation in Internet related activity is that users actively participate in shaping it. Its history shows how entrepreneurs exploited the early Internet and WWW related values of free and open communication to commercialize it within late capitalism, which introduced commercial dynamics and market inequities into its development. The contradictions between a utopian ideal of free and open communication shaped by its early developers and users and the Internet's subsequent commercialization by entrepreneurs for business, public sector and popular markets are influential in its ongoing development.

Chapter 3 introduces three main approaches to the social study of technology and moves beyond these to argue that technologies including the Internet are socially shaped and culturally informed. The three main approaches are technological determinism, social shaping and social constructivism. These perspectives are extended to show how technology gains meaning in different social contexts through the interaction of social values, cultural sensibilities and economic and political agendas materializing in specific socio-cultural forms. Technologies gain meaning in society by exploring the interdependency of the relations of production with the narratives and forms of participation of cultural forms. There is a need to explore the ways in which the Internet is materializing in an array of social and cultural forms to gain an understanding of the meaningfulness of the Internet within contemporary society.

Chapter 4 addresses the social environment of the Internet and considers whether the Internet is part of a broader social change that is resulting in an 'information society'. First, the discussion addresses the ways in which Internet-based communication interacts with notions of 'time and place' and 'the virtual and the real' and considers how these notions contribute to changing senses of identity, community and civil society. Some of the analysis tends to be overly optimistic, seeing the Internet as a source of liberation by taking social actors out of their established relations of community, institutions, time and place into virtual worlds, techno-spaces and cyber cultures. Pessimistic views, however, include a prognosis of isolated individuals, the break down of community and loss of social interaction. The chapter then addresses changes in economic, occupational spatial and cultural areas to consider if the Internet is part of a transformation that is resulting in an 'information society' or whether society is intermediated and informational without having undergone any fundamental transformations.

Chapter 5 addresses the ways in which the Internet and the transnational informational economy is interacting in the context of work by looking at, for instance, the renegotiation of time and place in tele-work and the renegotiation of gender roles seen in discourse on the demise of 'organizational man' and the rise of 'flexible woman'. Although the Internet is shaped by, and is shaping, new forms of work based on networks, some old work structures and practices are proving resistant to change. The extent, character and consequences of any of these changes are considered through the labour process and the relations between management and labour. There is also an exploration of the implicit promise of 'restored relationships' with a better work-life balance via the 'electronic cottage' and mobile work. These issues are strongly interlaced with the gendering of organizational cultures and women's access to, and experience of, work in an e-enabled economy. They show that the use of the Internet in the context of work reproduces existing social relations, inequalities and hier-archies as well as challenging work gender relations and inequalities.

Chapter 6 looks at how the 'logic of the Internet' is interacting with changes in the ideology and practice of many aspects of welfare and health provision, education, (local) government and citizenship. It addresses the provision and character of education, welfare and democratic process in the context of the consumerization of the public sphere and examines how the Internet and its networking capacity is being shaped to mitigate between consumer choice and welfare needs. This chapter extends the analysis to show how social values, working practices and technologies interact with the provision of public services and the practices of citizenship. It is also the arena in which issues of access, usage and design are visibly linked to concerns of inclusion and exclusion. Changes in the ideology of welfare – namely the move from a collectivist approach of universal provision to a consumerist welfare based on choice and conditionality – are becoming embedded in e-service delivery, e-citizenship and in e-participation, with some residual notion of social justice in those relationships. In this context, agency is an important aspect in ensuring quality of care, participation and equality in society.

The discussion of the dynamics of inclusion and exclusion in relation to the Internet in Chapter 7 brings together the issues raised above and identifies contemporary inequalities. The idea of a digital divide can be understood as the differentiation between the Internet-haves and the Internet-have-nots, which can feed into and reinforce existing sources of inequality and social exclusion. The discussion moves beyond issues of access to situate the digital divide in the multidimensional dynamics of exclusion. Factors within these dynamics are socio-economic position, ethnicity, family status, geographic location, language, as well as educa-tional capacity and digital literacy. The 'knowledge gap' and access to information is important in the dynamics of inclusion as they are used in life-long learning as resources for work and personal development. These dynamics are further complicated in the global digital divide, where lower Internet penetration in developing countries (although it can be uneven within these countries), combined with rapid changes of the Internet-based technological paradigm, requires that the less developed countries have to out-perform advanced economies just to stay where they are, thus foster-ing and reproducing global inequalities.

Chapter 8 discusses the ways in which the Internet is becoming embed-ded in everyday life, highlighting the ways in which social actors are negotiating their lived realities and cultural sensibilities in shaping the Internet through its use. Contemporary cultural change such as fragmen-tation, popular democratization and informalization influence the way the Internet is embedded in everyday life. The development of networked individualism is shaping everyday life and the Internet is used as a tool for communication in this context. However, networked individualism and networks are grounded in institutions and the concept of 'domestication' shows how the Internet is becoming part of everyday life through the social relations of households and their moral economies. The argument opens up this discussion to address how the differentiated use of the Internet is culturally informed, by analysing the use of digital communication technology in a small rural town, in the cosmopolitan condition, in diasporic communities and in the mobile routines of the daily lives of mothers and children. Very often, in everyday life, the socio-cultural forms of the Internet are a combination of old and new forms of participation.

Chapter 9 discusses cyber culture in the context of late modern culture. Cyber cultures have a material dimension in that they consist of computing artefacts and websites; they also are symbolic in that they exist in fiction, film and in people's imaginations; and they are lived through the cyber experiences of people participating in cyber culture. Nonetheless, the notion of the 'virtual' is important in understanding cyber cultures, so it is considered in relation to the ways in which, and to what degree, social actors play with virtual identities, virtual communities and subcultures, as well as virtual sexualities. The early rhetoric surrounding cyber culture emphasized the possibilities of liberation from traditional forms of identity, community and sexuality. Although there are some examples of liberation, these hopes have not reached their envisaged potential; for example, in relation to gender and ethnic identity or in the reinvigoration of community. The practices of online interaction limit total free-play in virtual worlds because values such as trust, reciprocity and honesty in communication remain important in Internet-based communication. Cyber cultures emerge as a negotiated reality mediated between imaginations, on and off-line experiences and social mores, being facilitated by machines, wires and websites.

Chapter 10 addresses new media in the context of a new communications environment. The media is a defining feature and institution of modern and late modern life. The focus on new media reiterates the tension between the consumerization of the Internet on the one hand and its historical legacy of free and unregulated communication on the other. The dynamics of this tension feed into the communication environment of the public sphere. The key characteristics of new media, namely digitization and convergence, are discussed in relation to interactivity in mediated forms of communication and the rise of networks in the reshaping of a communications environment. The cultural contexts of new media developments show a relative under-determination of new media when compared with traditional media, as the medium does allow users to participate more interactively in media forms. However, although there are some examples of innovative and participative new media, they are part of the media environment's culture of global capitalism. This is reproducing media concentration as well as generating new media nodes in the communications environment. The ubiquity of interactivity and more individualized use of new media raises questions on the quality of content and raises issues about online experience. For example, although social networking sites connect people with each other they also produce arenas of personalized and individualized entertainment, rather than cultural critique in an active public sphere. These issues situate the Internet in broader social and cultural change by exploring the ways in which new media is materializing in socio-cultural forms in everyday life and in broader institutional change.

In Chapter 11, the Conclusion, the analytical framework of the cultural form brings the main themes of the chapters together to discuss the characteristics of the relations of production, narratives of the medium and types of participation in the socio-cultural forms of the Internet. The relations of production are based in transnational informational capitalism, which is organized through networks. The narratives are about open and free communication based on interactive, flexible and networked communication. Forms of participation are based on the idea of users shaping the form, with freedom of communication and association. Overall, the interdependency of these three dimensions is producing the Internet as a socio-cultural form which is defined by its flexibility and adaptability to facilitate a range of socio-cultural forms. The socio-cultural shaping and materialization of the Internet in various forms and contexts of use mean it contains the contradictions of social life – therefore, one sees not freedom but the negotiation of constraints as people seek to sustain ways of life that are meaningful to them. In terms of the character of society, there have been some changes in the organization of capitalist society towards a networked, informational and intermediated society; however, there is continuity in social practices and cultural sensibilities that militate against the development of a narrow technocratic society. The focus, therefore, is on communication, with the evolvement of a highly communicative society in which the ability to connect is of paramount importance. Communication is cultural and the forms it takes both create and challenge institutions. The current communicative turn is both social and cultural and shapes the technologies which humans create. Given the contradictions of the Internet and of society, there is a need to secure culturally the ethos and capacity for everyone to be able to shape and participate in the forms of communication that the Internet allows.

2

The Cultural History of the Internet

Introduction

An exploration of the history and culture of the Internet provides insights into the relationship between society and technology. The argument in this chapter develops Dewey's (1939) point that society is made in and through communication, situating the Internet within social life and contemporary cultural change through an understanding that technology is socially shaped and culturally informed. This is done by looking at the ways in which the relations of production, the narratives and forms of participation have historically interacted to produce the Internet and the WWW. The history of the Internet enacts the complex and contradictory characteristics of technological and social change and shows how economics, politics and culture inform the development of technologies within specific socio-historical contexts. The relatively short but rapid history of the Internet, from its inception in 1962 in military research to its commercialized use in 1995, shows how entrepreneurs exploited its founding values of free and open communication to commercialize it within late capitalism.

A Framework for Historical Analysis

A history of the Internet requires an understanding of the ways in which the materiality of the technology was developed and shaped by social actors within networks of institutions and what gave that development its distinctive cultural characteristics (Wessels, 2007b). Principally, this means that an analyst needs to consider the process in which material, social and cultural factors interact to produce socio-technical change. Abrams (1982) argues that the 'idea of process and the study of process' offer ways to address how actors act in relation to given situations and socio-cultural frameworks that are historically formed and presented. This means addressing the 'awesome paradox' (Berger and Luckmann, 1967) of how human activity produces a world of things, such as the Internet, for instance, as social and cultural forms: a task that involves understanding 'the relationship of personal activity and experience on the one hand and social organization on the other as something that is continuously constructed in time' (Abrams, 1982, p. 16).

The focus on process in relation to the Internet is important because it encompasses the characteristics of socio-technical change, which Freeman argues is social and the result of human actions, decisions, expectations and institutions (Freeman, 1992b). Historical analysis, therefore, means exploring not only broad sweeps of change and the interaction of factors generating that change but also the process of innovation (Wessels, 2007b). Innovation refers to change that requires a significant amount of imagination, represents a relatively sharp break with established ways of doing things and creates a new capability of some kind. It is essential to distinguish between the conception of a new product or means of production – an invention – and the practical implementation of that conception – innovation. Overall, change with regard to technology is best understood as 'socio-technical' because technology is embedded within the dynamics of social change.

The process of technological innovation is embedded in particular institutional and commercial environments within society. In these various environments, social actors have access to skills in defining and solving technical problems as well as an economic ability to judge the cost-benefits of technical applications – all of which interact with the dynamics of the selective appropriation and adaptation of technology by user communities. Users and producers, who build knowledge and experience cumulatively, through learning by doing and learning by using, constitute this environment. Castells (1996) argues that the interactivity of actors, institutions, skills and so on form a milieu for innovation, which is as relevant to the 'digital revolution' as it was to the industrial revolution.

There is often debate about the actual meaning of 'revolution', with commentators disagreeing on what the definitive characteristics of revolution are and how to ascertain the time frames for fundamental change. Given this problem of definition, the concept of 'paradigm shift' is useful for identifying significant changes that produce new perspectives, production systems and patterns of consumption (Mansell and Steinmueller, 2002). A socio-technical paradigm is a coherent framework made up from a set of technologies, their social organization and application and related socio-economic and cultural values that constitute a mode of socio-technical activity within society. Thus, if a mode of production changes, including its technology, in ways that alter the social organization of production, distribution and consumption, then a paradigm shift will have occurred. This might not necessarily mean that there has been a fundamental change in society but it might indicate changes to the organization of social and economic activity within society.

Framing the History of the Internet

The development of the Internet provides insights into how it gained its specific characteristics. To address the social and cultural shaping of the Internet, the term 'Internet activities' is useful because it considers the relationship between production and consumption in the development of the Internet. A distinctive feature of Internet-related technologies is that they are more malleable, reconfigurable and dynamic than many industrial technologies. The significance of this feature, historically and conceptually, is that it allows for greater adaptation and interpretation within user–producer interactions in development processes (Dittrich et al., 2002). This adaptability relates to changing organizational, social, cultural and media forms based on networks mediated by the Internet. The details of these developments interact with broader socio-economic change; such as the way networked production processes support a global market economy underpinned by the current neo-liberal consensus and modus operandi (Wessels, 2007b). The social and cultural history of the Internet provide, on the one hand, a base from which to ascertain the capacities the Internet offers, with on the other hand an understanding of the ideas that shaped its form. Furthermore, it highlights the institutional frameworks in which the work involved in creating the Internet was instigated and developed – which is a key component in shaping the technology.

The concept of the cultural form addresses these interactions in the history of the Internet by tracing the interdependencies between the relations of production, the narratives of the form and the participative interaction in the form (Wessels, 2007b). Actors within socio-technical change populate these dimensions, and the dynamic of development is created by the agency within each dimension and between dimensions (see Figure 2.1). In some instances there is an overlap between the dimensions; for example, the narratives of the form can also be situated in the relations of production. In other cases there may be disjuncture between the dimensions, for instance, in scenarios of user take-up that do not dovetail with the envisaged purpose of the technology. An overarching characteristic of the development and use of the Internet is that it involves processes of 'social learning' (Williams et al., 2005) in which actors engage in and work with ideas, concepts and artefacts within and between the dimensions of a cultural form. They use a range of resources including finance, knowledge,

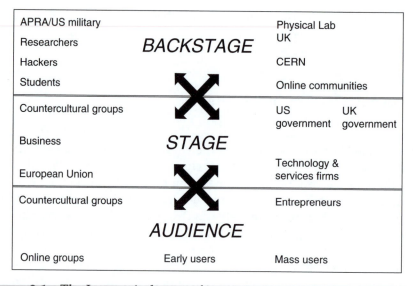

Figure 2.1   The Internet's theatre of innovation
Source: 'The Internet's Theatre of Innovation', adapted from Wessels 2007b, p. 43.

skills and experience, and capabilities to envisage new technology and its applications.

These resources and imaginations are not specific to one domain of the cultural form, but permeate the process by which technologies are transferred, adapted and taken up in user settings. Thus, the political and policy communities play a role in socio-technical change in the way they frame policy and engage with commercial and user groups in creating narratives of technology and society. Likewise, the commercial sector is an important resource in the large-scale production of technologies and in the marketing of new technological products and services. User communities are a resource in a unique way in shaping the Internet, through their activities as 'users as producers' and 'users as consumers' (Castells, 2001). This is because users as producers informed the early development of the Internet and users as consumers have been, and still are, important in shaping market trends that feed into ongoing developments.

The metaphor of the theatre illustrates the relationship between production and consumption in the innovation and development of new technologies (see Chapter 3). The backstage area is where actors configure as producer networks to work in specific projects of the development process. The stage area is where policy-making, industry and other discourse communities produce narratives that give meaning to Internet activities. In the audience domain, many types of user groups adopt, adapt, reject and shape the Internet's use in relation to user contexts and environments. Change derives from the ways in which these three dimensions become interdependent in particular developments that are informed by, and in turn inform, an overall trajectory of socio-technical change as part of broader social change. This approach to the history of the Internet avoids any narrow technological, economic or social determinism by addressing the ways in which social actors and institutions envisage and give meaning to the Internet in its material, social and symbolic terms.

The question, however, moves beyond the development of a new socio-technical and social phenomenon to the development of new forms of communication. Abbate (2000), for example, argues that 'between the 1960s and 1980s, computer technology underwent a dramatic transformation: the computer originally conceived as an isolated calculating device, was reborn as a means of communication' (p. 1). A central part of the early imagining of the Internet was focused on rethinking forms and structures of communication and the invention of the WWW was based on the ideal of providing free and open communication that overcame bureaucratic and hierarchical constraints. Silverstone's argument of 2005 reflects this focus when he suggests the use of ICT is part of a communication revolution, or at least signifies a communicative turn in contemporary social life. His suggestion needs to be understood in relation to Dewey's (1939) point that society is made in and through communication. Together these points indicate the need to question the ways in which social experience is communicated and mediated and how these processes inform social change. The logic for undertaking this type of analysis is that the facilitation of communication through ICT, as well as established forms of communication materializes in social and cultural forms that are situated in socio-economic trends, which are made meaningful through cultural and political frameworks.

By addressing the Internet as a cultural form, analysts can gauge the character of agency and structural factors that shape its trajectory. In so doing, cultural forms analysis can identify the perspectives that influence the development of the Internet and trace some of their contradictions. Castells (2001), for example, sees the Internet as a potential source of emancipation, which, if utilized in progressive social relations, can transform society. He argues that the

> story of the creation and development of the Internet is one of extraordinary adventure. It highlights people's capacity to transcend institutional goals, overcome bureaucratic barriers and subvert established barriers in the process of ushering in a new world. It also lends support to the view that cooperation and freedom of information may be more conducive to innovation than competition and property rights. (p. 9)

In a similar spirit, Berners-Lee (1999), the inventor of the WWW, states that

> Enquire ... Enquire within upon everything ... led me to a ... vision encompassing the decentralized organic growth of ideas, technology and society. The vision I have for the Web is about anything being connected with anything. It is a vision that provides us with new freedoms, and allows us to grow faster than we could when we were fettered by hierarchical classification systems into which we bound ourselves. (p. 1)

However, Robins and Webster (1999) provide a different perspective to these optimistic views. They start by seeing technology, including ICT as 'articulating the social relations of the societies in which they are mobilized ... [that includes] power relations' (Robins and Webster, 1999, p. 2). They argue that the Internet mediates capitalist social relations, and in this context it can be thought of in terms of the forward march of the long historical process of Enclosure, involving

> the further and rapid extension of market criteria and conditions. This process has both extensive and intensive dimensions. And it threatens to penetrate even deeper into private and previously sacrosanct realms of life (leisure, child-rearing, domestic activities, even identities). ... for the first time in human history, of the entire planet being organized around a single set of economic principles. (p. 7)

Robins and Webster address many of the fears articulated by E.M. Forster's short story *The Machine Stops* (1909). In this science fiction novella, Forster posits a situation in which human beings cannot live without technology and become trapped in it. The degree in which they are trapped within a technocratic world encompasses the conundrum that humans forget that they created the technology. Forster also predicts online life by describing video-conferencing as part of human communication, which in his rendition results in social alienation. Nonetheless, Forster, unlike Robins and Webster (1999), suggests that 'the machine' can be resisted and destroyed and that human spirit and sociability can find non-alienating forms of communication. These types of scenarios illustrate that it is the social relations in which technology is imagined, designed, developed and used that shape it and give it meaning.

Given the above point, Abbate (2000) warns against taking any dominant perspective by arguing that the Internet is constantly developing in line with its developers' commitment to flexibility and diversity in both technical design and organizational culture (p. 6). She further reaffirms that the Internet's identity as a communication medium was not inherent in the technology – rather, it was constructed through a series of social choices (ibid.). These choices are organized socially through a process of production, narrative and participation in theatres of innovation in which actors from various constituencies interact to produce change. The social and cultural dynamics of economic and technological change are therefore influential in shaping the ways that technologies, as social artefacts, are embedded within the social relations of society (see Chapter 3).

The Internet's Theatre of Innovation

To understand the history of the Internet it is important to address its theatre of innovation. This theatre involves social actors, resources (including material and intellectual) and the interplay of power within the economic, political and socio-cultural dynamics of innovation. Innovations and socio-technical changes are products of their social environments. They often involve painstaking research and development activities and the creation of the Internet is no exception to these types of processes (MacKenzie and Wajcman, 2002; Abbate, 2000; Naughton, 2000).

The 'relations of production' of the Internet is comprised of research centres and universities, government departments, user groups of varying kinds and the commercial sector. The narratives of the form evolve from both computer technologists wanting to set up networks of computers and military strategists wanting flexible networked communications for warfare. These narratives and emergent technologies are appropriated and adapted by student groups, hackers, countercultural and grass-root movements. Actors in these contexts develop narratives in line with their interests and shape the Internet further to their contexts of use. Once the concept and practice of networking computers were established, and continue to be developed, commercial entrepreneurs transferred the Internet (and continue to transfer subsequent innovations) to the mass market, where users as consumers further shape its development.

Actors involved in the early phases of the relations of production were based in United States government research agencies, think tanks and universities and in the British National Physical Foundation. The United States as an emergent super-power, amongst its other agendas, drew on the British experience of the value of computerization in code-breaking in World War II that resulted in the United States Defense Department setting up the Advanced Research Projects Agency (ARPA) in 1958. The aim of the Agency was to bring together research resources including expertise from academia to develop innovative technologies for military use. The political climate of that time, principally the Cold War, meant that the US government prioritized investment to build military capability and provided resources for research to support the improvement of military strength.

Narratives of that time were primarily from a government view of gaining military superiority over the Soviet Union. These narratives could be seen in scientific communities and more broadly in popular culture as well as in the political sphere. The launch of the Sputnik satellite in 1957 raised fears regarding the 'science gap' between the USSR and the US. Politically, events such as the 1961 shooting down of an American U-2 spy plane over the USSR, the rise of the Berlin Wall in 1961 and the Cuban Missile Crisis in 1962 generated a climate in which US military capability was seen as important. These fears, especially those surrounding the possibility of nuclear war, were represented in popular culture, seen, for instance, in novels and films such as *On the Beach, Fail-Safe* and *Dr Strangelove* (Abbate, 2000, p. 9).

In this context, communication systems were seen as an important element in a nuclear war strategy. Defence analysts argued that a robust, flexible communication system was needed to secure command and control functions under nuclear attack: a networked communication system would sustain military functionality by re-routing communications via other nodes not disabled by nuclear attack. The Information Processing Techniques Office (IPTO) within ARPA developed a computer network called ARPANET, which enabled the sharing of online computing time between computer centres and research groups. To build the network IPTO drew on packet switching, a telecommunication transmission technology (Abbate, 2000), developed by Baran at the Rand Corporation and Davies from the British National Physical Foundation. Packet switching enables any message from digitized speech to computer data to be sent in digital form; the binary numbers or 'bits' can manipulate information and send it in blocks.

Baran developed the idea of 'distributed communications' by building an 'intelligent' message-switching network with fast end-to-end transmission of messages using small, inexpensive switches (Baran, 1964). The idea of intelligence stems from the fact that each node in the network has to determine routes in the distribution of messages without human intervention. This means that the nodes have to be computers and not just telephone switches, so Baran envisaged an all-digital network involving computerized switches and digital transmission across the links (Abbate, 2000). Baran used small and inexpensive computers in his system as the use of fixed-sized packets simplified the design of the nodes; from a military perspective, breaking messages into packets and sending them through different routes helped to ensure that the messages could not easily be decoded by unauthorized personnel. A further overarching advantage was that packet switching enabled many users to share a single communication channel, which is an economical form of multiplexing, enabling efficient and flexible transmission of data. Together, these factors built in survivability in a communications system, something that was relevant in the Cold War era of nuclear threat (Baran, 1964).

In the United Kingdom, Davies's input to packet switching evolved in a different context to that of Baran in the United States. The Labour Prime Minister in 1964, Harold Wilson, set up a Ministry of Technology. One of the ministry's priorities was to secure the British computer industry with a view to developing Britain's technological and economic capability. Davies was interested in interactive computing and wanted to improve the ease of use of computers. Building on ideas of time-sharing, Davies sought to utilize packet switching to provide affordable user-friendly interactive computing rather than survivable military communications. In his prototype network, Mark 1, all terminals, printers and other peripheral devices were connected directly to the network, which involved redesigning the user interface and making it easier to use (Abbate, 2000, p. 32). Davies's target user groups were based in civil society and in the commercial sector and he envisaged that this technology could underpin, and contribute to, UK competitiveness in the computer market and other high-tech industries.

The indeterminacy of the innovation process can be seen in the early relationship between production, narratives and the participation of scientists in the development process. Thus, despite their innovative work, neither Davies nor Baran had sufficient resource to build networked computing. Instead, ARPA built the first large-scale packet switching network. The implementation of APRANET was by Bolt, Beranek and Newman and staffed by researchers from Massachusetts Institute of Technology (MIT), together with Harvard scientists and engineers. In 1972, the first successful demonstration of APRANET took place at an international conference in Washington DC. The next step was to build a network of networks and, in 1973, Kahn (ARPA) and Cerf (Stanford) produced a paper on basic Internet architecture. By 1975, ARPANET had been demonstrated and tested, and it was transferred to the Defense Communication Agency (DCA) for use in different branches of the armed forces (Castells, 2001). The Network Working Group, which was a cooperative technology group that included Crocker and Postel, designed an inter-network communication protocol. In 1978, Cerf, Lelann French Cyclades research group, Metcalf, Xerox Parc, Postel and Crocker from the University of California established Transmission Control Protocol/Internet Protocol (TCP/IP). These developments produced a networked computerized communications technology (ibid.).

Although the DCA had the ARPANET, it decided to develop its own dedicated network (MILNET) to ensure its communication systems were secure. Through this development, the Internet was released from military environments and moved to the US National Science Foundation (NSF). Following this move, ARPANET became ARPA-INTERNET and was dedicated to research, which gradually migrated to NSFNET. ARPANET was decommissioned in 1990 and NSFNET in 1995 because the Internet back-bone was increasingly provided by the commercial sector. The NSF's control was therefore short-lived due to the fact that the computer technology was in the public domain, and that the telecoms industry was fully dereg-ulated. In this context, the NSF quickly released the Internet into the public domain opening up the environment for the privatization of the Internet and in the early 1990s Internet Service Providers (ISP) started building their own networks (ibid.).

In relation to participation in the innovation process, the grass-roots tradition of computing and the work of graduate students and hackers are influential in the shaping of the Internet. Key contributions include Chicago students Christensen and Suess's program called MODEM for transferring files between personal computers (PCs) (1977) and a program for Bulletin Board Systems that allowed PCs to store and transmit messages (1978). Researchers built computer networks with Jennings developing FidoNet and Fuchs from City University (New York) and Freeman from Yale creat-ing BITNET. The development of UNIX at Bell Labs is a decisive aspect in the history of computer networking. Bell Labs released UNIX into univer-sity computing departments and in 1978 it distributed Unix-to-Unix CoPy (UUCP) that facilitated the copying of files between computers. Truscott, Ellis, Bellavin and Rockwell, who were all students at North Carolina, cre-ated a programme by which UNIX computers could communicate. Once improved and released, it formed Usenet News, a computer networks sep-arate from the ARPANET system. Usenet News arrived at the University of California (Berkeley) in 1980, where students gradually developed it and merged it with ARPANET forming the Internet. A central part of the development of the Internet within this grass-roots tradition was the Open-source movement. The ethos of this movement embodies the idea of 'copyleft', which means that anyone using and improving freely available software can and should distribute his or her improvements freely over the network (ibid.). Linux is a key example of such open-source development of code and computer operating systems.[1]

A further dimension feeding into the grass-roots sensibility was the cul-ture of individual freedom prevalent on university campuses in the 1960s and 1970s. In this environment, students and members of staff were exper-imenting with computing networks to build better and more usable net-works that would contribute to knowledge as well as for the 'pure joy of discovery' (p. 23). A dimension within these dynamics was the develop-ment of the personal computer. Computer scientists who had worked at ARPA and were embedded in 1960s' counterculture moved to Xerox Parc[2] and developed the personal computer there. They produced the Alto com-puter with mouse, keyboard and monitor as well as Dynabook (a proto-type laptop) and new forms of programming that made computing easier and more accessible. From within countercultural perspectives, personal computers were envisaged as having the potential to open minds and generate critique amongst the general populace, or masses (Bell, 2001). The grass-roots ethos also played into the way universities supported the diffusion of the Internet into community networks by working with community networks such as the Colorado, Blacksburg Electronic Village and Cleveland Freenet (ibid.).

The culture of hackers with their ethos of cooperation, open communication and freedom, is important in the Internet's development. Hacker culture comprises of networks of computer programmers who interact online on self-defined projects within an open-source approach to development. The freedom to pursue projects that were not determined by institutional or corporate agendas and their institutional autonomy meant that hackers could focus on improving the Internet. This freedom to create and to share knowledge in a gift economy[3] is sustained through peer recognition. Peers from the hacker community judge the significance of a 'gift',[4] which in the hacker community can be an improvement to code or aspects of hardware, in relation to the contribution it makes to the development of the Internet. The ingenuity of the giver is recognized and rewarded by building reputations through which individuals gain prestige in the hacker community. Underpinning this gift culture is the sense of fulfilment gained through creativity (Castells, 2001). The world of hackers is not, however, without conflict, as technological subcultures with their respective tribal elders (who are established hackers and act as mentors for younger hackers) fiercely debate technological issues that, in turn, promote development. Hacker culture is idealistic, with participants focusing on creating better Internet-related tools rather than commercial services (Raymond, cited in Castells, 2001). This idealism can also be seen in Stallman's political crusade for free speech in the computer age; he established the Free Software Foundation (FSF) and argued for the principle of free communication and use of software as a fundamental right. Hacker culture's open-source, peer-review model is a scalable method for achieving reliability and quality in technological developments (Castells, 2001).

The development of WWW is of primary importance in the broader social take-up and use of the Internet. The WWW refers to the set of information that is accessible by using computers and networks through a Universal Resource Identifier (URL), which identifies each unit of information. Berners-Lee, an English programmer working at CERN (Coseil Europeen pour La Research Nucleaire)[5] produced the WWW. He wrote 'Enquire' (a web-based program) in his spare time to help him remember the connections between people, computers and projects in the lab (Berners-Lee, 1999, p. 4). This led Berners-Lee to ask 'what if all information stored on computers everywhere were linked: suppose I program my computer to create a space in which anything could be linked to any-thing?' (p. 4). He then took this further, suggesting that, by being 'able to reference anything with equal ease, a computer could represent asso-ciations between things that might seem unrelated but somehow did, in fact, share a relationship' (p. 5), forming a web of information. He states that computers could not solve social problems but they could assist the human mind 'in that computers could follow and analyze the tentative connected relationships that define much of society's workings, unveiling entirely new ways to see the world' (p. 5).

There are precursors to Berners-Lee's work. In 1945, Bush, once Dean at MIT and then Head of the US Office of Scientific Research, wrote an article 'As We May Think' on the Memex machine which could cross-reference microfilm documents. Ted Nelson is another key visionary, and he wrote about 'Literary Machines' in 1965, arguing that computers would enable people to write and publish in a new, non-linear format, which he called 'hypertext'. He described a project called Xanadu in which the entire world's information would be published in hypertext (p. 6). Nelson's dream was of a utopian society in which all information could be shared among people who communicate as equals. However, he never managed to secure funding for such a project. Engelbart, a researcher at Stanford University, built a demonstrator collaborative workspace called OLS (Online System) in the 1960s. His vision was similar in that he thought hypertext could be used as a tool in group-work and, using electronic mail and hypertext links, he designed the mouse – now a key feature of personal computing – and demonstrated its use. These developments, alongside the work of Barran, Davies, Cerf and Kahn, set the scene for Berners-Lee to develop the WWW.

Berners-Lee brought together hypertext and the Internet to build the WWW, and the first browser was released by CERN over the Internet in August 1991. Berners-Lee argues that, throughout the Web's history, there are parallels between technical design and social principles (p. 225). For instance, Berners-Lee designed the Web on universalistic (with lower case u) principles to build an environment that enabled people to think and discuss diverse issues from a range of perspectives in an open and accepting way (p. 226). He argues that both philosophies allow the devel-opment of decentralized systems, whether they are systems of computers, knowledge or people. Berners-Lee's values provide a narrative that focuses on the forms of participation in the WWW, in which

hope in life comes from the interconnections among all the people in the world. We believe that if we work for what we think individually is good then we as a whole will achieve more power, more understanding, more harmony as we continue the journey. We don't find the individual being subjugated by the whole. We don't find the needs of the whole being subjugated by the increasing power of the individual. But we might see more understanding in the struggles between these extremes. (Berners-Lee, 1999, p. 228)

Berners-Lee understands freedom in the Internet in two ways. First, freedom is experienced in terms of sending any content anywhere in the network in packets. Second, it provides a freedom of association based on mutual respect with an ethos of collective endeavour that goes beyond singular individual effort to build for the common good in ways that are unconstrained by bureaucratic regimes (p. 227). The Internet when seen from this perspective of the Web is a textual, audio-visual and social network that challenges a hierarchical bureaucratic model of communication.

From the discussion so far, it can be seen that the overarching 'architecture of openness' is a key aspect in the development of the Internet. This openness allows the Internet to be shaped by users who, through their use, become its producers too. For instance, nodes are easy and cheap to establish and, through open cooperation, a variety of spontaneous applications resulted in email, bulletin boards, chat rooms, the modem and hypertext. As Castells (2001) suggests, users are often the key producers of technology and, with the Internet, new uses and modifications are fed back in real time by users, enabling the Internet to develop rapidly. A related dimension to this is that this instantaneous response generates an environment where doing and learning are dynamically interlinked, a dynamic that keeps the Internet growing at a fast pace (ibid.). The character of this mode of participation in the Internet as a form of communication, and in its innovation process, continues in its development.

Taking the above characteristic of participation in Internet communication, virtual communitarians shaped the nature of that participation further in social and cultural forms. Virtual communitarians who as early users of the Internet sought to use it in ways to generate egalitarian and alternative communities. Their culture generated a context in which the Internet moved beyond its specialist employment to more general social use. These early users of networked computing outside of university or hacker environments created virtual communities, using the term popularized by Rheingold (1993). The values of these communities shaped the ethos, practices and organization of forms of online communities, such as messaging, mailing lists, chat rooms, multi-user games, MUDS, conferences and conference systems (c.f. Rheingold, 1993; Castells, 2001). Some of the early participants like SF-Lovers (Science Fiction Lovers – an early online community) were technologically sophisticated, but from the 1980s onwards, users were not necessarily skilled programmers in developing virtual communities (c.f. Rheingold, 1993; Castells, 2001). This trend of widening participation was further supported with the advent and roll-out of the WWW in the 1990s because the WWW enabled everyday users with only limited technical knowledge to use the Internet in innovative ways.

Castells (2001) points out that the communitarians contributed to the shape and evolution of the Internet, including its commercial manifestations in decisive ways – for example, the earliest Bulletin Board Services (BBS) in the San Francisco Bay area was the sex-oriented system Kinky Komputer, which spearheaded a form of online practice (private and commercial) that continues till today. Other developments include the work of the Institute for Global Communication (IGC) that focused on socially responsible agendas such as protecting the environment and preserving world peace. For example, it set up the first women's computer network (La Neta), which was used by the Mexican Zapatistas to build international solidarity on behalf of Indian Communities. Other community networks such as the one created in Seattle by Schuler called the Seattle Community Network or Digital City Amsterdam sought to renew or enhance citizen participation. Another historically specific use of Internet-based networks was the way in which Russian academics used the Internet to organize activities for democracy and freedom during the *perestroika* period of dismantling the Soviet Union (ibid.).

These online communities had a similar ethos and sensibility to that of 1960s and post-1960s countercultural movements. This was seen especially in the US – in the San Francisco Bay area; for example, there were a variety of online groups, such as Homebrew Computer Club and the Community Memory projects. In 1985, the Whole Earth 'Lectronic Link (WELL)[6] set up an innovative conference system led by Brand (a biologist and artist who created the Whole Earth Catalogue) and Brillinat (a member of Hog Farm Commune and one of the organizers of the Woodstock festival). Similar to Brand and Brillinat, many WELL members lived in rural communes and were PC hackers and/or were part of the fan culture Deadheads.[7] Other examples include Jenning's anarchist agenda in FidoNet and Amsterdam's Digital City's roots in the squatters' movement in the 1970s. These types of online developments tended to spring from a sense of thwarted communal aspirations that were located in the failure of countercultural community-based endeavours (ibid.).

Although the early virtual communities set a precedent for the development of online communities, subsequent online community-based activities expanded beyond countercultures. A variety of communities emerged that were based on a range of values and interests. The proliferation and diversity of online communities illustrate that there is no unified Internet communal culture (ibid.), rather the flexibility of the Internet allows for a range of communities of interest. Thus, as Jones (1995) emphasizes, the social and situated characteristics of culture are influential in shaping virtual culture and, as a consequence, produce a diversity of virtual communities. For example, MUDS form sites for those involved in role-taking and fake identities, the French Minitel gained popularity through its user-shaped Messageries Roses system and social movements, including right-wing extremist ones, use the flexibility of the Internet to form online presences and constituencies. Although there is diversity amongst virtual communities, Castells (2001) points out that online communities share two features. First is a horizontal free communication that advocates global free speech in an environment dominated by media conglomerates and government bureaucracies which censor communication. Second is the practice of 'self-directed networking' in which individuals find, or produce, their own network in which to self-publish and self-organize. The communitarian culture's appropriation of the Internet embraces diversity and reinforces the role of the Internet as a tool for horizontal communication and a medium for free speech. Thus, culture and technology combine to facilitate networking that is self-directed and can organize communities of interest in the generation of meaning.

The community-based take-up and use of the Internet did raise concerns about the quality of the Internet's future. Fears from within the Internet community about the ad hoc and anarchic development of the Internet prompted the founding of organization of the Internet Society (ISOC) in 1992. The aim of this not-for-profit organization is to provide leadership and guidelines for Internet standards, education and policy to ensure that the open development of the Internet is for the benefit of people across the world. The setting up of the ISOC at that time set a legal framework for development of the Internet. Those within the ISOC were just beginning to exploit the Internet commercially (pre-Bill Gates) and having a standards organization protected them, whereas ad hoc development would not. The quality of the open development of the Internet was, and continues to be, protected through the ISOC and it also provides steering on policy and educational issues regarding the Internet's ongoing shaping. The ethos of self-regulation within the Internet community shapes the way in which regulation of the Internet has developed. For instance, the creation of ICANN (Internet Corporation for Assigned Names and Numbers) emerged from other Internet community organizations that sought to develop policies to ensure that the Internet's development would maintain its foundational ethos. Building on the work of Postel in Internet Assigned Numbers Authority (IANA) and his small team of dedicated staff, ICANN's mandate is to support one global interoperable Internet in the model of stakeholder representation. This type of self-organized regulation is a check to threats to Internet operations from powerful commercial interests as well as ensuring privacy and security for all Internet users.

Although those engaging in virtual communitarian projects extended the use of the Internet into social contexts more generally, it was entrepreneurs who had the vision and capacity to introduce and extend the Internet into mass culture and use. CompuServe (founded in 1969) was the first major commercial online service provider dominating the field in the 1980s and maintaining its significance until the mid-1990s. Its entrepreneurial culture underpinned development producing a range of services such as the chat system 'CB Simulator', a range of online financial services and moderated forums. As the WWW grew in popularity, companies migrated to Web-based services and in 1997 CompuServe converted its forums to HTLM web standards.

Another significant player in the commercialization of the Internet is Bill Gates, who used his entrepreneurial skills to form Microsoft. Gates, however, was not a producer of the Internet in technical terms. Neither did he contribute to the development of the Internet by being a hacker or being involved with the virtual communitarians. It was, in fact, the opposite – although Gates identified how to exploit the Internet's openness and culture in commercial terms, he thought 'hackers were thieves' (Castells, 2001). In his 'Open letter to Hobbyists', Gates argued that proprietary rights meant that he had the right to invest technological innovation in the pursuit of profit. Actors working within this entrepreneurial culture pushed the Internet out into broader society and set an agenda for commercializing the process of technical innovation in computing, without sharing its founding values (ibid.). As Castells argues, business drove the expansion and diffusion of the Internet through commercialization, which happened very quickly during the 1990s (p. 55).

The specific characteristics of entrepreneurs and the environment in which they operate enabled them to develop the potential of the Internet for mass use. The environment in which much of this early entrepreneurial activity took place was in and around Silicon Valley in the US. In Silicon Valley there was a concentration of technical actors, knowledge and entrepreneurs that provided the expertise and resource for exploiting the Internet in commercial terms. Another distinctive factor is that these entrepreneurs sought to make money out of 'ideas' rather than natural resources or products. They generated ideas and visions of the possibilities of the Internet and sold those intangible goods rather than any tangible material product or capital resource. Another distinctive factor is that these entrepreneurs did not take any risks in terms of putting their own money into developments; rather they persuaded venture capitalists to invest finance and resource to develop their ideas and visions. Castells argues that the defining feature of Silicon Valley's entrepreneurial culture is how ideas and creative imagination, something he terms as 'mind-power' is transformed into, and used for 'money-making'.

Within entrepreneurial culture, the activity of 'money-making' and the building of capital are the criteria for success. This success is linked to the idea of freedom, defined in relation to the dynamics of the corporate world, in which 'the only way to be freed from capital is to attract capital' (Castells, 2001, p. 57). The quest for money often manifests itself in 'workaholism' in which the reward is external in the form of money itself. This is qualitatively different to the puritan ethic of the early industrialists in which individuals worked hard to improve the self and to seek salvation within Protestantism (Weber, trans. Parsons, 1930). The ethos of the Silicon Valley entrepreneurs was instead immediate gratification that cut across ethnic lines in a sphere of individuals, who were instrumental in exploiting the Internet for their own material gain and who did so in a fiercely individualistic way (Castells, 2001).

The skill of the Internet entrepreneurs was, and is, their almost charismatic ability to envision and sell cyber futures to investors based on their firm conviction that they can form such futures. By this envisaging, they draw in venture capitalists to invest in their ideas to produce tangible goods and services, as well as intangible aspirational lifestyle frameworks for different consumer sensibilities. The combination of actors, both individuals and organizations, from the spheres of invention and innovation, technological development and venture capital produce 'the Internet entrepreneur' (Castells, 2001, p. 58). The 'Internet entrepreneur' is therefore not a person but a social phenomenon (ibid.), although this phenomenon is often popularly perceived as a person with keen vision, such as Bill Gates (see 'The Road Ahead', 1995). The Internet entrepreneur as an individualistic and market focused actor would not have developed a socio-technical system based on principles of openness and sharing-principles that underpin the Internet. However, their role and their capacity to commercialize the Internet is a significant aspect of its history. This entrepreneurial culture interacted with the meritocratic culture of academic and computing research, hacker culture and virtual communitarian culture in the multilayered cultural dynamics of the innovation of the Internet. The cultural dynamics that gave the Internet its socio-technical form gave it the potential to diversify into social and cultural forms (Castells, 2001, p. 37).

Change, however, is an intrinsic part of the history of the Internet, extending beyond its process of innovation. Since its introduction to general society in 1995, its shape and use are continually being adapted, seen, for instance, in emergent trends of 4G mobile phones, peering technologies, mapping and remediation in alternative media such as podcasting,[8] blogs[9] and vlogs[10] as well as Web 2.0.[11] The openness of the Internet allows it to be shaped by users who, through their use, become its producers too. The concept of Web 2.0, sometimes referred to as the 'Social Web' or 'social computing' serves to highlight the idea of a second-generation of web-based communities that aim to facilitate (co-) creativity, collaboration and sharing amongst users. The relatively low cost and ease of use means that Web 2.0 services are opening up new ways for mainstream Internet users to share, adapt and create content. The defining feature of most Web 2.0 services is a cluster of dynamic social networks that form a 'participative web' through the active engagement of its users (Frissen, 2008). Web 2.0 encompasses a wide range of applications, such as blogs, wikis, social networking sites, podcasts, social bookmarking sites, auction sites, online games and peer-to-peer services. These services allow users to publish, distribute and share pieces of content, examples include blogs, Flickr, YouTube. They also allow people to work or play together seen in, for example, Second Life, Habbo Hotel. They can also create a collective body of knowledge such as Wikipedia. Furthermore, they facilitate users to attach their own interpretations to bits of information in the form of 'social bookmarks' or 'tags', for example de.li.cious and to produce and share reviews and preferences such as Amazon, Last.fm, TripAdvisor. Particularly successful are social networking sites such as Facebook and MySpace that offer an attractive and accessible platform for users to interact and to share social capital (ibid.).

Although the Web is opening up for popular use there is a tension in its development. This tension is based on the contradiction between the utopian ideal of free and open communication shaped by its users and the way the Internet has been commercialized for business, public sector and popular markets. These contradictions are seen, for example, in the controlling aspects of new forms of flexible work, and in the tension between values of unregulated communication and censorship in relation to Internet pornography. It is also seen in the way the promise of emancipation in cyber culture is curtailed through the commoditization of culture. Part of the development of the Internet involves actors producing measures, both on- and off-line, to counter disadvantages of the Internet whilst taking advantage of its interactive and networking communication.

Analysis: Linking the Details of the Innovation of the Internet with Social Change

The framework of the cultural form shows how the early phase of the Internet's innovation was socially shaped and culturally informed. The cultural form concept also takes our analysis beyond the early shaping of the Internet into its ongoing developments. To locate the Internet, and its development, more broadly within social life there is a need, theoretically, to explore the relationship between the Internet and society. The link is located in the relationship between communication and technology as expressed and materialized through the Internet. To address this relationship with society, theoretically, it is informative to draw on two perspectives: one that 'society exists in and through communication' (Dewey, 1939) and the other that technologies express a social vision, create powerful symbols and engage us in forms of life (Pfaffenberger, 1988). Thus, the Internet as a technological artefact expresses a social vision of communication; it creates powerful symbols such as networked computer communication and engages us in forms of life that integrate online communication with off-line activities. The overarching use of the Internet is communication and through the processes communication society is constituted (c.f. Dewey, 1939). It is through this dynamic that commentators can start to trace and analyse the relationship of the Internet and society, a dynamic that materializes as socio-cultural forms and is thus open to sociological inquiry.

A further aspect of understanding the dynamics of the Internet and society is, therefore, the ways in which Internet activities are involved in social change, and how their characteristics shape and are shaped in social change. The dynamics of social change including technology is a key focus of the social sciences, seen, for example, in the works of Marx, Durkheim and Weber who all address in various ways the transformations from feudal agrarian society to industrial capitalist society in the Western world. Similarly, theorists such as Bell (1974) and Lash and Urry (1987) focus on changes from industrial to post-industrial society that include the social, cultural and technological aspects of that change. In general terms, the ways in which technologies were used in industrialization, albeit somewhat differently in post-industrialization, resulted in transforming the processes of production and distribution, and generated new products and practices as well as new patterns of usage and consumption. However, it was not the technologies that generated change; rather it was the way in which the technology was appropriated within sets of social relations. For example, in the industrial revolution, the power of elites embedded within the political strategies of imperialist ambition and inter-imperialist conflict was influential in exploiting technology in new production processes. This influence by powerful states resulted in wealth moving to them and tied into rapid urbanization, new class formations and new forms of inequality (Castells, 1996).

It was the configuration of social, political and economic factors, rather than the technology itself that produced environments in which technology could be exploited for economic, political and social purposes. Taking this broader approach, Robins and Webster (1999) see the Internet as part of a view of a long revolution of capitalist development starting from the Enclosures Acts of Parliament (1750 to 1850). They take a Luddite view that extends beyond a movement against technology *per se* to a protest against wider changes to ways of life through new social mobilizations of *laissez-faire* capitalism. Thus, 'the global network society' is the latest context in which social relations are reconfigured in capitalist and market oriented ways.

Although these are broad approaches to sweeps of changes, any understanding of the Internet needs to take into account the ways in which it is adopted (or not) and how it becomes meaningful in social life, which together shapes its ongoing development (Wessels, 2007b). The use and development of ICT in everyday life (Silverstone, 2005; Haddon, 2004) and in institutional and organizational settings (Cornford and Pollock, 2003; Mansell and Steinmueller, 2000; Wessels, 2007b) show that the uptake of technology is rarely a straightforward transfer and take-up process. Rather, the nature of change in terms of socio-technical change occurs through a process of social engagement, adaptations and resistances with new technologies (Silverstone, 2005). This process counters any discourses of revolutionary change based on a narrow definition of Internet technology that posits a technologically led transformation of social life through convergence or over-determination (ibid.).

Although social change is not technically determined, it is also not economically or socially determined (Silverstone, 2005; Haddon, 2004; Mansell and Steinmueller, 2000; Wessels, 2007b). Instead, the dynamics of innovation and social change is culturally a complex, contested and iterative process. Although some aspects of technological change may be fairly rapid, social and cultural change usually occur more slowly (Silverstone, 2005). Silverstone points out that the lack of synchronization between social and technological change reflects the complexity and indeterminacy of the social. He argues that this is particularly the case with regard to the practices of everyday life: everyday life is something that has to be actively managed by social actors and it provides sites in which technology becomes appropriated in distinct and often creative ways (ibid.; c.f. Haddon, 2004). The everyday consists not just of the domestic private realm but also interacts with public life, whether in the realm of politics, culture or work. The indeterminacy of the social, therefore, is also reflected in the more formal domains of work, politics and public services, as well as organized leisure time (McLoughlin, 1999; Dutton, ed., 2001; Bell, 2001; Wessels, 2007b). The cultural dynamics of the production and consumption of the Internet means that the history of the Internet is a 'contested, temporal and emergent' process (Clifford, 1984, p. 19).

Conclusion

The history of the innovation of the Internet to the point of its commercialization shows how the Internet is socially shaped and culturally informed

(Castells, 2001). The relations of production involve military, academic and think-tank research centres, hackers, grass-roots user groups and entrepreneurs. The narratives focus on flexible, interactive and networked computer communication, which moved from military motivations to (lower case) universalistic principles and then to market consumerism. The characteristics of participation include cooperative open-source development, openness and freedom and interactivity and flexibility. The social contexts and cultural ethos of each phase of the development of the Internet have combined to form an open and networked communication system. The flexibility of the form within the dynamics of social change is generating scope for the formation of new socio-cultural forms. The flexibility of its design and its openness of use means that the Internet has the potential to be part of a wide range of socio-cultural forms. Its founding features of open communication within a philosophy of freedom continue to shape its development in combination with commercialization. The interaction of these values, features and processes are embedded in broader socio-cultural contexts of changing communication environments within the social relations of late modern society. To return to the point of the 'awesome paradox' of how human activity produces a world of things, the historical process of the innovation of the Internet produced characteristics that actors are currently engaging in and negotiating, and in so doing, their activity continues to shape it.

3

Cultural Forms and Socio-Technical Change

Introduction

This chapter sets out a theoretical framework that aims to address the ways in which technology is socially shaped *and* culturally informed (Castells, 2001). First the chapter summarizes how the social sciences have addressed socio-technical change. Those taking a technological determinist perspective claim that technology determines the social and social change, which leaves little room for social agency in socio-technical change. By contrast, social shaping approaches argue that economic and social factors such as the organization of work or gender roles shape technology. Social constructivism goes further, arguing that technology is fully social. Approaches within the fields of innovation, management and organizational studies are more specific. A key theme in innovation studies is that technological change is situated within institutional change, and management studies highlight the ways in which technology interacts with organizational change. Although these approaches are insightful, they do not fully address the ways in which the materiality of a technology such as the Internet and its character of communication and services are socially shaped *and* culturally informed.

To address this point the chapter outlines a conceptual framework for understanding how technology gains its material form and meaning through innovation processes shaped by social values, cultural sensibilities and political agendas. The framework is premised on the meaningfulness of social action in the production and consumption of (digital) technology. The concepts that make up this framework include the integration of technologies in social and cultural forms constituted through the relations of production, narratives and policies and user participation. Innovative action is understood as a performance in which new technologies and envisaged services are creatively imagined and staged in relation to social values, cultural narratives and contexts of use. Innovation takes

30

place in various types of 'transformational spaces' such as product and/ or service workshops, prototyping trials and user-based contexts. In these spaces social actors ask 'what if' questions in developing and appropriating new services and technologies. These activities take place in a broader 'theatre of innovation' made up of institutions, developers and researchers, service providers, policy-makers and user groups. By understanding the processes of innovation as the institutionalization of socio-cultural forms, the social, political and cultural aspects of innovation can be addressed, thus elucidating the richness and complexity of the development of the Internet as socio-cultural forms.

Addressing Technology and Social Change

Those working within the social sciences were initially reluctant to analyse the characteristics of technical change, as the 'black box' of technology was thought to be outside the specialized competence of most economists and sociologists, requiring the expertise of engineers and scientists (Freeman, 1994). Nonetheless, historically within the social sciences, commentators have addressed the relationship between technology and society. Marx, for example, recognizes the importance of technology for understanding class relationships in his examination of the relationship between labour and technological production in the form of automated and powered machinery (Marx, 1976). White's (1978) technical determinist approach argues that the development of feudalism as a social system was the direct product of the stirrup. Technology also figures in recent post-modernist descriptions of society – for example, Poster (1990) argues that new forms of social reality and social life are emerging due to the increasing mediation of communications by electronic devices.

These approaches differ from one another in various ways, but display a similar interest in the relationship between technology and society by focusing on the influence of technology upon social structure rather than the social constitution of technology. They are examples of technological determinism. Theoretically, proponents of technological determinism argue that technology is an autonomous force that acts on society and produces social change. Thus technology caused social change and defines society. There are two main strands within this theory: one is a 'hard' perspective where technology is the only factor in change; the other is a 'soft' perspective that posits that technology is highly influential in social change. White's technological determinism is an extreme formulation of the hard approach, asserting that technology causes social development, whereas Marx (1976) also takes into account economic factors as well as technology in the relations of production and hence veers more towards a soft form of determinism. Poster

(1990) argues that the spread of information technologies is one element of 'the post-modern experience',[1] which, through the spread of simulation,[2] for example, contributes to altering social relations. However, across a range of hard and soft approaches, these sociological approaches use a study of technology to observe the constitution and organization of the structural arrangements of society, rather than concern for the constitution and organization of technology *per se* (Button, 1996).

Deconstructing the Relationship between Technology and Social Change

The development of 'social shaping of technology' approaches created interest in technology as an arena where issues such as labour and gender relationships are played out. MacKenzie and Wajcman define technology as referring to

> ... a set of physical objects (cars, vacuum cleaners, computers), human activities such as steel making (which includes what steel workers do as well as the furnaces they use), and knowledge (technology refers to what people know as well as what they do). (MacKenzie and Wajcman, 1985, p. 3.)

Proponents of this approach argue that, as the technology can be shaped the 'content' of technology is open for sociological scrutiny. This 'content' of technology is understood as the materiality, social activity and knowledge that constitute a technology. Examples of social shaping approaches include Hughes's (1998) study of Edison's development of the light bulb, where he identifies the influence of economic factors in technological innovation. Cockburn's (1985) study of compositors in the printing trade identifies the ways in which gender dynamics resulted in technology becoming the property of men through the exclusion of women from technical jobs. Social shaping approaches also contribute to understanding the innovation process by which they highlight the social dynamics of change, arguing that

- Innovation is a complex social activity – a process of struggle as well as a technical process. It involves processes of interest articulation, and learning processes.
- This framework highlights the types of expertise possessed by different actors in the innovation process and the flows of information between them.
- Innovation is not a linear process, but an iterative, or spiral process. It takes place through interactions across a network of actors.

- All this gives rise to significant differences in the form and content of the emerging technology. (Williams and Edge, 1992, p. 18.)

Williams and Edge argue that traditional approaches to innovation separate technologies from their social concepts and fail to identify the social arrangements within which technology emerges and becomes embedded. Thus, for example, Webb (1991) analyses the relationship between supplier and user firms in a variety of new technologies, including ICT-based products. Webb emphasizes that product development is not simply a question of deploying technical know-how but involves other types of expertise, such as marketing, and argues that 'social interactions amongst particular occupational groups within and between firms, their cultures and orientation, all influence product design and choice' (p. 21). Williams et al. (2005) follow this approach to show how technological change involves processes of social learning, whereby developers and users learn to appropriate and shape technology for specific contexts of use.

Social constructivists argue that technology is grounded in, and constituted by, socially operative forces. Bijker et al. (1987),[3] for example, draw on social studies of science to identify three stages in the social construction of technology. The first stage is demonstrating that technology is open to different interpretations. The second stage is mapping out the mechanisms through which debate is closed through the stabilization of the artefact, not only by 'solving' problems but also by having relevant groups see that the problems have been solved. The third stage is seeing how the content of the artefact is related to the social. In relation to this last point, Woolgar (1991) advocates an approach that focuses on the discursive and interpretive practices of constructing technology, arguing that 'what we apprehend this word is correct as technology is to be constructed as text, the production and consumption of which is on a par with our own writing and reading practices' (p. 9).

Woolgar's approach leads Winner (1985) to argue that 'technology can have politics'. In his study of the Moses Bridge, which connects Long Island to Jones Beach in Manhattan, Winner points out that the way the bridge was built precluded the use of public transport, which excluded 'blacks', as habitual users of public transport, from Jones Beach. He states that the technology (the bridge), therefore, excludes black people from the beach as a leisure area, meaning that 'whites' using their private cars could retain exclusive access to the beach and enjoy its leisure facilities. Woolgar (1991) argues that this technology can therefore be read in two ways: as a way of transporting people or as a way of playing out racial prejudice. Woolgar's interest is in the persuasiveness of the text, that is, what makes one reading of the text more persuasive than another. Law (1987) demonstrates another dimension of social constructivism by focusing on the construction process. He argues that technology is an emergent phenomenon that requires associative activities to be enacted through an 'actor-network' Latour supports Law'a position by arguing that an 'actor-network' involves

> 'actor', 'agent', or 'actant' without making any assumptions about who they may be and what properties they are endowed with ... they can be anything – individual ('Peter') or collective ('the crowd'), figurative (anthropomorphic or zoomorphic) or nonfigurative ('fate'). (Latour, 1987, p. 12.)

Law (1987) argues that 'stability and form of artefacts should be seen as a function of the interaction of heterogeneous elements as these are shaped and assimilated into a network' (p. 25). He argues that artefacts result from the elements that make up a network.

In general, social constructivist theorists emphasize the way that technology is socially constructed whereas, conversely, the proponents of social shaping highlight the way in which social factors shape technology. Molina (1995) attempts to move beyond social shaping and constructivist approaches and towards institutional and organizational approaches to technology in his conceptualization of 'socio-technological constituencies'. He analyses the ways in which actors, resources and technologies configure to develop new technologies, showing that they form constituencies to do so. This formation of socio-technical constituencies shows how both technological and social constituents are inseparable in innovation processes. Molina's perspective is a broadly social networking one, but differs from actor–network theories because his approach does not place the animate and the inanimate in the same category. Nonetheless, he defines the link between culture and action as one in which rules guide or direct action, which in a Wittgenstein (1958) approach is empirically invalid, and in a Bourdieu (1977) perspective is tautological. Although these approaches deconstruct technology in relation to the social in varying ways, they lose some details of associating technology and social worlds, whether through not fully accounting for any interactional work (Garfinkel and Wiley, 1980), the role of organizations (McLoughlin, 1999), human and institutional dynamics (Mansell and Silverstone, 1996), or through cultural factors of the production and use of technology within society.

Associating Technology and Social Worlds: Work in Institutionalizing Technology

In a critique of constructivist approaches Garfinkel argues that these approaches remove the phenomenon from the realm of the social world (cited in Button, 1996), which reveals a more general need to address the details of the link between social factors and technology. Garfinkel (ibid.) proposes that, to explore the cultural worldliness of phenomena, production should be considered. He addresses his concern about constructivism from ethnomethodology's emphasis on the work involved in the production of cultural objects and artefacts, including the work of the occupations involved (Garfinkel, 1984[4]). This ethnomethodological view stresses the ways in which actions and interactions produce cultural objects in ways that are 'accountable'. Significantly, this starts to provide an explanation of why an artefact emerges in the form it does and at the time it does. This is because the accountability of the actions that produce artefacts is realized within sets of relations produced by the social actors themselves.

Researchers within the ethnomethodology tradition focus on details of actors' work and interactions in producing technology. This approach entails undertaking detailed observations of the actions and interactions of actors as they develop and use technology indexically and reflexively in social contexts. Approaches within ethnomethodology are often used to inform the design of technology by detailing the actions and interactions of the users of technology within specific contexts (Hartwood et al., 2002). The focus of these approaches is on the way in which actors produce orderly and accountable social action (including action that incorporates technology) through the action itself. This micro approach does not address areas at the meso level, such as the role of technology in organizations, or concerns at the macro level such as the function of technology within the broader environment of the (socio-economic) relations of production.

Orlikowski's (1992) work begins to examine the meso level by addressing technology in relation to organizations.[5] She argues that technology is created and changed by human action and is used by humans to accomplish action, and she calls this recursive notion of technology the 'duality of technology'. The interaction of technology and organizations is a function of the different actors and socio-historical contexts implicated in its development and use, thus technology is a product of human action, which also assumes structural properties (p. 405). Orlikowski (1992, 1994) draws on Giddens's structuration theory,[6] which posits that agency and structure are not independent, and argues that, within this framework,[7] the ongoing social action of agents habitually draws on technology that in turn objectifies and institutionalizes it.[8] She sees human action as knowledgeable and reflexive and notes that, although there is flexibility in the design and use of technology, influencing factors (whether external or internal) mean that the interpretive flexibility of any given technology is not infinite. There is, however, a lack of clarity regarding the precise influence of structure and agency in her analysis, which reflects reformulations, including that of Giddens,[9] regarding the relations between structure and agency.

There is still debate at a theoretical level regarding the appropriate conceptualization of relations between the two, as well as discussion on the prior or interrelated question of how 'agency' and 'structure' should be defined in the first place. Thus, Layder (1981), for example, regards Giddens's conception of structure as lacking any autonomous properties or pre-given facticity, and Bryant and Jary (1991) have detected a persistent bias towards agency in Giddens's formulation. Without understanding the precise nature of action and structure, especially if actions are seen as capabilities rather than intentions, it is difficult to understand the dynamics of change. Given this, Archer states that 'the theory of structuration remains incomplete because it provides an insufficient account of mechanisms of stable replication versus the genesis of new social forms' (Archer 1992, p. 131). When the problem of conceptualizing relations between structure and agency in the theory is applied to technology and social action, it reproduces the theory's inherent ambiguity – the ambiguity of analysing relative influences of action and the structuring components of technology-in-use.

Mansell and Silverstone (1996) set an agenda for framing research questions in studies of ICTs, which seeks to gain a more nuanced understanding of the relationship between technological change and institutional structures. They draw on Freeman, who argues that all innovations are 'social and not natural phenomena; all of them the result of human actions, human decisions, human expectations, human institutions' (Freeman, 1992b, p. 224). Mansell and Silverstone (eds, 1996) develop this view, maintaining that 'the analysis of the determinates of technical change cannot be divorced from the analysis of institutional change' (p. 15). They draw on functionalist accounts that address social activity by referring to its consequences for the operation of some other activity, institution, or society as a whole.[10] Mansell and Silversone adopt Merton's middle-range theory as an organizational tool to aid them in constructing 'minor working hypotheses' within 'master conceptual schemes' needed to address technological and institutional change. They address the issue of change through 'differentiation', which is used widely in theories of social change (Smelser, 1959; Parsons, 1951). Differentiation refers to a process whereby sets of social activities performed by one social institution split up between different institutions, representing an increasing specialization of parts of society, resulting in greater heterogeneity within society.

Mansell and Silverstone (1996) use this 'soft' functionalist framework to explore the institutional–technological change dynamic and adapt this overall ethos to a range of scenarios from the development of a European Information Society (Mansell and Steinmuller, 2000) to the appropriation and use of technologies in everyday life (Haddon, 2004). Mansell and Steinmuller (2000), for example, counter the view that information society developments are inevitable and take a single evolutionary pathway. Instead, they show that the ongoing development of a European Information Society is the result of a range of competing visions and strategies held by various social actors in Europe and across globe. Silverstone and Hirsch (1992) develops the concept of domestication to address the ways in which technologies become accepted and used, or become rejected, within the complexities and routines of everyday life[11] (also see Berker et al., 2005). These approaches counter accounts of a rational and linear innovation process, which is monocausal and technically determined (Berker et al., 2006; Mansell and Steinmuller, 2000) and, in different ways, analyse various aspects of the social and institutional dynamics of technological innovation.

Addressing the Cultural Dynamics of Technological Change

Addressing the richness of the dynamics of technological change involves considering the link between technological forms and human culture. Geertz's (1973) semiotic concept of culture stresses that human action is meaningful because social actors weave 'webs of significance' within their various activities. By understanding human action as symbolic (i.e. meaningful), the complexity of the link between technical forms and human culture can start to be considered in all its 'cultural this-worldliness' (c.f. Garfinkel and Wiley, 1980). Culture adds a symbolic level to our social, institutional and material understanding of the development of technologies – digital or otherwise – and it involves moving beyond technical determinism and technical somnambulism, as Pfaffenberger (1988) argues

> In the somnambulistic view, 'making' concerns only engineers and 'doing' concerns only users. Hidden from view is the entire network of social and political relations that are tied to making and are influenced by doing. In the technological determinist view, the technology ... is seen as something apart from this network. Technology is thus, in this view, an independent variable to which forms of social relations and politics stand as dependent variables. So there is indeed a hidden unity underlying these positions that seems to stand in apparent contradiction: technology, under the sway of Western culture, is seen as a disembodied entity, emptied of social relations. ... It stands before us, in other words, in what Marx would call fetished form: what in reality is produced by relations among people appears before us in a fantastic form as relations among things. (p. 242)

In taking a cultural approach to innovation, the emphasis is on symbolic action, and the analysis is particularly directed towards human action as it attains meaning and is interpreted. Innovation, therefore, is understood by the ways in which change and transformation occurs through action that is meaningful. The process of understanding the meaningfulness of technological change involves considering how humans act in meaningful ways, which in turn leads to situating meaning in social forms, cultural values and technology. Given this framework of analysis, it follows that one needs to address the way in which humans change established patterns of actions by, for example, asking 'what if' questions in the process of change which involve envisaging new ways of doing things. Furthermore, these processes must be understood contextually, since research and development (R&D) projects and technology-in-use adaptations, are situated within a broader social and institutional environment. These broader environments generate resource and relevance as well as the context in which meaningfulness of technological change materializes into various social and cultural forms.

Dilthey's (1914–1936) analysis of meaning is helpful for understanding the ways in which humans make sense of situations and act meaningfully in their varied and diverse social worlds. He argues that meaning involves understanding that there is a distinction between static models of thought and action such as cosmologies, theologies, philosophical systems, ethical systems and ideologies, and the dynamic lived *Weltschauung*. This *Weltschauung* consists of a *Weltbild*, that is, a body of knowledge and belief about what is cognitively taken to be the 'real world'. A set of value judgements is raised upon this, expressing the relation of the adherents to their world and the meaning (*Bedeutung*) which they find in it. This, in turn, supports a more or less coherent system of ends, ideals and principles of conduct, which are the points of contact between the *Weltanschauung* and praxis, the socio-cultural interaction, making it a force in the construction of human projects, and of society at large. Dilthey (1957) argues that *Weltanschauung* is not a permanent, fixed structure of eternal ideas but itself represents, at any given moment, a dispensable stage in humans' unending struggle to find a convincing solution to the 'riddles of life' (Dilthey 1914–1936, *Gesammelte Scriften* VIII, p. 237). This concept of meaning indicates that action as praxis involves humans working within their understanding of a set of social and material conditions and actively interpreting the value and meaning of these conditions with relation to sets of principles. The meaningfulness of specific contexts, and the ways in which they are interpreted, form the cultural framework for considering social and technological change.

As Dilthey (1957, 1914–1936) suggests, meaning is situated in social experience, and therefore understanding technological change involves considering the dynamic interplay of social forms, cultural values and technology. Pfaffenberger (1988) addresses this point by arguing that

> technology is humanised nature [which] is to insist that it is a fundamentally
> social phenomenon: it is a social construction of nature around us and within
> us, and once achieved, it expresses an embedded social vision, and it engages
> us in what Marx would call a form of life. The interpenetration of culture and
> nature here described is, in short, of the sort that Mauss (1967) would read-
> ily call total: any behaviour that is also, political, social and symbolic. It has a
> legal dimension, it has a history, it entails a set of social relationships and it has
> meaning. (p. 244.)

This conceptualization encompasses the social relations of the formation of
technologies, which can therefore address the social, political and cultural
dynamics of embedding ICT in forms of communication. Understanding
the complexity of this link requires understanding the ways in which cultural forms are envisaged and materialized within the social drama of
innovation. This provides a framework for the social relations and cultural
dimensions of technology, and the characteristics of the interaction of technology with social forms and systems of meaning to create new technological forms. The processes within these frameworks are especially relevant
because the characteristic action within innovation is that of 'performance',
where social, political and cultural values are constantly 'in play' in relation
to material and technological artefacts and the conventions of communication. The actual performance of the innovation enacts – dramatizes – the
complex links between human culture and technological forms.

If the understanding is that technological change is interdependent with
social and institutional change, then the meaningfulness of that change
is understood through culture. Chaney (1993) argues that cultural change
refers to differences in the ways that social projects are discursively understood in particular historical contexts. Part of cultural change involves
understanding the way in which change is contested and represented. One
particular approach to cultural change takes a dramatist frame of reference (Burke, 1989), which addresses the cultural frames and social stages
of the process of change. This focus provides a framework for the analysis
of social order as being reflexive. For example, in envisaging new forms of
communication, social actors reflect on and experiment with cultural conventions, which are 'distinctive forms of symbolic imagination embodied
in material practices [that] are aspects of the institutionalization of a more-
or-less coherent order' (Chaney, 1993, p. 15). Developers and users of ICT
interpret and play with these conventions, revealing social patterns and
mores, and in so doing shape technologies reflexively. As meaning is generated through performance, interpretation is contingent on, and infinitely

capable of, reconsideration (ibid.). The recognition that interpretation is a social practice politicizes the constitutive significance of cultural imagery, rather than atomizing meaning. Thus, as Chaney argues, 'if a form of life is a way of using a set of implements and resources then the order through which cultural imagery represents types of order is a distinctive way of being in the world' (p. 15) and creates languages in the formulation of social projects. How people change the way they communicate, therefore, does not simply mean changing the technological aspects of communication. Rather, it involves integrating social values and cultural meaning within communication technology holistically as a social and cultural practice that materialize as socio-cultural forms.

The use of implements, artefacts and resources in, for instance, a communication system and the re-imagining of new forms of communication require some analysis of the way that actions affect situations. As Burke (1989) argues, the image of action as performance highlights how actions affect situations, which allows for the ways in which actors create the meanings of situations and form actions that are strategic. This perspective allows action the potential to be dramatic because it includes conflict, purpose, reflection and choice, and actors frame events in the formulation of experience and through symbols. The interpretation and framing of events, such as the development of Internet related services, are characterized in terms of sets of relationships where modes of performance involve 'an assumption to an audience for the way in which communication is carried out, above and beyond its referential content' (Bauman, 1977, p. 11). Thus, as new forms of Internet services are being created, there is a reflexive concern with forms of communication as they attain meaning in social and cultural contexts. The characteristics of performance are realized in social dramas that give a sense of 'experiential matrix' for the generation of various genres of cultural performance (Turner, 1974, p. 78). Turner argues that drama involves modes of transformation of both performer and setting and requires playing with forms of experience.

The relevance of this concept of drama to studies of socio-technical change is that it can address the transformations of products and social practices into new 'production functions' and 'symbolic goods and services' within specific contexts of development and use. Turner stresses that the truly spontaneous unit of human social performance is not a role-playing sequence, but rather that action through social drama results in the suspension of normative role-playing, in which passionate activity abolishes the usual distinction between flow and reflection. This is because it becomes a matter of urgency in a social drama to be reflexive about the cause and motive of action, which affects the social fabric. It is in the social drama that *Weltanschauung* becomes visible, if only fragmentarily, as factors give meaning to deeds that at first sight seem meaningless. The point that Turner makes is that the performative genres (such as socio-technical change) are, as it were, secreted from the social drama,[12] and in turn surround it and feed their performed meanings back into it. In this sense, the process of socio-technical change is embedded in the dynamics of the relationship between socio-cultural landscapes and technical developments in a variety of innovation projects and technology-in-use contexts.

To reiterate, the theoretical framework being developed here aims to address the cultural dynamics of technological change without losing the technology's content or giving too much influence to overly determined action. The framework does this by arguing that action is meaningful and produces artefacts through cultural frameworks in social dramas. As socio-technical change involves questioning the existing technological and social order, and the processes of innovation occur in cultural frameworks, action gains meaning from the context of situations and the interpretations in use. In this context, action has a strategizing element to it within any given situation, which as Gusfield (1989) argues, is the crux of human drama. Therefore, when action is understood as performance within social dramas, it is a way of affecting a situation.[13]

More specifically, Burke (1989) argues that members of social groups understand their social world through their symbolic order[14] and come to see that order through 'performance'. Performance is therefore a source of representation and transformation and a dialectic of 'flow' – spontaneous movement in which action and awareness are one – as well as reflexivity in which the central meanings, values and goals of culture are seen in action (Schechner and Appel, 1990, p. 1). As indicated above, drama involves modes of transformation of both performer and setting and requires playing with forms of social experience. Turner's (1974) focus on performance and social drama shows that there is a continuous, dynamic process linking performative behaviour (art, ritual, play) with social and ethical structures, and considers the way in which social actors think about and organize their lives and specify individual and group values. An innovation process exhibits further characteristics of performance – that performance is an art, which is open, unfinished, de-centred, liminal and, for Turner, is a paradigm for process. The practice of innovation is performative because it involves artefacts and culture being 'in play' in the process of change.

People in innovation projects or in technology-in-use contexts experiment with ideas and materials in relation to their orientations to perceived social and cultural values. There is an ever-present potential for conflict, since actors in these innovation dramas have different ideas and interpretations of the development and use of technologies. Thus, social dramas constitute transformation and reflexivity in spheres of life and life worlds, which is a defining feature of social and technological change. At this point, one can understand innovation and social order as reflexive, because the practice of innovation tends to break with some aspects of established ways of 'doing things', that is social conventions, in seeking to envisage new social and cultural forms. The concepts of drama and action, when utilized within ethnographies of performance, therefore help to identify the symbolic relevance of specific cultural constellations of communication which give meaning to particular communities as well as elucidate the reflexive constitution of social order (Chaney, 1993). It is precisely this last point that helps address the problem of social action and technological change, in that, innovative actions involve questioning the existing order of things and processes of innovation occur in cultural frameworks.

A key aspect in the performance of innovative dramas is 'transformational spaces'. These spaces can be understood through a theatrical metaphor, where actors devise transformational spaces. Examples include technology development workshops in which developers play with narratives, products and social conventions of imagined audiences to creatively think through new cultural forms. Another example is the spaces created in the home, such as a corner of the living room, where families learn to appropriate and shape technologies for their own purposes. These types of workshops operate as a 'transformational space' by being part of a workshop-rehearsal process that is liminoid (Schechner, 1977). Liminoid or liminal means a space that is 'betwixt and between' the fixed world from which material is extracted and the fixed score of a performance text (Turner, 1974; Schechner, 1977). Within socio-technical change involving, for example, the Internet, this is realized in the interdependency of ICT, narratives of the role of communication and characteristics of participation in communication and services. It is liminoid because it is 'in-between' existing communications systems, conventions, guidelines and visions of possible future forms of communication. There is, therefore, a potential for transformation of ICT because in these spaces it is not constrained by established conventions, and actors can interpret and 'play with' narratives and artefacts of a nascent ICT form.

To expand the understanding of transformational spaces, Turner's idea of liminality (1974) is linked with Stanislavski's (1946) magic 'if'. Thus, when ICT development workshops and user contexts of technology-in-use are seen as rehearsals, the use of 'if' is a way of researching a physical environment, effects and relationships – everything that will sooner or later be fixed in the performance of a cultural form. The work done in the contexts of these different types of rehearsals is 'real work' because it is where actors shape the technology by seriously problematizing the artefact and use context. Often, however, a casual observer of these rehearsals may feel that the work is 'as if' in nature, something tentative, subjunctive: 'let's try that', 'this could work', 'what would happen if?' Workshops and user scenarios are in a sense playful because the techniques of 'as if' flourish in games, role exchanges and improvisations, and participants contribute 'stuff from all over'. Rehearsals, whether workshops or user contexts find, reveal and express material, and give potential technologies and services performative shape.

These performances are not *ad hoc* occurrences because they are realized through innovation dramas of particular cultural forms. Cultural forms, like most conceptual tools, have been used in a variety of ways[15] and can be applied to the analysis of the form and content of social dramas. This is because action, performances and dramas are not random events; rather they are constituted through the drama's relations of production, through the narratives of the play and through the participation between producer, performer and audiences (Chaney, 1990). The cultural form addresses these aspects and their relationships in the dynamics of change.

Williams's (1974) concern is to resist cruder forms of technological determinism, and in his study of television he situates the technology within cultural conventions that stem partly from other narrative traditions and partly from wider cultural concerns. The cultural form is, therefore, both more than and less than a particular technology. Although Williams places culture at the centre of analysis, he does not use Geertz's semiotic concept of culture; nonetheless, he does address cultural conventions in the generation of meanings of media technologies. However, he is positioned away from media and cultural theorists such as Hall because he makes culture central to the processes of struggles over collective meaning[16] and thus meaning becomes significant in itself. Other approaches to cultural forms include the works of scholars at the Birmingham Centre for Contemporary Cultural Studies (CCCS) writing in relation to developments in cultural analysis within an English tradition,[17] American functionalism[18] and the Critical Theory[19] of the Frankfurt School.[20] Academics at the Centre, including Hall,[21] approach culture through the idea of hegemony,[22] which means the ways in which power is exercised though ideological and political means to gain the consent of the mass of the population for the existing (capitalist) order.

Hegemony posits an ideological determinist stance to culture, but the CCCS approach seeks to account for a degree of negotiation in determining cultural meanings, whilst maintaining some constraints on voluntarism. There is, however, a contradiction between needing to retain a core of prescriptive determinism while recognizing creative cultural strategies in constituting distinctive social worlds.[23] As Chaney (1994) argues, there is a 'problem with theories of hegemony as with all prescriptive versions of social determinism, in that they try to close off the processes of the production of meaning. Such theories cannot allow for the freeplay of irony or reflexivity in cultural discourse' (p. 48). Although Chaney argues that there is a necessary interdependence of culture and society, this must not been seen as a relationship in which one governs or determines the other, with all that implies in terms of functionalism or hidden purposes. Rather, one can only understand the 'dynamic intensity of the meaning of cultural practices by reference to social concerns; participating in and/or enjoying some cultural object is a form of social action' (p. 49).

As this discussion indicates, the concepts of culture and cultural forms have been defined and utilized in different ways. However, one particular definition of cultural forms is useful for understanding socio-technical change:

> ...three interdependent elements...These elements are: first, the relations of production – that is the social organization of producing and distributing, obviously including specific features of the technology of expression, cultural phenomena; secondly, characteristic modes of narration – that is the themes, styles and narrative organization of the form; and thirdly, the type of participative interaction between producer, performer and audience that is characteristically provided within a particular form – more generally, the social bonds, the nature of the collectivity, that is implied and generated within the performance. (Chaney, 1990, p. 51)

This conceptualization examines the interdependency of production, narrative and participation that shapes the innovation of new technological systems, which express particular social and cultural sensibilities when in use. The specific context of production, the context of the formation of specific narratives and the contexts of participation in the form enable an understanding of how ICT develops as cultural forms to gain specific characteristics. This involves understanding the interdependency of the production of ICT, the narratives of communication and services and the communicative interaction and participation of people with technology and technological services.

The cultural form acts as an organizing principle for understanding socio-technical change and situates performance within the production, narrative and participation aspects of innovation and change. Change can only be said to have occurred if the production, narrative and participation become interdependent, that is, for production and consumption to be articulated through narratives that hold meaning for both producers and consumers. To address the emergence of the Internet as a new communication media, the interdependency of its production, the characteristics of its narratives and the participative interaction between producers, performers and audiences all need to be understood. Chaney's concept of the cultural form within a semiotic cultural approach provides a framework for understanding the cultural dynamics of innovation. The ways in which new social and cultural forms are realized in symbolic action enables an understanding of how the Internet and ICT emerge in their distinctive socio-cultural forms.

This cultural forms approach facilitates an appreciation of the cultural contexts of innovation processes and the ways in which the development of new artefacts and services is embedded within broader socio-cultural trends. Figure 3.1 indicates the spaces and the interactions of, and between, the relations of production, the narratives and the forms of participation. These spaces and interactions can be populated with various groups and perspectives involved in any R&D project and user context in an innovation process. It shows the potential that these actors have to form specific configurations in the various transformational spaces of innovation processes.

The three aspects of the cultural form are drawn into a broader innovation environment in which production, narrative and participation are generally organized. This broader environment is understood through a metaphor of theatre, and specifically as a 'theatre of innovation'; represented by Figure 3.1. The figure illustrates where central actors of an innovation drama are placed: those within the relations of production are primarily seen as 'backstage'; those involved in the formation of narratives, policy and commerce are located on the 'stage'; and participants in public, semi-public and private realms form 'audiences'. These actors move in and out of rehearsals such as workshops and user contexts in the areas of backstage, stage and audience, which are interlinked in the innovation drama and process. Thus, those involved in the relations of production, in the formation of narratives and as audiences move between these spaces, and the meanings and knowledge gained through these interactions shape

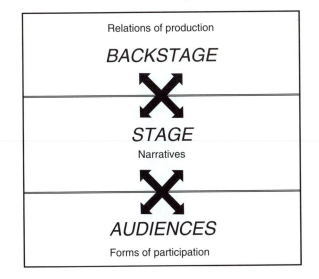

Figure 3.1   The theatre of innovation
Source: Wessels, 2000a.

new ICT and communications systems. The arrows show the interactions between these aspects, with interactions occurring in each area of the theatre as well as between areas. Innovation, however, only occurs when there is interdependence between all three areas and all interactions are symbolically framed in the process of change. For example, interactions within the relations of production are formed in transformational spaces of developers testing 'demos', which relate to those producing narratives in forming policy or marketing frameworks on stage and with audiences when ICT is tested, marketed and used with user groups. These various types of interactions with audiences using new ICT and ICT services produce other transformational spaces in the ongoing development process.

The cultural form is a conceptual framework for analysing the relationship between the Internet and contemporary society. A tool of inquiry can be adapted to various contexts of production and use; for example, it can be used to understand how police services are developing ICT in their public communication strategies and activities (Wessels, 2007b). In this example, the research explores the interaction between the production of new forms of public communication, the narratives of police services and the types of public–police interactions that frame the development of ICT in policing contexts. The conceptual framework can be applied to e-government in a similar way. It can also address changing consumer practices in everyday life by focusing on participative practices of the everyday and how that interacts with the development of products that are given meaning in the discourses of everyday life. Likewise the concept can be applied to the socio-cultural context of work and to the field of culture and entertainment.

Conclusion

The argument in this book is that the innovation of the Internet and ICT as socio-cultural forms involves complex links between human culture and technological forms. The link between values and technologies is traced, showing that this link is constituted through narratives, production and participation. The work of actors differentially situated in the innovation drama gives the process dramatic and symbolic meaning through their interpretations of values, technologies and social conventions. The economic, social and political are all juggled to produce a new communication media that has meaning in contemporary society. This is done through performance in transformational spaces within the broad theatre of emerging cultural forms and shows how technology is socially shaped and culturally informed (Castells, 2001).

4

The Socio-Cultural Environment of the Internet

Introduction

This chapter discusses some of the key themes involved in understanding the social environment of the Internet and takes the themes forward as a framework for analysing whether the Internet is part of broader social change that is transforming society to an 'information society'. Early perspectives of the Internet address the ways in which new forms of Internet-based communication interact with changing experiences of 'time and place' and 'the virtual and the real'. They explore the ways where these experiences are part of changing senses of identity, community and civil society. Some of the analysis tends to be optimistic, viewing the Internet as a potential source of liberation by taking social actors out of their traditional social relations of identity, community and time and place into virtual worlds, techno-spaces and cyber cultures. Pessimistic views include a prognosis of isolated individuals and the breakdown of community as a result of the loss of face-to-face social interaction. Having situated the Internet within a changing social environment, the chapter moves on to ask whether it is part of a broader social transformation that is resulting in an 'information society', or whether society is intermediated and informational in new ways without having undergone any fundamental transformation. The chapter follows Lyon (1988), by treating the 'information society' as 'problematic' – a 'rudimentary organisation of a field of phenomena which yields problems for investigation' (Abrams, 1982, p. 5).

Social Landscape of the Internet

The social landscape of the Internet is constituted through the interdependency of its production, narratives and participation in social and cultural forms. The landscape is diverse and is neither socially nor technologically determined. A central theme of this landscape is that, over time, the process of change is producing new forms of sociability through the 'affordance' (which is a technical term for the possibilities) of the technology as well as adaptations made through use. These new forms of sociability and communication are constitutive of new socio-cultural forms.

In the mid-1990s there were fears that the Internet and mediated communication would result in actors losing interpersonal skills and would reduce face-to-face interaction and local community activity.[1] Stoll (1995) sums up this anxiety by saying that he feels his days go by – 'dribble' – through his modem. To understand how mediated communication interacts with forms of sociability, Jones (1995a) distinguishes between the 'transmission and ritual' and 'transmission and transportation' views of communication. Transportation refers to how much we can communicate, or 'get across' most efficiently, economically and rapidly – and thus Stoll (1995) points out that information is transported via the modem and the Internet. Ritual acknowledges that communication involves a 'sacred ceremony that draws persons together in fellowship and commonality' (Jones, 1995b, p. 15), which is lacking in Internet communication, causing Stoll (1995) to feel that the days go by virtually without his presence.

The Internet materializes in, and is symbolized through, the personal computer, keyboard and mouse. These are integrated into telecoms and computer industries, into various domestic and public spaces and routines and, as such, are adapted to existing spaces as well as shaping a variety of new spaces. The flexibility of the Internet opens up possibilities in the formation of socio-cultural forms, with the character of participation also shaping their social and symbolic meaning – whether bringing people together in respect and dialogue or drawing them apart, alienating each from one another and commodifying relationships. Although the Internet is opening new forms of communication, it is its use, its ritualized and instrumental communication and types of sociability that is central in understanding the social environment of the Internet.

The remote character of Internet communication and the flexibility of the form create contexts in which actors re-experience time and space. The Internet extends Giddens's (1984) notion of the disembedding of time and space because its communication is instantaneous, interactive and global. Communication is no longer located in fixed time or space, which relates to the mobile characteristic of the late modern condition (Sennett, 1998; Urry, 2000). A consequence of these trends is that late modernity is characterized by the fragmentation of time and space and, in this context, individuals reflexively construct and narrate their lives. A pervasive sense of displacement and divergence and, in relation to this, the undermining of established traditions and habitués is creating life experience in which all 'that is solid melts into air' (Berman, 1982). To counter this, there is a longing for community, small-scale discussion and leisurely engagement in social and cultural life (Innis, 1951, 1952a, b). Within these broader trends, and feeding into them, the Internet generates a new sense of temporal and spatial demands – always being available anywhere and responding immediately to communication within a '24/7' global world. The Internet provides spaces for 'being' such as Internet Relay chat, Usenet groups and social networking sites (SNS). This, certainly in the first two cases and in some instances in the last case, however, can take the form of 'lurking', which is biased towards an isolated form of being. Lurking denotes a passive and non-interactive reading on an online conference, newsgroup or Bulletin Board Service (BBS). Jones (1995a) argues that this parallels Hoggart's old men in reading rooms by being a place to be among people but not with them. The importance of ritual in communication to secure the individual's sense of self, the adaptability of Internet technologies and the sense of mobility through online connectivity are all aspects being negotiated in the social landscape of the Internet.

In late modernity, the narration of community and individual identity within society is one in which community is seen to belong to individuals, rather than individuals belonging to community, as is the case in traditional understandings of community (ibid.). Cyber-optimists such as Rheingold (1993) argue that the Internet could recreate community and would go beyond traditional community by overcoming the constraints of time and space to enable everyone to communicate, whenever and wherever they are. The Internet constructs community out of communication rather than inhabitancy and being, in which individuals select whom they communicate with in line with their interests. In this sense communities are like 'committees' or 'teams' rather than individuals forming community from shared local life (Castells, 2001). Although there are agreed principles of engagement in online communities, participation in them is based on instrumental and/or popular cultural individualized choices rather than situated and affective action based in place-bound communities. It is within the narrative of choice and interest-based networks that Rheingold set up Electric Minds Inc., a media company to create the Social Web, a global brand for community (Rheingold, 1993).

This dynamic of community as a brand and as belonging to individuals is resulting in the rise of marketing and pseudo-communities through which individuals select affiliations and lifestyles in ways to create and display their identities and networks. Online communities are imagined as running parallel to ongoing situated lives and are made up of individuals who share interests for a particular time (Castells, 2001). Membership of online communities can be transitory, with individuals participating for however long they wish. The spaces of communication online also provide arenas for the construction and enactment of identities which, given the remote and mediated character of communication, are virtual. Virtual identity has the potential to free actors from a prescribed and established identity, they can re-narrate themselves and re-imagine identity as well as disclose whatever information (or mis-information) they wish about themselves. These constructions vary in form and substance, with actors choosing from personal, symbolic and social tropes, conventions and representations. The construction of these communities and identities is situated between the private experience of consumer culture and public structures of multinational power ('Finsinger and Pauly, 1986). Finsinger and Pauly argue that these constructions are crafted out of spaces between the proximate communities of everyday life and the everywhere communities of popular culture, which are imagined, nostalgically, by referring to people's pre-industrial past and futuristically with images of post-industrial projections. The use of the Internet to foster, or manufacture, senses of connection and community is especially responsive to the fragmentations of late modern life in which time, space and relationships are often emptied of meaning and are experienced as a series of fragments (Innis, 2004).

The mobile, multicultural and individualistic characteristics of late modern society raises the issue of how civic life can be sustained and how it will flourish. Within the ideal of civil society there is a profound moral political belief in the achievement of a good society. A central part of the formation of active civil society is that it should provide arenas for public debates on issues of society. These debates ideally seek to foster dialogue between self-interest and understanding otherness in terms of defining a collective good, which supports democracy and democratic processes. The media (traditional and new) underpin civil society as they produce communication environments for dialogue and debate by their staging of 'private troubles and public issues' (Mills, 1959). Silverstone (2007) argues that engagement in media and its representational practices require an orientation of 'proper distance' that ensures both understanding and respect of diversity and difference.

However, the media also trades in the spectacular, the populist, and so can be exploitative (ibid.). An early example of exploitative practice on the Internet is online pornography. Despite the difficulties of identifying the domain of jurisdiction vis-à-vis the Internet's lack of geographic existence and judging what is offensive across cultures, the Communications Decency Act passed into law in the US in 1996. This set out what actions are acceptable in the online world and the responsibilities individuals have when they are online (Carey, 1993). It also questioned the assumption that individuals have separate online and off-line lives and identities, so cyberspace began to be seen as a bodied place. Providing users self-regulate, follow online etiquette and abide by the law, Internet related communication can serve civil society by providing a communications channel through which individuals engage freely with a diversity of 'others' that allows for multiple realities and identities (c.f. Turkle, 1995). Silverstone (2007) argues the case for a genuine plurality in the communications environment to support an engaged and civilized society. These approaches challenge the traditional notion of civil society which requires unity and shuns multiplicity, by arguing that a communications environment needs to hear the other and welcome the other in ongoing dialogue (ibid.).

The Internet, as part of the communications environment, has the potential to enhance democratic process. The networked logic of the Internet could provide fora for debates and a means to exchange information as well as facilitate interactive communication among citizens, and between citizens and their representatives (Barney, 2004). However, the problem with regard to citizenship and public engagement is not only related to the Internet and its usage, but also to late modern life in which actors need the ability to transcend their own positions to respond responsibly in relation to collective social issues (Jones, 1995a). The Internet has the potential to act as a virtual public sphere, but its claim to freedom does not guarantee it an existence beyond its users' activities, which delimits its impact and influence in democratic processes (Papacharissi, 2002). The virtual public sphere's relative autonomy and lack of formal links into established democratic processes limits participation to solely online expression. This diminishes the impact of having one's voice heard, leaving Dewey's (1939) call for citizens having a responsible share of democratic processes unheeded. In this context, the Internet affords only a framework for communication. From this perspective, the Internet is just a representation of multiple realities and identities, which limits agendas of public debate through which individuals might transcend their everyday lives.

Relationships between the Internet and Society

As the development and use of the Internet continues and expands across society, it is clear that a straightforward dichotomy between the online and the off-line does not reflect the character of the relationship between the Internet and society. Castells (2001) addresses the online/off-line dichotomy by questioning the assumption that virtual communities (primarily based on online communication) are the culmination of a historical process that separates locality and sociability in the formation of community. This process is said to produce new selective patterns of social relations that substitute territorially bound forms of human interaction, increase social isolation and generate the break down of local social communication and family life. Furthermore, the Internet allows faceless individuals to practice random sociability whilst abandoning face-to-face interaction in local situated settings. However, with the expansion of the Internet into various social contexts, patterns of sociability emerge that weave the Internet into intermediated and situated life.

Castells, therefore, suggests that, rather than looking at a dichotomy between 'the virtual' and 'the real', research should address the social reality of the Internet's 'virtuality'. Research shows that use of the Internet is often instrumental in character and is closely connected to work, family life and everyday life. For instance, 85% of Internet usage comprises email for work-related communication and for keeping in touch with family and friends (Wellman and Haythornthwaite, 2002). Furthermore, SNS offer popular communicative spaces for expressions of friendliness amongst peer-groups. Actors appropriate the Internet in various and diverse social practices, which creates new socio-cultural forms and patterns of interaction and communication. For instance, the Internet provides opportunities for role-playing and experimentation with identity, which commentators argue is creating virtual identities that are seen as 'fake'. However, most online role-playing and identity building is done by teenagers and is an extension of off-line adolescent practices (Castells, 2001). Baym (1998) found that most users create online selves consistent with their off-line identities. Research shows that, in use, the Internet is an extension of life, in all its dimensions, and with all its modalities, in which the 'real fights back' (Turkle, 1995). Nonetheless, the ethos of the early development of the Internet – openness and freedom – continues and can be seen in Barlow's libertarian Electronic Frontier Foundation which fosters unbounded sociability within a virtual community, as well as in the flexibility of Web-based communications via mobile phones and other Internet-enabled communication.

However, the process of commercialization generates pressures that influence the way the Internet develops in certain markets. Marketing interacts with the ways in which Internet-based products and services are appropriated, adapted or resisted by actors. These patterns of use influence the development of the Internet. Users, who inhabit certain roles and have distinct identities, (Livingstone, 2002) are to some degree producers as well as consumers. There is some degree of freedom in the ways in which consumer usage shapes the Internet, especially in relation to its shorter, highly distributed user–producer value chain. However, within this decentralized dynamic there are contradictory influences that generate a centralizing dynamic of the Internet. Thus, although as consumers, users can and do shape the Internet, the market expertise and power of techno-elites also create frameworks of development for user choices.

These dynamics blur any straightforward understanding of the virtual and the real, since the spheres of civil life and everyday life situate the contexts of Internet use more broadly within social and cultural dynamics. The way in which the Internet gets taken up reflects class differences, for instance those of a higher social status tend to have more geographically dispersed friends and family and email is a good way to keep in touch in this context. A study of Internet use and social interaction by Katz et al. (2001) found higher or equal level of community and political involvement among Internet-users compared to non-users. Their findings show that users of the Internet tend to have larger social networks than non-users when variables are managed. The Internet, in this context, seems to have a positive effect on social interaction as it enables wider networks of friends, increases exposure to information of various sorts and, through communication and information exchange, encourages people to attend more events and activities, both formal and informal. Their research shows that the Internet does not necessarily lower social interaction and increase social isolation but, when individuals who are already well connected take up the Internet, it can support their social activities.

The Transformation of Sociability: Networked Individualism and Networked Social Movements

A key part of late modernity, which also informs the formation of virtual community, is the displacement from community to network in terms of communities based on the sharing of values and social organization, and networks built on choices and strategies of social actors, families, individuals or social groups. Wellman and Haythornthwaite (2002), for instance, identify networks of interpersonal ties that provide sociability, support, information and a sense of belonging and social identity. A key transformation from place-based community is the development of weak and strong networks in which users adapt ICT to meet the needs of network sociability. Although theories of social capital point to the development of trust and relationships for the bonding of individuals as a prerequisite to crosscutting bridging networks for collective support and action this does not translate in any straightforward way to the Internet. Within communicative action, the practice of using the Internet is often experienced as a communication hybrid between physical space and cyberspace. This leads to an array of networks that reflect a diversity of social forms, some new, such as more individualized family life: families of choice; specialized communities; and portfolios of sociability (ibid.). These new configurations may not provide sources of secure social support and could introduce fragility in forms of social support in late modernity. Nonetheless, these new types of sociability do offer ways in which individuals and groups can celebrate diversity, plurality and choice.

The development of networks as a social form relates to the rise of individualism. Beck (1992) and Giddens (1991) claim that in late modernity one sees a system of social relationships centred on the individual that engenders a privatization of sociability. The Internet becomes embedded in this social form because networked individualism is a social pattern, not a collection of isolated individuals (see Chapter 8). Rather, individuals build their networks, online and off-line, on the basis of their interests, values, affinities, projects and cultures. Because of the flexibility and communication power of the Internet, online social interaction plays an increasing role in social organization as a whole. Online networks, when their practice is stabilized, may build virtual communities which are not necessarily less intense or less effective in binding and mobilizing than traditional place-based community (Castells, 2001).

There are threats to sociability through networks, communities of choice and online communication, in that what may emerge are patterns of inclusion and exclusion that are not progressive, inducing what Putnam (2000)[2] calls 'cyberbalkanization'. However, the network as a social form adapts and people are interacting to develop new forms of communication that provide support in an intermediated, informational society inhabited through mobility and in enclaves (Turner, 2007) of various forms. Thus, for example, from the technological point of view, wireless Internet and Web 2.0 may support new forms of sociability from bottom-up social and cultural developments materializing in social networking site such as Facebook, as a socio-cultural form that emanated from the student community (see Chapters 8, 9 and 10).

The use of a network extends to social movements which, in late modernity, involve purposive collective action that aims to transform the values and institutions of society which, to varying degrees, manifest themselves on and through communication on the Internet (Castells, 2001). Examples include movements based around labour, the environment, women, human rights, ethnic identities, religions and nationalism. Castells points out that there are four reasons for social movements to use the Internet. First, social movements in the information age are mobilized around cultural values. Second, social movements in the network society are filling a gap left by the crisis in vertically integrated organizations inherited from the industrial era. Third, the globalization of social movements is historically distinct due to globalization itself. Fourth, the global environment in which many civil society activists work requires them to 'act local and think global'. This dynamic is seen in at least six major social movements in global action: human rights, women, the environment, labour, religions and peace (Cohen and Rai, 2000).

Another emerging trend is the rise of citizen networks. Starting in the mid-1980s, developing in the 1990s and continuing today, many local communities are online and have a Web presence. These citizen networks are often linked with local institutions, municipal governments and grass-root citizen participation in local democratic processes. This activity generates information exchange, political organization and fora for debates, producing a form of democracy in cyberspace. Part of this process has fostered social entrepreneurs who work to process new forms of citizen engagement and self-representation (Castells, 2001). Examples include Cleveland Freenet and the Public Electronic Network in the US, Iperbole in Bologna, Italy and Amsterdam's Digital City in the Netherlands. Citizen networks usually provide information from local authorities as well as other civic associations, in effect producing an e-bulletin board of city life (ibid.). They also organize the horizontal exchange of information and conversation amongst network participants and they provide access to the Internet for those without it. A typical example of this type of network in the East End of London (UK) is Newham Online (Wessels, 2000a; Harrison and Wessels, 2005). This network seeks to foster participation, enhance local democracy and provide training, access to education and jobs; it has spread to new media industries, e-museum projects; young people online; and a local interactive digital television service (Harrison and Wessels, 2005). This type of networking activity is expanding globally, varying according to local context, cultures and levels of economic and technical development. For example, in North East India, the e-Arik project uses ICT to support agriculture in rural India. The WIDNET programme is an ICT based initiative of Zambia Association for Research and Development (ZARD) that seeks to promote and support women in Zambia. The Cell Bazaar service in Bangladesh facilitates online trade for buyers and sellers in a mobile marketplace. In Turkey, the Strengthening Networks in Turkey: Young Human Network project (SNiT) and the Mediterranean Youth Technology Club (MYTecC) are further examples. These types of developments, however, are dependent on an active local and regional civic society. The shaping of this civic society relates to, and feeds into broader society-level changes to which the discussion now turns.

The Social Dynamics of the Internet and Conceptualizing Information Society

The social environment of the Internet raises the issue of whether this environment constitutes an information society. Lyon (1988) addresses Toffler's (1980) argument and questions whether society is in a third wave. Toffler argues that change occurs in waves, with the first wave being agricultural, the second wave industrial and the third wave is the information society. Lyon suggests that the notion of information society has its roots in the concepts of leisure, service and post-industrial society. The question is whether post-industrial society has been superseded by an information society. Bell (1974) uses the notion of an axial principle to define the character of society, which acts as an energizing principle for all the other dimensions of society. Bell argues that the axial principle in post-industrial society is 'theoretical knowledge', and given this science and technology becomes more important in the economy, which results in a rise of professional, scientific and technical groups in society.

In relation to an information society, the question is whether information and its circulation via ICT is a central dynamic in changing social relations and society. When this is translated theoretically, the question is whether information is an axial principle within the dynamics of social change. However, Bell's approach does not fully account for the social relations of production and consumption of social change and how class-based distinctions are influential in shaping society. Lyon (1988) argues that by not addressing social relations Bell's analysis underestimates the resilience of some existing patterns of social relations and the extent to which new conflicts and struggles could arise in the information society. To understand post-industrial society, analysts seek to identify who holds the theoretical knowledge and which groups carry out practical tasks determined by theoreticians and what the structures are for doing so. To consider the information society, researchers need to address whether information, and its use through ICT, is a key dynamic in socio-economic relations. And if it is, how is it changing the social relations of production and consumption in society?

Touraine (1971) raises the issue of class dynamics and reasserts the question of class conflict by arguing that there is a major cleavage between a technocratic class and disparate social groupings whose lifestyles and livelihoods are governed by technology. The dominant class of technocrats holds power through its knowledge and its control of information, and the rise of social forecasters and planners forms a new stratum wielding power through their knowledge and planning capacity. Perkin (1989) argues that certified expertise is the 'organizing principle of post-war society', in which the 'expert' displaces once-dominant groups, with an ethos of service, certification and efficiency. Gouldner (1979) goes further, identifying a new class 'composed of intellectuals and technical intelligentsia'. This new class is divided in various ways with, on the one hand, some members taking technocratic and conformist positions whereas, on the other hand, are a number of humanist intellectuals taking a critical and emancipator stance. The contours of this distinction help to identify those who have the knowledge and power to shape social and economic developments. It may also indicate who are in subordinate positions and how this is materializing in working conditions and in class- or status-based social formations. The development of techno-elites or technocrats (Robins and Webster, 1999) is a significant factor because they have powerful leverage over social, economic and political affairs. These elites are empowered by their communication skills, analytical abilities, foresight and capability to formulate strategic policies; these skills are often obtained through privileged education, shared clubs, boardrooms and access to ICT (ibid.). The rise of theoretical knowledge, the reconfiguration of class positions, and new sources of power give some indication of social change. This, however, raises the issue of what are the specific aspects and necessary prerequisites of an information society (Webster, 1995).

Technological innovation is often cited as defining the information society because developments in ICT-based information management and communications have led to the pervasive implementation of ICT throughout social life. Within this technological determinist perspective, a convergence argument about the networking of computers is compared to the provision of electricity in that the 'information grid' is considered analogous to the electrical supply (ibid.). The development of technology is seen as an evolutionary process in which Integrated Services Digital Networks (ISDNs) provides the basis of an information society. Once these information networks are established, they become the highways of the information age in the same way that roads, railways and canals were the highways of the industrial era: thus 'computer technology is to the information age what mechanization was to the industrial revolution' (Naisbitt, 1984, p. 28). This determinist approach towards technology simplifies the process of change and posits that society becomes an information society when there is a critical level of technology take up (Webster, 1995). This is a reductionist approach because it does not consider the complexity of social change and that technological change requires institutional change.

Freeman (1992, 1994) counters this strong technological determinist view, arguing that it is the way in which technology is embedded within innovation cycles that gives it meaning in socio-economic change. Researchers at the Science Policy Research Unit (SPRU) (based at the University of Sussex, UK) take a neo-Schumpeterian approach to socio-technical change. Their approach combines Schumpeter's theory of innovation with Kondratieff's theme of 'long waves' of economic development to explain how ICT represents the establishment of a new epoch. This perspective avoids a reductionist technological determinism by analysing change through techno-economic paradigms (Freeman, 1992b, 1994). Freeman (in Mansell and Steinmuller, 2000) argues that an information-based economy is set to mature early in the twenty-first century and supports Piore and Sabel's (1984) argument that much of this economy will be characterized by flexible specialization in which small production units respond rapidly to niche markets with customized products made by adaptable, multi-skilled craftspeople. This type of production is related to the idea of a network – both the network as an organizational form (Castells, 2001; see chapter 5) – and as a networked society (Castells, 1996). Castells (1996) argues that the rise of networks that link people, institutions and countries characterize contemporary society. The purpose of these networks is for information to flow in what Castells defines as an 'informationalized society' – one in which 'information generation, processing, and transmission become the fundamental sources of power and productivity' (p. 21). The significance of this for Castells is that it is 'the new information technology paradigm (which) provides the material basis for (the network's) pervasive expansion throughout the entire social structure' (p. 469). Thus, the network underpins and is the infrastructure of society. However, this raises questions regarding the character of those networks' social relations, the role of institutions and information as a commodity within them.

Fuchs (2007a) addresses this question, arguing dialectically between the dynamics of old and new social relations. Fuchs defines a networked society as comprising transnational network capital or transnational informational capitalism. His main argument is that networked ICT provides the technological infrastructure that facilitates a global network of capitalism. However, he does not abstract this out of social relations, because networked capitalism involves regimes of accumulation, regulation and discipline. These economic, institutional and cultural factors make use of ICT to coordinate global production, distribution and consumption and require new strategies for executing corporate and political power and domination. Some of these strategies involve restructuring the organization of capital. This includes the rise of dynamic nodes of production that can be formed and reformed within a more fluid economic, political and cultural global marketplace. However, this capitalism retains many of its traditional features, principally that it is based on structural inequalities. There are central hubs such as global cities and technopoles that have the power and resources to centralize the production, control and flows of economic, political and cultural capital (ibid.). Therefore, networks are used in economic activity and society is still characterized by the social relations of capitalism. Both Marxist perspectives and Post-industrial approaches suggest that there are changes to some degree in the patterns of production and consumption. Some scholars seek to measure change based on categories of economic activity and occupation, which are considered below before returning to the issue of the social relations and restructured capitalism.

Machlup (1962) sought to assess the size and growth of the information industries by establishing measures of the information society in economic terms. He identified five broad industry groups: education; media of communication (radio, TV, advertising); information machines (computer equipment, musical instruments); information services (law, insurance, medicine); and other information activities (R&D, non-profit activities). He argued that as early as 1958, 29% of US GNP came from the knowledge industries. This led management commentators such as Drucker (1969), to argue that knowledge is the foundation of the economy, with the shift from an economy of goods to an economy of knowledge, with its organization being the prime creator of wealth (Porat, 1977). There is, however, as Webster (1995) states a methodological problem of categorization in that the secondary information sector work-related outputs are divided between informational and non-informational domains, but the division between 'thinking' and 'doing' is ambiguous. For example, where is the division between 'thinking' and 'doing' in the operation of computer numerical control systems of line management functions that are an integral element of the production process? The second difficulty is that the aggregated data homogenize a vast range of economic activities and Webster argues that informational activities vary qualitatively: for example, four million sales of *The Sun* newspaper cannot be equated with, or considered more informational than, the 200,000 circulation of the *Financial Times*, even though the sales are doubtless of more economic value. On top of the ambiguities of measuring information work there is the issue of identifying 'at what point on the economic graph does one enter an information society?' (p. 56).

Another main argument focuses on the occupational profile within societies, and contends that there is an 'information society' when the majority of occupations are based on informational work (ibid.). This argument asserts that the 'information society' has arrived when clerks, teachers, lawyers and entertainers outnumber coalminers, steelworkers, dockworkers and builders, and it is frequently combined with economic measures (Porat 1977a, b; Stonier, 1983). The recognition of the changing distribution of occupations is a central aspect in sociological approaches that argue for a post-industrial society, which have also informed debates regarding the information society. Bell (1974) argues for a 'white collar society', in which there is a rise of service-related work, including informational work, with a corresponding decline of industrial labour. Changes in occupational structures, he argues, is resulting in changes in the social realm, such as the end of class-based political conflict, the development of a more-communal consciousness and the development of equality between the sexes (see Chapter 5). Many of the discussions regarding the information society fuse with those of the emergence of a post-industrial society but neither approach adequately identifies a new society that is either an information society or a post-industrial society (Webster, 1995).

There is a methodological issue regarding the ways in which workers are assigned particular occupational categories. Porat (1977a, b) develops three broad areas of work into which he can fit 400 different occupations, while Jonscher (1983) simplifies occupational categorization further by having two sectors: one the 'information' sector and the other the 'production' sector. This does not reflect the nature and range of occupations, nor does it express what informational work is, or the degrees to which different types of work are informational. Neither does it provide insights about the gradations of informational jobs, some of which are more routine, and some of which have strategic and managerial responsibilities (Webster, 1995). It therefore fails to identify the hierarchies and associated variations in power and esteem of workers differentially positioned within the economy and within organizational structures. The few ethnographies of working lives, such as the work of Terkel (1977) and the more recent study by Woodfield (2000) show the complexity and blurring of straightforward categories of occupation in relation to skill-sets and routines as well as gender in 'high-tech' companies (see Chapter 5).

The drive to networked communication and networked organization of economic production has a spatial dimension to it which, when taken with other dimensions of change, starts to allude to the richness needed to define the information society. The logic of networks is that they connect locations globally, overriding the industrial organization of space and time, thereby introducing the capacity to alter the organization of capitalism. Goddard (1992) shows how four interrelated elements in the transition to an informational economy are related spatially via networks:

1. Information is a 'key strategic resource' on which the world economy is dependent.
2. Computer and communication technologies provide the infrastructure that enables information to be processed and distributed.
3. There is a rapid growth of the 'tradable information sector' seen in the expansion of new media, and online bases of information as well as in reorganization of the world's financial system with the development of high finance trading.
4. The growing 'informatization' of the economy is, with supporting policy and infrastructures, facilitating the integration of national and regional economies (cited by Webster 1995, p. 18).

Therefore, from a geographical perspective, Goddard (1992) argues that when these trends are taken together, they emphasize the centrality of information networks linking together locations within and between towns, regions, nations, continents and the world. In part this addresses Webster's (1995) point that networks have been part of social life in both traditional and industrial societies, which means addressing how new ICT-based networks are significant in forming an information society. In a geographical sense one can see changes that interact with the economy, which impact on national and regional society. Part of the social dimension of this trend is the cultural characteristics of the various flows of information and how these interact with contemporary culture.

An important part of contemporary culture is the pervasiveness of the media in daily life that spans public and private spheres, circulating a large amount of information. In Westernized countries there is a high penetration of television and radio and new media. In contemporary society, social experience is mediated (Smith, 1988) with actors adapting, rejecting, interpreting and using media in different ways (Silverstone, 2005; Harrison and Wessels, 2005). The mobile phone, for instance, is a central communications medium in organizing everyday personal and work life as well as circulating information and news[3] (Haddon, 2004, 2008). The media's informational reach is extensive, informing but not necessarily determining style and aesthetics of individuals, homes and lifestyles within the symbolic realm (Webster, 1995). The intrusion of information in these realms is accomplished by the global advertising business, publishing empires, the fashion industry and worldwide agencies of media production.

With regard to this trend, some commentators argue that there is an 'explosion of signification' which indicates the emergence of an information society. In particular, Baudrillard (1994) argues that the 'death of the sign' has occurred in media-saturated society with the circulation of more and more information that has less and less meaning. This means that clothes used to signify status, a political statement a political philosophy, and television news reflected world events (Webster, 1995). However, the way in which the reach of media has expanded and has reworked symbols means that signs no longer signify an established symbolic order and social meaning – thereby potentially emptying meaning from representation. Many actors in the Western world, therefore, experience social life as hyper-reality, as spectacle and artificiality, which Poster (1990) defines as a new 'mode of information'. Although there is a proliferation of media-generated images, it is the way in which these are interpreted and adapted in social life that grounds them and gives them significance within social formations, hence they are one aspect of the ways in which life becomes meaningful – they are part of culture, rather than necessarily determining culture.

In broader terms the discussion so far indicates that patterns of production, distribution and consumption are changing and that ICT forms part of those changes. These changes are configured around a rethinking of the use of information in economic and cultural life in which they retain the features of social relations based on capitalism. To trace some of these trends spanning both continuity and change, Fuchs (2008) argues that society based on informational capitalism is a class society because capital accumulation achieved through knowledge is a stratifying, class-forming process. He catches the current ambiguities of change by pointing out that knowledge labour is simultaneously a non-class and a class, based on the argument that economic class is a relational economic category.[4] He defines knowledge labour in a similar fashion to the theorists discussed above – as labour that produces information, communication, social relationships and ICT. Given this definition, knowledge labour is not a separate class, but an economic production process constituting a vertical sector of the economy. This quaternary sector produces knowledge and, in these terms, knowledge labour is a non-class.

The crux of his argument is that, by viewing knowledge as a broad social category instead of a narrow sector-specific economic category, it becomes evident that it lies at the heart of class formation in informational capitalism. Knowledge forms part of the commons of society, it is a social product which is produced and consumed by all and includes educational knowledge, entertainment knowledge, practical knowledge, technological knowledge and public infrastructures (institutions in the areas of health, education, medical services, social services, culture, media and politics). There is therefore a blurring of clear, observable class distinctions because most people contribute to the production and reproduction of the commons but, nonetheless, global capital exploits surplus value. Therefore, although there is some evidence of changing occupational categories and cultural change, broadly speaking the social relations of capital are being reproduced in new forms. These theorizations give some indication of the complexity of researching and understanding social change.

To be more specific and with respect to the difficulties of observing and understanding social and technological change, Mansell and Steinmuller (2000) argue that assessing change to an information society is difficult because the transformations that are occurring in the use of the ICT infrastructure are so pervasive. From their research of developments towards an information society in Europe, they find that the use of new ICT and services is influencing not only costs of inputs and the nature of the outputs in the economy, but also the way in which work is organized and skills are articulated. If researchers want to assess the potential effects of a specific feature of information society developments, such as the growth in e-commerce, it is necessary for them to take into account the possible implications that e-commerce will have on existing ways of doing business, the organization of work and the use of leisure time. They see an associating structural transformation of the labour force with the spread of ICT infrastructure. This leads to a growth in the service economy, along with a growing need for technological advances to improve service activity and productivity. These service outputs are extremely malleable and services change rapidly, including changes in the way labour is organized that involve innovations, such as call-centres, user-support hotlines and direct marketing automation.

Mansell and Steinmuller argue that changes in the economy cannot be attributed exclusively to the development of ICT and the diffusion of new services. Ever-increasing levels of education and the expansion of specialized labour make it possible to engage in a growing variety of activities that are connected with, or ancillary to, the production of goods and services. These trends are reshaping some aspects of the division of labour, with former management functions conducted on the shop floor and individual workers and teams taking responsibility for the flow of production (Sennet, 1998, 2001). The upgrading of job descriptions is linked to a new division of labour. Given these organizational and technological changes, Mansell and Steinmuller (2000) argue that there are changing requirements for skills, and that there is a need to understand exactly what skills are required and how they are acquired. These skills need to be measured without oversimplifying their characteristics.

They also argue that in Europe, the voluntary sector is a source of new jobs as well as offering opportunities for individuals to gain new skills, thus contributing to social well-being. Other important actors are local government and their regional partnerships, which are producing innovations in a variety of e-services and e-inclusion programmes (Harrison and Wessels, 2005; Wessels, 2008). Regional and municipal governments are taking a proactive role in fostering new businesses, including those involving the Internet and the production of informational and creative content. Both the voluntary sector and civic government efforts are key components of virtual community strategies which may well be effective in ensuring that the movement to an information society can benefit all. Mansell and Steinmuller (2000) argue, however, that the development of an information society is extremely difficult to predict and that it needs new forms of measurement and better understanding. They argue that R&D has to be carved out from incumbent legacies and must embrace insurgent strategies – not only for economic competitiveness and improving political engagement but also to facilitate a virtual community strategy to underpin an ICT-literate society. Mansell and Steinmuller continue by arguing that these dimensions of change involve the mobilization of society across all dimensions and require an expansion of the vision of information society by dynamic players and emergent communities. This observation suggests that analysis of information society involves addressing broader social and economic issues as they interact with cultural and political dynamics. This requires analysis to explore developments that use ICT and expand the use of networks, identify their characteristics and understand how they may, or may not be changing society. The social landscape of the Internet, therefore, is significant in understanding the ways in which the character-istics of the Internet are taken up and adapted across the dimensions of social life and society.[5]

Conclusion

The social landscape of the Internet is made up of various relations between the technology and social practices that are expressive of the broader rela-tionship between the two. The social landscape in which the Internet is materializing is one that is flexible, adaptable and communicative. The dis-embedding of time and space and the rise of mediated and remote com-munications in a more mobile society means that individuals find new ways to participate and express community as well as constructing and reconstructing forms and expressions of identity. Networked individual-ism is a social form of late modernity that bridges many established and emerging social and cultural forms – hence the dualism of the virtual and the real, the online and the off-line are mitigated through social agency.[6]

The dynamics of these broad themes are also interpolated into socio-economic trends. The organization of capitalism is adapted to exploit infor-mation as a commodity globally resulting in networked transnational capitalism. The character of work is changing in this environment with work being more explicitly focused on information in its various guises. However, inequalities remain and, although there is a re-labelling of jobs, income-based and elite positional distinctions remain. These inequalities are often related to underlying contradictions and a definition of informa-tion society based on Bell's post-industrial thesis does not fully address these inequalities as it does not focus on the capitalist relations of production. This is significant because – as in other spheres of life – work and the economy bridge both legacy systems and evolving new forms. One, therefore, sees continuities of old institutions – senses of community and identity; work and economy; and ideals of civil society, social movements and democratic engagement. One also sees how these institutions are being reconfigured by the agency of individuals and organizations and their appropriation of ICT. One can say that the changes in late modernity represent a change in forms of communication (Silverstone, 2005) but the continuities in soci-ety mean that the concept and actuality of an information society remain 'problematic'.

5

Work and the Internet

Introduction

The topic of work and the Internet expands some of the themes identified in the previous chapter, such as the renegotiation of time and place seen in notions of flexible, virtual and mobile work. Bearing in mind the difficulty of defining a new economy and informational capitalism (Braithwaite and Drahos, 2000) the economy is nonetheless increasingly being managed through the use of the Internet-based networks. However, the extent, character and consequences of any of these changes are questioned by assessing the ways in which the work has and has not changed. This includes addressing the characteristics of relationship between management and labour and asking whether work remains not only highly controlled but also increasingly unprotected through contract-based work. These discussions lead to a critical assessment of the implicit promise of the 'restored relationship' in a better work–life balance with electronic cottage and flexible forms of work. These issues are strongly interlaced with the gendering of organizational cultures. Women's access to, and experience of, work in an e-enabled economy, shows that the use of the Internet in the context of work reproduces existing social relations, inequalities and hierarchies as well as challenging them. These aspects need to be understood in the broader context of how the Internet as a socio-cultural form is interacting with work and the organization of economic life. This involves addressing the relations of production within modes of production and the narratives that express those relations as well as the characteristics of participation in forms of work.

Relations of Production: The Changing Context of Work

To understand the experience of work and the way it may or may not be changing means understanding broader changes in the social relations of the economic and business spheres. The general context is the move from Fordist to post-Fordist modes of production which are reshaping both work and social and cultural life, including, for instance, the readjustment of women's roles in the workplace and their related roles in everyday life. Fordism refers to the use of the assembly lines, standardization and mass markets based on class that primarily characterized production and consumption between the 1940s and the 1960s. However, with recession in national economies within manufacturing and industrial sectors and the emergence of globalization in the mid-1970s, Fordism was undermined. Post-Fordism signifies a change to more flexible production for niche markets based on consumer typologies and preferences. Production is often based on 'just-in-time' processes that are, in part, enabled through ICT on a global scale. It also involves a rise of white-collar and service sector jobs in which there is a feminization of the workforce. Shifts to post-Fordism produce new dynamics in relation to social inclusion and exclusion, which also interact with aspects of the digital divide such as needing the relevant skills to work in the new economy. Post-Fordism is closely interrelated with consumer society and ongoing developments in patterns of consumption. These trends are part of the globalization of the economy in which the production and consumption of goods is organized on a global scale. The current informational capitalism (Castells, 1996) or transnational informational capitalism (Fuchs, 2007a) underpinning globalization means that there is an inequity within the system that not only affects producers and consumers but also shapes the character of work and types of occupations and reward structures. By addressing the question of change through a Fordist/post-Fordist lens, the analysis is one of social shaping rather than taking a form of technological determinism.

McLoughlin (1999) develops a critique of post-industrial theories of society and related information society discourse. He asserts that post-industrial and information society arguments posit that technology is a determining factor in social change, including that of work and organization. These accounts tend to have positive views of ICT arguing that its use can improve working environments. Part of an improved context of work includes an expanded range of highly skilled and enriching jobs, more autonomous and less alienating forms of work, and more harmonious and consensual relations between management and labour (ibid., p. 48). From a post-industrial perspective, the motivation for firms to implement technology is to improve their competitive position (Wilkinson, 1983) and any other consequences or utilizations are, on the whole, seen as incidental (McLoughlin, 1999).

Labour process theorists critique the post-industrial theorists' optimistic and positive scenarios of ICT-enabled work in the information society paradigm. In general terms, critical commentators question whether the emerging use of ICT within new forms of production is different from the predominant post-Fordist mass production paradigm. They also raise the issue that the use of ICT is ushering in new forms of electronic surveillance in the workplace. Many of the critical perspectives stem from the work of Braverman (1974) who developed a Marxist approach to changing trends in modes of production and related patterns of consumption. Whereas Bell and other post-industrial writers concentrate on the internal logic of the move from an industrial mode of production to a post-industrial one, Braverman locates change within the capitalist mode of production (Knights et al., 1985; Knights and Wilmott, 1988; Thompson, 1989). Critical approaches point to continuity in many aspects of work rather than to any radical transformations in the social relations of economic and working life.

A key theme within critical perspectives stresses the ways in which management seeks to maintain control over workers, which is based on a principal argument within Marxism that there is fundamental conflict between labour and capital. This conflict is structural and is located in the relationship between the few who own the means of production and the masses who do not and who are therefore forced to sell their labour. The private owners of the means of production want to maximize profits, and part of ensuring good returns from their investments entails controlling the workers and their levels of productivity. This means that the main role of management is to have 'control over the labour process' (Braverman, 1974, p. 63). Given this need to control labour within the capitalist process, labour process theorists ask if relations between labour and management have changed in the organization of work within information society scenarios. They argue that the process of re-labelling jobs into an expanding stratum of information and knowledge workers hides continuity within labour and managerial relations. Therefore, although economists such as Porat (1977) produce statistics based on changing job titles, labour process theorists address the ways in which work continues to be controlled through deskilling (in which work is fragmented and workers lose the integrated skills and comprehensive knowledge of crafts persons) – with skilled job titles masking deskilled jobs.

Labour process theory posits that ICT and the Internet are being used to enhance ways of controlling the workforce. In industrial contexts, control of the workforce was achieved through the scientific management techniques of 'Taylorism'[1] and 'Fordism'.[2] Key principles of these techniques are the separation of 'conception', the mental labour of planning and decision-making, from 'execution', the exercise of manual labour. These systems require direct personal supervision of workers. However, the use of ICT can eliminate the need for direct personal supervision of workers as management can use ICT to control and deskill workers by either automating out the need for direct human intervention or by using ICT to break down jobs into fragmented work processes that each requires little conceptual ability. Looking at the developments of ICT from this perspective, there is little evidence of any radical break from the past, rather there is the maintenance and continued centralized control of labour by management using ICT (McLoughlin, 1999, p. 49). Through networked technologies, this control is extended outside of the factory and office to mobile workers, homeworkers and outsourced functionaries. Braverman's (1974) argument can therefore be extended to ICT, in that ICT can negate 'the control functions of the worker, insofar as is possible, and their transfer to a device which is controlled, again insofar as is possible, by management from outside the direct process' (ibid., p. 115).

The materialization of labour relations, ICT and work in the relations of production emerges in organizational forms. A significant aspect of the global economy is e-business, which is 'any business activity whose performance of the key operations of management, finance, innovation, production, distribution, sales, employee relations and customer relations takes place predominantly by/on the Internet or other networks of computer networks, regardless of the kind of connection between the virtual and physical dimensions of the firm' (Castells, 2001, p. 66). Castells argues that 'by using the Internet as a fundamental medium of communication and information processing, business adopts the network as its organizational form' (ibid.). He defines the network enterprise as a 'lean agency of economic activity, built around specific business projects, which is enacted by networks of various composition and origin: the network is the enterprise' (ibid., p. 67). The firm continues to be the unit of accumulation of capital, property rights and strategic management, but networks perform the business practice. Networks are flexible and adaptable and can therefore meet the requirements of continuous innovation and the rapidly changing demands of the global economy. The role of the Internet in these kinds of network enterprises is that it enables 'scalability, interactivity, and management of flexibility, branding, and customization in a networked business world' (ibid.).

The way in which the network materializes in practice is varied and is open to debate. However, the notion of virtual working can act as a sensitizing concept for discussing any possible changes in the character of work. Jackson (1999) identifies the key themes in the literature on virtual working, which are

- The collapse of hierarchy and an erosion of boundaries, both within and between companies;
- A concentration on 'information processing', in which teams and individuals, using ICT, create and manipulate information-based, 'virtual' products;

- The use of networked ICT to empower consumers, providing new ways of interacting with businesses and greater access to information about their products;
- A movement away from employment relations, towards more arm's-length, contractual relationships with workers;
- Transient, project-based work systems, involving networks of co-workers, suppliers and associated companies;
- Flexibility in time and space, with interactions mediated by cyberspace;
- Reduced use of 'centres', buildings and offices;
- A sense of disembodiment, with imagery emphasizing a lack of physicality and corporeality;
- An emphasis on continuous innovation and learning, and a capacity rapidly to reinvent business models. (Jackson, 1999, p. 13)

The above trends embody many of the characteristics of the relationship between the Internet and society: the emphasis on the circulation and use of information, networking, the renegotiation of time and space, senses of the virtual and the real, ongoing learning through the life-course and a shorter value chain between consumers and producers. Understanding if and how these trends are materializing and gaining meaning in contemporary life involves addressing the narratives of work and the ways in which workers participate and negotiate in new forms of work. As the discussion below shows, Jackson's (ibid.) definition of a virtual organization in real terms is complex and is not easily developed.

Narratives Regarding Work in the e-Economy

Castells (2001) argues that companies depend on the quality and autonomy of labour. The e-economy needs workers who can succeed in a digital informational environment. Workers, therefore, have to be able to navigate – both technically and in terms of content – vast amounts of information, organize it, focus it and transform it into specific knowledge, appropriate for the task and purpose of the work process (ibid.). Castells argues that this kind of labour needs to be highly educated and able to take initiative. Labour in this context must be able to re-programme itself, in skills, knowledge and thinking, according to changing tasks in evolving business environments. This type of labour, defined as 'self-programmable', requires a certain type of education through which the stock of knowledge and information accumulated in the worker's experience can be expanded and modified throughout his or her working life. The combination of these factors is resulting in what is termed the 'knowledge-worker', which involves ongoing, self-directed 'e-learning' in professional life. The heightened levels of autonomy and involvement in project-based patterns of work are often combined in a light-touch form of cooperative ownerships. These factors induce workers to have a total commitment to business projects that extend well beyond contractual arrangements. For example, professionals working in and around Silicon Valley regularly work approximately 65 hours per week and, at times of project delivery, these professionals will work around the clock until the deadline is met (ibid.).

Not all labour, of course, is within the professional strata. For instance, immigration is a key source of talent across the labour market on the one hand, and on the other hand, there is generic labour, which is not 'self-programmable' including, for instance, those employed in call centres as well as routine manual work. In most domains of labour the characteristic of labour relations is flexibility – and the notion of 'flexibility' is a key element in the narrative of work in the e-economy. Carnoy (2000) argues that flexibility within the labour market manifests itself in several forms of employment relations, such as self-employment, part-time work, temporary work, subcontracting, consulting and in new contractual forms of commercial employment. The various employment patterns and the differing character of working practices, as well as the individualization of working life means that knowledge-workers are not a homogeneous group (Huws et al., 1990, p. 103). Flexible working can therefore be narrated from the point of view of the elite flexible worker who can dictate his or her terms of employment or from a teleworker parent who has to combine work and family obligations (Galpin and Sims, 1999). Reich (1997) labels this distinction in the contemporary labour market evocatively as that of an elite and a peasantry. In less evocative terms, the European Commission (1994) places teleworkers into two groups: middle-class, self-motivated individuals or low-wage relatively unskilled workers who are desperate for work and, therefore, open to exploitation. Galpin and Sims (1999) talk about this distinction in terms of a skilled elite core referred to as knowledge-workers and an unskilled group known as 'operatives'.

Changes to notions of an ideal worker in the high-tech sector serve as a good template for understanding the narratives that underpin telework. The rise of the 'hybrid worker', as someone who has both social and technical skills, in software organizations in the mid-1980s signified a changing narrative of the characteristics of workers (Woodfield, 2000). The rise of key words such as flexibility, service, customization and communication found in commercial narratives for achieving success in the market generates a rethinking of skills and aptitudes (ibid.). For example, Deakin (1984) argues that 'advice, the translation and communication of ideas and the provision of intelligent information' (ibid., p. 17) are important in the high-tech sector. Woodfield (ibid.) argues that progressive organizations address the softer skills in pursuing commercial success because intangibles are an important part of the value chain within the ICT and service sectors. A consequence of this change is that these skills are seen to dovetail with gendered characteristics. Woodfield (2000) states that women's socialization shapes them to be more empathetic, to share information and foster cooperative working, and have better interpersonal skills (c.f. Hochschild, 1983; Frenier, 1997; Tannen, 1995). Turkle (1985) adds to this view from a programming perspective. She asserts that women have a 'soft mastery' of computing due to their gendered development path which ensures that they learn the softer skills of negotiation, compromise and give and take (ibid., p. 108). The narrative of work in the new economy is one of softer skills, flexibility and cooperative working, which manifests itself differently across levels of knowledge workers and operatives.

The concept of teleworking from home is located within the popular narrative of a rural idyll in which the work–life balance is regained through evoking a romantic notion of the tele-cottage or electronic cottage (Toffler, 1980). The imagery behind it is that teleworking reduces employers' costs by transferring overhead costs to employees and enables greater flexibility in the workforce. The restored work–life relationship promises that workers will have less commuting time, more flexibility, greater adaptability of working hours across their life course and a better ability to balance working life with domestic life. It is also argued that these adaptations increase productivity, lower office and travel costs and generate a higher morale among employees. However, this optimistic view has to be tempered, as there are constraints and disadvantages to teleworking from both management and worker perspectives. From a management perspective, managers are concerned that they will have less control over their employees when they are not physically present in the office, which also raises questions about the ubiquity of electronic surveillance in the workplace. On the other hand, workers often feel isolated, and many are anxious about being overlooked in the allocation of assignments or promotions because they are less visible. Furthermore, many home-workers find that they work very long hours due to the difficulties of managing the work–home boundary. Thompson (1985) sums up this cottage industry as 'not only roses and thatch, but also long hours of toil by the dim light of rush candles for inadequate subsistence wages', which may be updated with 'backache and eyestrain of long hours keying-in at the visual display unit' (p. 22). These concerns can lead to resistance to teleworking, with both managers and employees wanting to retain more place-based patterns of work.

These narratives about working life in the advanced economies interact with and impact upon existing gender relations. Gender relations within industrial society are based on the man being the main wage earner with the woman largely undertaking domestic work and participating in paid employment only in a part-time and/or low-level capacity. The trend towards flexibility in labour relations and the emphasis on softer skills within post-industrial contexts is characterized as the demise of 'organization man' with the rise of 'flexible woman' – representing a move from an industrial pattern of work to a post-industrial or information society pattern of work (Castells, 2001). Evidence of this trend can be seen in California, one of the highest take-up areas of ICT related work, where only 33% of Californian workers fit into industrial patterns of work (ibid.). Although European labour markets are less flexible, the overall trend points to this labour marker heading in the same direction as the United States. The narrative of work in post-industrial and information society is composed of work flexibility, variable employment patterns, diversity of working conditions and the individualization of labour. Castells argues that these are systemic features of e-business. Flexible labour practices are part of a new form of social structure, which Castells characterizes as network society.

These narratives underpin some of the changing contexts of work that relate to the 'technological-cum-economic imperative' (Freeman, 1994) of improving productivity through the application of ICT paradigms in business. The social aspects of these technological and economic drives include

1. Under-employment, due to replacing people with machines (Bell, 1974; Freeman, 1997).
2. Deskilling, in which computerized functions enable the same jobs to be performed by people with lower skill levels (Braverman, 1974; Attewell, 1987).
3. Increased stress, through the speeding up of work and heightening time pressures (Attewell, 1987).
4. Surveillance, by increasing the monitoring and electronic surveillance of the workplace (Attewell, 1987; Zuboff, 1988).

Dutton (2001) challenges the pursuit for competitive advantage through ICT by focusing on social concerns of the consequences of economically driven change. He addresses some of the issues concerning participation in the workplace.

Participation in the Workplace

Dutton (2001) critically explores developments within workplaces, which form intersections between the practice of work, the narratives of working life and broader organizational, social and economic change. Dutton argues that the nature of workplace is shaped by technology and work practices in three distinct ways:

1. The dynamics of the increasing centrality of ICT in the workplace.
2. The changing composition of the workforce.
3. The relocation of work across time and space.

An overarching theme across these dimensions of change is that of flexibility in the workplace, which Dutton argues is more than technological change in that it requires social and cultural change.

It is the way in which technology becomes appropriated, used (or not) and resisted that shapes it within its contexts of use. The take-up and adaptation of technology is an iterative, contested and complex process (Cornford et al., 2004). Analysis that addresses the impact of ICTs on work, in a determinist way, overestimates the influences of management strategies, such as moves towards virtual organizations, and underestimates the role of users, whose habits, skills and attitudes shape the production and use of ICTs in ways that support or constrain tele-access strategies (Dutton, 2001, p. 152). The idea of contexts of work points to the way in which the workplace not only varies in form but is also located and shaped within a framework comprised of the goals and strategies of broader economic actors; the public at large as customers and users of ICT; and the workers themselves – their skills, knowledge and expectations. It is the dynamics of these actors and their actions that shape the characteristics of change.

Dutton argues that researchers, and anyone involved in producing technological and organizational change, must understand 'users'. This term covers an array of user-groups, from organizations, their managers and workers, to everyday technology and media users. Lievrouw and Livingstone (2006) expand on this point by arguing that users have particular social characteristics and identities, such as parent, child, nurse, doctor, administrator and so on. The various situations of distinctive groups of users in social relations of work contexts are important in understanding the way in which technology gets taken up and appropriated. Given the process of technological appropriation, the analysis of the use of ICT at work needs to consider organizational change and the ways in which different types of workers adapt the technology within new forms of work.

One example of organizational change is the development of the networked office. This is a central aspect of tele-access within a range of organizational forms related to work practice. The drive to implement networked computers with word-processing functions in offices is based on the quest to improve efficiency. It is aligned with a narrative of using ICT to integrate and distribute information and activities. The use of ICT is seen to circumvent and overcome place-bound and geographical constraints in the organization of work (Uhlig et al., 1979). Although this vision is as yet imperfectly realized, its rationale is interacting with existing work relations producing a range of consequences. One primary consequence is some 'deskilling' of office workers who are seen as mere cogs in a 'distributed' assembly line with, on the other hand, the emergence of highly skilled information workers who act as gatekeepers in the office domain. Another aspect is that in the implementation and rationalization of technology in the office some routine office tasks have been reduced. Furthermore, the use of ICT to 'automate' (Zuboff, 1988) the office has reproduced the existing hierarchical and patriarchal structures of office work, which maintains the *status quo* within labour relations.

In general terms, early adaptations of ICT in the office tended to 'automate' existing working practices. However, through engaging with the ICT some managers and employees started to think about the way they worked, and how they could use ICT to change their working practices and environments, thus pushing towards 'informating' the office (ibid.). In this context, workers started to use ICT in different ways and in so doing challenged established roles and practices within organizations. This together with ICT infrastructure for tele-access and management strategies fed into the development of networked forms of organization and work practices. The combination of the changing character of some working practices with attempts to improve efficiency and the development of an ICT infrastructure gave rise to the concept of 'alternative officing', which acted as a catalyst in the deconstruction of traditional conceptions of the office and its reconfiguration.

Dutton (2001) argues that re-engineering office work into alternative officing involves three core factors. First, there is the drive to economize through standardizing offices, which seeks to reduce costs per employee through modular open office designs or cubicles. Second, there is the development of sharing facilities, by which individuals and teams share office space, using a 'first come first served basis', by 'hotelling' or 'hot-desking'. Third, organizations use space outside their physical environment, such as the home, tele-centres, satellite offices, customer premises, mobile offices and corporately provided mobile devices. The development of tele-access has also generated a new category of workers, namely teleworkers. The rise of teleworkers as a type covers a vast array of work profiles and patterns, such as remote work from electronic-cottages, call centres, home and other outsourced arrangements; mobile workers who communicate via mobile ICT; those who mix office and mobile work (Wessels et al., 2008); as well as those working from alternative offices. All of these forms extend the reach of the office in space and time. Common to all these patterns is that workers have a range of ICT-related communication and information skills. These generic skills are, however, located within a diverse range of work environments, professions and work-specific skills.

The case of tele-homework is one example of new forms of work. Haddon (1998) and Haddon and Silverstone (1993, 1994) differentiate tele-homework from traditional homeworking. Traditional homeworking involves small-scale manufacturing or the provision of services in the home, whereas tele-homeworking involves some processing of information, ranging from professional tasks to clerical ones. However, and in relation to the problem of defining informational work, Haddon and Silverstone (ibid.), point out that this is only a guide because the boundaries of telework are not clear. What Haddon and Silverstone illustrate is the way in which roles and responsibilities of professional and white-collar levels are blurred in telework. On the one hand, clerical work is becoming increasingly professional with the expansion of skills and training within the clerical role and, on the other hand, many professionals, such as academics, work from home, and are 'teleworking'. Broadly speaking, therefore, information processing using ICT is part of work in general, including small businesses and traditional homework.

Haddon and Silverstone identify three main types of terms of employment in tele-homework. One type is the employer-organized schemes, which are very often relevant to female employees who are expecting or have children and want to spend more time at home with them. Another type is when individuals request that they telework in organizations without broader schemes and are granted an individual telework arrangement. Yet another type is one where workers become self-employed and undertake contract work for the organization (ibid.). Very often, becoming self-employed is a strategy that older workers take if they feel marginalized or are overlooked in the job market. All of these terms provide flexible working arrangements but, apart from the employer-organized schemes, they leave many workers without adequate union protection and job security.

Call centres are also part of the broader trend of 'distributed work' (Dutton, 2001, p. 152). Goddard and Richardson (1996) argue that a significant aspect of the use of ICT in work is the 'spatial re-organization of the functions and personnel' of a firm or organization (cited in Dutton, 2001, p. 152). As Moss (1987), Goddard (1994) and Goddard and Richardson (1996) point out, this process of spatial reorganization started in the 1970s, primarily in the banking and finance sector, including insurance companies and some other firms. Organizations relocated clerical staff from 'back offices' at headquarter-sites in central business areas in cities to sites outside of those central areas. Out-of-town sites are less expensive than business districts within city centres; in particular, the cost of buildings and human resources are lower. This spatial reorganization with its underpinning economic rationale is played out beyond the city and its periphery to

wider global, geographical dimensions. Very often, this involves organizations based in Western economies using labour and space in less-developed
economies because both of these resources are cheaper there. For example,
Dutton (2001) cites the way in which companies employ computer programmers in India where wages and site-costs are lower than in Western
advanced economies. The distribution of call-centres follows a similar logic,
albeit involving more routine work and less skilled labour. This type of
arrangement is usually understood as 'outsourcing' and is a form of the
de-centralization of organizational functions. Some geographically distributed firms also centralize administration functions, such as accounting and
billing, by outsourcing these aspects of their work to a central hub (Dutton,
2001, p. 153).

The call centre is part of the spatial re-organization of work; it origin-
ates in the finance, insurance and travel industries and spread into many
other sectors, including the public sector. The development of telephones
and ICT in telework is heightened in call centres; On the one hand, these
centres are enabled by ICT infrastructure providing access to information
and, on the other hand, customer interactions are via the telephone, and
increasingly email and Web-based transactions. Call centres, through ICT,
handle large volumes of interactions and often operate on a 24/7 basis.
They can do this partly because of where they are located: often in places
where labour is relatively cheap, and where there is an appropriate ICT
infrastructure, such as less-developed countries like India (Taylor, 2005)
and de-industrialized regions in Western economies, such as Northern
England (Richardson and Belt, 2001).

Richardson and Belt explore the training of call centre workers. They note
that many of the workers are sourced from de-industrialized areas, which
are characterized by high levels of long-term unemployment and low educational attainment. Given this background and the employers' need for
cheap labour, Richardson and Belt explore the character of pre-training
courses that individuals undertake prior to actual call centre training.
They found that potential workers are trained to have a customer-oriented
focus, and to have a friendly manner and pleasant phone etiquette. In these
pre-training centres they also learn work discipline. Both the training and
the work are highly monitored and centrally controlled, with calls regularly listened to and recorded. Not only are call centre staff monitored but
customers' calls are also rated to filter out high cost, low yield customers.
Stringent targets are set and performance is logged and monitored. In addition, timing of work practices are strictly allocated and policed, removing
any opportunity for initiatives from the workers. From these observations,
Richardson and Belt argue that call centre workers' work, although mediated through ICT, is 'aestheticized' in a similar way to that of sales staff
in department stores. Furthermore, call centre work is tightly controlled

through forms of remotely facilitated management techniques such as the monitoring of calls and performance.

Participation and Organizational Issues

The organization is the most dominant form in which work in contemporary life is managed and conducted. Each organization, in various ways, is composed of structures, workers, production and market-oriented functions, labour, including management, professional and routine workers, and information and communications systems. An important aspect of organizations is their culture, and organizational culture gives meaning to the organization and those working within it. The central thrust of organizational studies is focused on the organization itself; however, the focus for understanding telework is both addressing the organization and its relationship with the environment. Manning (1982), for example, argues that, organizations structure their environments, and the relationship between technology and organizations can be extended into its environment, which is important in the rise of remote and mobile work. Case studies suggest that a technological determinist approach does not capture the way in which technology is negotiated in struggles over the control of working practices between workers and management (Dutton, 2001). These negotiations also highlight that management visions are adapted in the process and actuality of working practices. Nonetheless, to underestimate the influence of organizational structures and process is to miss an important factor in the dynamics of telework because they are influential in shaping the parameters of work and its practices.

The negotiations surrounding the introduction, development and establishment of new organizational forms and ICT raise issues regarding the openness of an organization's culture. Dutton (2001) argues that many management strategists take for granted that all workers are 'high-tech, ICT-centric users' (p. 155). However, research shows that this is far from the case, with many workers within an organization not fully accepting the technology. Many of the concerns workers have relate to effects of the innovative use of ICT on productivity, privacy and the quality of the working environment (ibid.). These concerns are not solely related to technology but are also directed at the organizational change and work practice that accompanies any technological change.

The resistance to change can stem from managers' and supervisors' fears of losing control over staff working remotely, and consequences of this fear can lead to tighter monitoring and control through the imposition of targets and similar methods. Another consequence of these types of fears is that remote work can lead managers to trust and hence use, subcontractors more because this relationship can be controlled through specific contract arrangements. In this context, workers are monitored for having to meet their targets and build their individual portfolios in accordance with agreed specifications (Lauden, 1986).[3] This can lead workers to be judged on the outputs of their work, rather than by their work experience or practices. For example, many telework schemes are focused on sales and personal incentives rather than skills that often underpin productivity such as tacit knowledge and team-building capabilities. The target type of monitoring of worker-productivity extends to the allocation of rewards, with reward and promotion being based on performance measured against targets.

These processes have a combined effect of rendering workers less secure in their jobs and undermining union representation and organization where it is present. This is especially seen in the rise of subcontracted and casual work. Many workers also feel that the skills and knowledge they have, that is, their tacit knowledge, is not recognized by management. This has two main consequences for them:

1. They feel that these tacit skills are important as they often underpin their work, both in relation to productivity and in relation to quality, which feeds into market feedback and suggestions for innovation.
2. They fear that they might be overlooked for promotion because these tacit skills are not visible or valued.

This is also related to perceptions of not being 'seen in the office', which they feel impacts on their chances of promotion and, given the project-based organization of work, they also fear that they may get overlooked in the formation of new project teams. In general terms, forms of worker resistance are related to flaws in management strategies (Dutton, 2001). On the one hand, workers have to be autonomous and take self-directed roles, that is, be self-programmable but, on the other hand, competitive pressures (within the neo-liberal consensus) cause private and public enterprises to offer employees less secure forms of employment. These can take the form of lower pay rises and rewards and more flexible hours, while demanding more from their employees in terms of travel, personal commitment, time and managerial skills, together with self-direction and motivation, often in mobile and remote working conditions.

Negotiations also involve managing risks in ICT-based work and communication within the workplace. For instance, there is the problem of 'information overload' in which workers receive and have to manage a constant influx of large amounts of information. This means workers have to sift through a huge amount of information, make decisions about what information is relevant and then turn that information into knowledge of various sorts. If workers feel pressured and lack skills needed to assess the validity and reliability of the information, they are at risk of generating mistakes in the system. In this context, there is an ever-present risk of misinformation which if continually circulated can create 'misinformation systems' (Alcoff, 1969). Another risk in ICT communication is 'inappropriate substitutions', which happen because social cues found in situated interaction are lost in computer mediated communication (CMC). Although CMC can facilitate communication by reducing status differentials to promote open communication, there is a danger that emails might be misinterpreted. In general terms, 'email frenzy' can lead to misunderstandings because it lacks the 'tones' and 'cues' of face-to-face communication. For effective communication human contact is often critical.

On top of the above areas of negotiation, widespread use of ICT also generates concerns about privacy and electronic surveillance. Although management often overestimates the efficiency of workplace e-surveillance and underestimates the ability of employees to bypass systems designed to control their work (Attewell, 1987), nonetheless, personal locators, call monitors and mobile phones extend management control outside the walls of an office (Dutton, 2001). This can be another source of anxiety and struggle for worker discretion, especially for mobile workers working in sensitive community settings, such as key workers in the social care sector (Wessels et al., 2008). The combination of the factors discussed in this section illustrate the ways in which both ICT and new working practices are negotiated and socially shaped in relation to organizational cultures. Part of organizational culture includes the gendering of the workplace, to which the discussion now turns.

Participation and Gender

A key feature missing from Braverman's analysis is the question of gender relations in the workplace. Feminist writers (Thompson, 1989; Beechey, 1982; Knights and Willmott, 1988) point out that conflict within the workplace takes place not just in the context of labour and capital but is also related to gender inequalities. In the context of a wider sexual division of labour, feminists argue that management use technology to maintain men's control of women in the workplace, thus maintaining women's subordinate position in labour relations (Barker and Downing, 1985; Cockburn, 1983, 1985; Wajcman, 1991). Management techniques, for example, seek to replace traditional men's work by technology and cheaper female labour. Aligned to this strategy is the way in which 'skilled' and 'unskilled' are socially defined and rewarded, with technology being appropriated in workplace negotiations of the relative value of labour power. Part of these processes includes the ways in which men may seek to retain control of their status in the workplace through reasserting, or redefining traditional images of what constitute 'man's work' (McLoughlin, 1999).

Studies that address the social shaping of technology show that patriarchal relations are important in shaping technology (Mackenzie and Wajcman, 1985). This is seen in the early history of computing, when there was a male predominance of computer departments, computer clubs, electronic discussion groups, video arcades and ICT firms that indicate that ICT is a male domain. However, this ignores the extent to which women work with ICT in the workplace and at home, which shapes their competencies with computing. Furthermore, it also renders invisible the ways in which children's socialization, education and engagement in culture can shape gender affinities towards technical artefacts (Webster, 1996). Moving on to address gender and work in the e-economy means considering the interaction of gender relations in the workplace and the dynamics of gender and technology. Given the rise in telework, the development of networks and flexible forms of work, the role and position of women in the labour pool is significant. The rise of flexible work on the one hand might help women to balance their domestic and working lives; on the other hand, achieving this balance is difficult.

Women have relatively low rates of participation in the labour market for designing and developing computer-based systems. Precise rates vary but, as a guide, the rates are 20% in the United Kingdom, 15% The Netherlands (NL), 24% Sweden and Denmark, 30% Finland, 25% Australia and 30% in the United States (Webster in Dutton, 2001, p. 167). These figures suggest that policies aiming to propel women into high-value ICT jobs have failed (Millar and Jagger, 2001). Whereas participation rates in the research, design and creative sectors within ICT is low, women form the majority of employees in ICT manufacturing and assembly jobs. These jobs are not well rewarded and are routine, being distinct from higher-value research, design and creative work. Furthermore, opportunities to develop higher skills are limited in assembly type jobs. This type of work is also separate geographically, as the bulk of ICT assembly-type work is in developing countries and free trade zones, or done in pockets of homework, where cheap female labour is available (Webster, 1995).

Woodfield's (2000) study on women working in 'high tech' companies shows how the need for softer skills, communication skills and flexibility may be advantageous for women. However, existing managerial conventions such as job evaluations and career manoeuvring are still biased towards male-oriented work practices. Although much ICT-based work requires the softer skills of good communication competencies, relational and organization skills, many organizations are unclear about how to measure and reward these capabilities. So, even if women are socialized to have a better quality and higher level of such softer skills, reward and promotion structures tend not to measure or recognize these attributes. Instead, the male-oriented culture of many organizations works through more established practices such as presenteeism, 'old-boy' type networking and production-related outputs (Woodfield, 2000). An exception is public sector employment in the United Kingdom, which tends to have better policies in relation to equal opportunities in the workplace. These equal opportunities policies support women working in telework or in ICT-based departments and centres. Given this context, women in the public sector are more positive than men about ICT in the workplace (Dunkle, 1991). However, apart from within the public sector, opportunities for women to advance in the high-tech sector are undermined by patriarchal structures, even though they have the relevant skills and are flexible (Woodfield, 2000).

Factors such as finding ways to manage work and domestic duties at home are especially problematic for women (Haddon and Silverstone, 1994). Much of women's tele homework is low-paid and casual, and they have little support from management or from organized trade unions (Webster, 2001). In addition, many women do not like working at home all week because they find it isolating. They experience difficulties in maintaining work relations with colleagues as well as lacking stimulation to feed motivation. Many labour and trade unions are not in favour of the development of teleworking in the form of homeworking, pointing out the risks of generating 'sweated labour' and the difficulties of monitoring wage levels or working conditions within homeworking environments. These are very important issues for women and they also extend to men. Lipsig-Mumme (1991) raises a concern that flexible employment patterns will lead to the gradual break-up of full-time unionized jobs, as more fragmentary employment patterns enable employers to shift responsibility for costs back to workers including women employees. This expands to the whole of the workforce because not only are workers' rights threatened but unionism as a movement is threatened in the longer term, thereby undermining restraints on working terms and conditions.

These dynamics underpinning and shaping telework are producing an inequitable and insecure context for those in the workforce. Producer and user organizations are failing to provide a supportive culture for women (and other less powerful groups in the economy, such as younger and older people as well minority groups). A further consequence is the risk of not identifying the talents and creativity of women, limiting opportunities for them to participate in the higher value and creative sectors of the economy.[4] Taking these trends together, ICT and flexible work have not on the whole improved the quality of women's participation in the labour market. Rather the capitalist relations that appropriate the Internet exploit women's position in society that is still influenced by patriarchy.

Conclusion

The current reorganization of capitalism is involving the use of ICT in various forms of organizational change that encompass negotiations in working practices. Post-industrial theories and proponents of information society developments tend to posit a positive situation in which ICT is ushering in a new society that promises more knowledge-based work for a broader and higher skilled workforce. However, when looking at the relations of production one sees continuity in the social relations of capital with management maintaining control over labour. There have been adaptations in the characteristics of the production process so that capital can meet the continuous innovation and rapidly changing market demands of the global economy. This includes moves towards virtual organizations, characterized by networks of communication and production that are flexible and responsive to market trends. These take various forms from electronic cottages to call centres. Narratives of work and workers within this networked organization include flexible patterns of work and teleworkers. The emphasis is on softer skills and more collaborative forms of work within networks.

However, when one considers the character of participation in the social relations of work based on these narratives, a more complex picture arises. Participation in working life is diverse and gendered, with distinctions between knowledge workers and operatives, involving deskilling as well as reskilling. Resistances to change involve struggles over control of working practices and the technology within them. Some of the new forms of work when combined with the ethos informational capitalism are undermining worker protections, such as the threats to trade unionism. These dynamics suggest that workplaces are being culturally shaped in the ways various workers negotiate the meaning of their work and indicates that the relationship between technology and organization in a not universalistic or 'culture free'. Rather, the interdependency of the three dimensions of the Internet as a socio-cultural form in this context suggests that capital has found new ways to restructure itself, and its use of ICT is changing some of the ways people work, which is negotiated by both labour and management. There are some benefits to flexible work but the promise of the restored relationship of a better work–life balance has not generally materialized for most workers.

6

Public Policy and the Internet

Introduction

The aim of this chapter is to introduce the ways in which the 'logic of the Internet' is interacting with changes in the ideology and practice of many aspects of welfare and health provision, education, (local) government, political process and citizenship. This domain extends the analysis to show how social values, working practices and technologies interact in the provision of public services and in the practices of citizenship. It is also the arena in which issues of access, usage and design are visibly linked to concerns of inclusion and exclusion in key areas of social well-being. The chapter shows how changes in the ideology of welfare – namely the move from a collectivist approach of universal provision to a consumerist welfare based on choice and conditionality – are becoming embedded in e-service delivery, e-citizenship and in e-participation with some residual notion of social justice in those relationships. In this context, issues of equality, agency and policy are important in ensuring quality of care and participation in e-services and e-government.

The Logic of the Internet in Public Policy

To explore the way in which the Internet is interacting with various dimensions of public policy means addressing the characteristics of broader changes in the socio-economic and political aspects of social life. The key relationship to address is the dynamics of transnational informational capitalism, its ICT infrastructure and trends towards post-Fordist welfare. The history of state welfare provision is linked to the organization of capital and practices of democracy and is part of the 'implicit social contract' (Moore, 1978) between labour and capital. Changes in the organization of capital in Fordism produced relatively well-paid workers who could afford mass-produced goods and ushered in the consumer economy (Steinert, 2007). Welfare state provision based on the insurance principle was one of the pre-conditions of this mode of production with its morale of working hard to gain rewards in consumer society (ibid.). Post-Fordism, the rapid acceleration of globalizing capitalism alongside Thatcherism and Reaganism and the fall of socialism in Eastern Europe all undermined previous corporatist settlements and created new social relations and divisions. These changes created a social split between those with the resource to participate in society as consumers and those who cannot and are therefore surplus. The reorganization of capitalism with its new 'shareholder' orientation and the rise of consultants in international corporations have also reduced obligations to a place or a country. Two main consequences of these changes are as follows: first, the exclusion of those unfit for the market (ibid.); and second, nation state governments having less power, resource and influence to mitigate a settlement between capital and labour, which erodes the provision of welfare (Barney, 2004). The combination of these factors is producing what some commentators term as 'exclusive society' (Taylor et al., 1996; Young, 2000). The exclusive society within the restructuring of capital is affecting the lives of people across socio-economic strata (Room, 1995; Steinert and Pilgram, 2007). The dynamics of this change within the ethos of neo-liberalism is, on the one hand, generating new forms of poverty and marginalization and, on the other hand, creating new demands on the provision of education and training and support for periods of unemployment.

Public policy has to address exclusion across a range of dimensions. Citizenship in part shapes public policy (Roche, 1992) and the rise of the classic welfare state evolved alongside the development of citizenship. Marshall (1950) argues that citizenship moved beyond civil and political citizenship to social citizenship, which seeks to ensure social rights for every citizen. The notion of social citizenship underpins the provision of welfare. However, with the rise of neo-liberalism and the turn to a free market ideology, this notion of social citizenship is being undermined (Roche, 1992). Liberal individualism shapes current notions of citizenship. This means seeing individuals as consumers of services, who exercise choice and who have rights to public services, on the one hand whilst, being members of a collective with responsibilities to that collective through the state on the other (Prior et al., 1995). There are however difficulties in reconciling individual choice with duties and obligations to a collective.

One of the consequences of this conflict becomes clear when it is considered alongside Silverstone and Hirsch's (1992) argument that consumerism is something that must be studied not only from the consumer's point of view but also as an extension of society. They argue that consumerism sustains the constitution of society through inequalities of class, status and power, which raise difficulties in balancing individual choice with collective good in quests for social cohesion and equality of opportunity. The concept of consumerism within public policy interacts with the Internet in a particular way. It is located in the generation of pseudo markets in welfare in which services operate along market oriented business lines. The availability of information is a central component in the logic of the market: information is integral to producers and service providers' marketing strategies because consumers cannot make decisions regarding products and services without information. The argument is that only informed consumers can make effective choices and hence get what they want. This pressure on producers and service providers to supply information when combined with user feedback mechanisms, whether through consumer choice, service satisfaction surveys or self-publishing consumer fora, produces a form of accountability based on market principles. However, in the pseudo markets of welfare, this process does not address the problem of needs in relation to choice generating threats to those less informed and vulnerable who are at risk of exclusions. Nonetheless, despite these risks, ICT is seen as a good medium for providing information and fostering interactive communication. This politicizes ICT because access to ICT is a requirement in ensuring inclusion and participation in public policy.

The logic behind the development of Internet-related technologies is based on the concept of the network and the restructuring of welfare based on patterns of post-Fordist production and consumption. In the first instance, Castells argues that three

> independent processes came together, ushering in a new social structure predominantly based on networks: the needs of the economy for managing flexibility and for the globalization of capital, production and trade; the demands of society in which the values of individual freedom and open communication became paramount; and the extraordinary advances in computing and telecommunications made possible by the micro-electronics revolution. (Castells, 2001, p. 2)

To recap, a network is 'a lean agency of economic activity built around specific business projects, which are enacted by networks of various composition and origin' (p. 67). The form of innovation within this environment is generated through open-source networks of cooperation in which product and process constantly innovate themselves in the common interest of increasing returns for all those participating in the network (pp. 101–102). The flexibility of networks and the ethos of individual freedom support current developments in public policy. Jessop (1994), for example, argues that a Schumpeterian Workfare State is emerging that aims to promote product, process, organizational and market innovation in open economies where social policy is subordinated to the needs of labour flexibility and/or the constraints of international competition. This differs from the governmental version of Fordism, which is standardization in the form of

Weberian bureaucracy. Burrows and Loader (1994) point out that models derived from regulation theory, the idea of flexible specialization and the notion of the flexible firm are all apparent in the restructuring of welfare (also see Gould, 1993). The main argument is that, if

> Fordism is represented by a homology between mass production, mass consumption, modernist cultural forms and the mass provision of public provision of welfare then post-Fordism is characterized by an emerging coalition between flexible production, different and segmented consumption patterns, post modernist cultural forms and a restructured welfare state. (Burrows and Loader, 1994, p. 1)

Hogget (1987, 1990, 1991) addresses the relationship between socio-economic restructuring and developments in the public sector. He compares the emergence of the flexible firm in the private sector with its decentralized forms, team-working, franchising and technological basis to the welfare state's decentralized and quasi-market strategies. Hogget argues that the new forces of production make possible emerging forms of control that involve a move from bureaucratic power towards 'remote' control. He asserts that social control will be managed through self-regulating systems involving remote rather than proximate monitoring and intervention. In this scenario, the 'incorporational' social control strategies of the 1960s and 1970s are replaced by 'exclusion'. Hoggett, therefore, follows those who suggest that a two-tier welfare system may develop with a concomitant development of an underclass, whose members are excluded from primary labour markets (Hoggett, 1994, p. 46).

Post-Fordist analyses of the restructuring of welfare are useful in identifying some of the key factors shaping change as well as the characteristics of developments. However, there are other significant factors in the dynamics of change. Williams (1993, 1994) argues that post-Fordist analysis is too dependent upon an 'unreconstructed political economy', which concentrates almost exclusively on social class. She argues that there is a lack of any appropriate consideration about social relations based upon gender, 'race', age and disability. For Williams, post-Fordist analyses fail to recognize the significance of non-class-based collectivities as agents of change and as foci of struggle that systematically challenge the social relations of welfare. These struggles cannot solely be regarded as responses to a crisis in Fordism but they also reflect challenges to the embeddedness of racism and patriarchy in the classic welfare state. These observations and analysis opens up space for acknowledging human agency and political struggle in patterns of social change.

Williams (1994) also raises issues surrounding the complex and often contradictory nature of neo-liberalism with respect to notions of diversity, difference and differentiation. She identifies three competing notions of diversity and difference as they apply to the restructuring of welfare. The first arises from the market-oriented conception of the consumer, with individual preferences being met by a differentiated 'mixed economy' of welfare. The second is derived from the requirement in health and social care reorganization that 'purchasers' of services should assess the individual needs of welfare recipients. Although this is related to a quasi-market conception, it is complicated by the related necessity of local authorities to produce community care plans in consultation with health authorities and users to identify their population's needs. Unlike the first two points, which may be seen as 'diversity from above', the third conception is characterized as coming from below.[1] The combination of these factors also point to some instances of bridging between neo-liberals and those working in the welfare sector who recognize that conventional welfare models can fail in some areas of persistent poverty or in cases of state failure (Wildavsky, 1975).

Networks are seen to have the potential to bridge pressures from above in the provision of flexible, differentiated and consumer-based welfare services, as well as pressures from below through welfare users themselves. Williams (1994) outlines how the dynamics of the three competing notions of difference and diversity interact in welfare restructuring. First is the conception of the welfare user as a consumer whose preferences are met by a 'mixed economy' of welfare. Second, the struggle over welfare services or regimes has moved beyond organized working-class determinants to include other social groups (Baggulay, 1994). Third, in the reorganization of health and social care, service providers act as 'purchasers' of services via a mechanism of assessing the individual needs of welfare recipients. In practical terms, practitioners negotiate these dimensions of care in their everyday working practices and their development of new networks of health and social care (Wessels et al., 2008). The agency of practitioners in these contexts is located between market-driven approaches and the ethos of providing good quality care, which raise tensions in ensuring universal provision free at the point of delivery (ibid.).

The broad context of public policy and social change shows how neo-liberalism and the rise of consumer society have undermined the classic welfare state. The language of individual choice and the rise of market mechanisms in public policy suit the use of the Internet as providing a technological underpinning for networked services. On the one hand, the development of networked public services has the potential to provide opportunities for more responsive service provision to meet the needs of a diversity of service users. On the other hand, given that networks are 'lean organizations', the development of post-Fordist models of welfare may generate gaps in service provision in which the most vulnerable are at risk of forms of exclusion. Public policy in open societies is shaped through democratic processes, it is therefore important to consider the way in which the Internet is interacting with political processes before considering specific areas of public policy.

Internet and Political Process

Parliamentary democracy is the central mode of representative politics in modern open societies, and it is dependent on 'efficient, multi-directional flows of information' (Coleman et al., 1999, p. 3). Coleman et al. argue that citizens need information to make choices about who represents them. There is, however, a pervasive disinterest in politics and general public apathy, often cited as a 'crisis in political communication' (Blumler and Gurevitch, 1995). This context has triggered an interest in improving participation in political processes and interactivity in the democratic process. The Internet is seen as an ideal information and communication tool to improve citizens' access to information (Barney, 2004). Part of such access means ensuring that information is made available to citizens, including public records and non-classified information. One advantage of the Internet is that its interactivity makes it possible for citizens to request information, voice their opinion and request a personalized answer from their representatives. Given that representative government can lead to passivity amongst the citizenry, the interactivity of the Internet can facilitate the re-engagement of citizens in collective civic action that may feed into the political process, such as, for example, the US based non-profit liberal public policy advocacy network Moveon.org. Another example is the Australian based GetUp, which is a community based political organization that uses the Internet to develop a 'progressive Australia'. This type of grass-roots activity is part of the wider political environment and these examples show that interactivity via the Internet can help citizens engage in political action.

However, as described in Chapters 2 and 3, developing technology involves addressing institutional arrangements and users' practices. Therefore, the development of the Internet in political communication requires addressing the institutional and cultural aspects of fostering engagement in political processes. First, as Coleman et al. (1999) show (through case studies), there are various forms of representative institutions with particular histories that influence the development and use of ICT. For example, the 'Westminster model' of the UK Parliament is rooted in its historical antecedents, with practices forged out of tradition. In this context, the institution is seen as being 'backward' in terms of technological innovation. Some members of parliament are frustrated by the lack of development, whereas others resist the uptake of new technologies in fear of them being disruptive to established practices. Many visions for implementing ICT in Westminster prove too ambitious, given the difficulties of organizational change within traditional political culture.

In contrast, the Australian Parliament is also based on the Westminster Model, yet it is one of the most technologically advanced legislatures in the world (p. 7). The modern and more progressive culture of this younger parliament has enabled ICT to be implemented in an organization open to change. Another distinctive example is that of South Africa, where democracy was hard and violently fought for. This history leads to a concerted effort to ensure that legislators are closely connected to the voting populace. However, the key limitation of ICT in this context is that its infrastructure and access is not universal or evenly distributed across the population. This democratic divide within a broader digital divide (Norris, 2000) undermines the potential of ICT to connect people with their representatives. The importance of history and culture in shaping the Internet in political environments is also seen in the post-communist societies of Eastern Europe. In Slovenia, for example, parliament sought to use ICT to create transparency in political processes after years of state secrecy. However, the legacy of state centrism is still evident in the design and practices of that parliament's website (ibid.).

The significance of political culture in informing the use of the Internet in political communication is also apparent within election processes. Comparative research by Kluver et al. (2007) explores a range of dimensions that shape and influence online communication in national elections. They compare web campaigns in 19 countries from across Europe, Asia and Australasia.[2] The study built on previous work by Norris (2000, 2001) which suggests that levels of economic and technological development are important indicators in the take-up of ICT in political processes. It also draws on research that identifies differences between countries, showing, for example that UK online campaigning has a party-centric focus, whereas in the United States the online focus is candidate-centric (Gibson et al., 2003). Kluver et al. (2007) address two main areas: political development covering variations in political institutions and political culture focusing on citizens' attitudes and voting behaviour.

The relationship between political institutions in producing informational products and citizens as audiences and participants is in part generated in web-spheres. Political web-spheres involve four main practices: informing, involving, connecting and mobilizing (Foot and Schneider, 2006); for example, campaign web-spheres will typically have candidate biography, policy information and contact details. Comparing web-spheres in different national contexts reveals that political culture is a key influence in the development and take-up of online political communication.

Kluver et al.'s (2007) research found that previously identified factors such as human, technological and political development have little significance on the practices of web-spheres. Rather, political culture measured in terms of an index of participation and engagement proves to be significant across all four practices for all countries. For example, strong campaigning influences the high use of political web-spheres in Czechoslovakia, whereas the passive political culture in Slovenia was influential in the low use of web-spheres (ibid.). The dynamics of political culture are therefore informing and shaping the take-up and use of the Internet in political communication.

These examples show how technology is socially shaped and culturally informed. It indicates that improving political communication involves not just technological change but also organizational and cultural change in a context of universal access to ICT. Another dimension to these constraints limiting the potential of the Internet is that, although the Internet is another source of information provision, it is often just used in the same manner of traditional post and reply. Research found that websites that are not 'user-friendly' alongside service, that it is slow in replying to email and online requests for information offer little advantage over traditional mail (Coleman et al., 1999). Important features in the take-up of online political communication are interesting genres in web-spheres and the responsiveness of services supporting the site. Although there are some examples of good practice, there is also continuity in the lack of responsiveness found in traditional political practices. In countries where there is a strong political culture, websites are more successful, but the broader issue of political distrust, crises in political legitimacy and citizen disaffection vis-à-vis their representatives is limiting the use of web-spheres. Given this sociocultural and political context, the interactive multi-directional media provided by the Internet has limited user uptake. In other words, the Internet cannot provide a technological fix for the crisis of democracy.

Another factor that hampers the usefulness of online political communication is the broader media environment that frames what Castells (2001) calls 'media politics'. The main thrust of his argument is that media politics is hugely influential in shaping people's political opinions and their electoral behaviour. Media politics tends to focus on political personalities and the ability of political actors to use the media effectively. Media politics is highly personalized and organized around the image of politicians and political candidates. A consequence of these dynamics is that media politics can lead to the prevalence of 'scandal politics' (Thompson, 2000) by leaking information and counter information about political players. Given the new media dimension of the Internet (see Chapter 10), the Internet is potentially another platform for the politics of scandal, rather than strengthening democracy by fostering the knowledge and participation of the citizens in policy processes. The character of political culture is therefore significant and needs to be addressed to re-engage citizens, and this also involves building appropriate institutional frameworks to improve communication with citizens. Within a coherent political and communication strategy, the interactive and flexible characteristics of the Internet can act as a useful tool to improve political engagement. The Internet can provide direct access to the information, foster interactivity with politicians and circumvent the spectacle of media politics.

The Internet in Public Services and Democratic Processes

Access is a key resource in politics and public services, which is why tele-democracy proposals such as the idea of a 'public information utility' have been promoted for many years (Sackman and Nie, 1970). These proposals are controversial because of fears that media consultants could manipulate public opinion (Lauden, 1977) and that inequalities might emerge in accessing services. Furthermore, narrow understandings of information do not acknowledge the fact that information is created and distributed through organizations via a range of platforms including printed media, electronic media and the new Internet media as well as through information workers of various types. By looking at the way in which policy-makers and public sector organizations are thinking about the use of the Internet in the public realm, one can start to understand the processes through which the Internet develops as a socio-cultural form in this context.

This framework opens up analysis to the processes of participation in contemporary life. Bellamy and Taylor (1997) argue that there are five sets of relationships lying at the heart of an information polity. These are

1. Internal relationships in the machinery of government.
2. The relationships of government organizations to consumers of their services.
3. The relationship of government to citizens of the state.
4. The relationships between governments and the providers of ICT infrastructure, equipment and services.
5. The relationship between existing information systems, patterns of communication and technical infrastructures to the polity's 'appreciative system' – the value system within the polity which attaches importance to some practices and agendas for change rather than others.

Although the rhetoric surrounding the development of e-government and tele-democracy has been in circulation for quite a while, the actual implementation and take-up of such services is still ongoing (Guthrie and Dutton, 1991; Cornford et al., 2004). In general terms, the implementation of ICT in the public realm is proving to be complex (Dutton, 2001). One of the main difficulties is that support for e-services is often based on an assumption of lowering public spending (Cornford et al., 2004); however, any delivery of services electronically involves some form of process re-engineering, which is expensive. Also, gaining efficiencies in public services through service re-engineering is more complex than in the private sector because public services have to provide services in relation to need as well as choice, it has to contribute to the public good and ensure democratic process. In recent political culture there has been, and there continues to be, drives to make government more 'business like', often within a neo-liberal ethos of 'efficiency, effectiveness and value for money' made popular during 1980s through Reaganism in the United States and Thatcherism in the United Kingdom. This, however, has to be balanced with the need to contribute to the general well-being and public good of national populations.

There is concern within all levels of government and public services to structural and technological reform. Many public sector employees are sceptical about e-services in case they deepen inequalities in access rather than enhance the quality of service and democratic process. The concerns about ICT include the rise of elites who are not public servants and are not held accountable to the electorate. For example, there are fears about the rise of a 'technocratic elite' who might exercise greater autonomy and control over decisions in the public sector due to their technological knowledge. There is also the possibility of the emergence of an 'economic elite' who are driven by military and industrial needs regarding ICT and who may shape the public sector along those lines. Another sector of the economic elites involves the marketing strategists who may manipulate public preferences to suit the people they are accountable to in their large multinational corporations. Finally, there is concern about the use of technology as 'reinforcement', in which ICT is a malleable resource controlled by a dominant coalition of interests, reinforcing the prevailing power structure of the political system (Dutton, 2001). However, as ethnographic research by Wessels (2007b) shows the diversity of interests and systems of accountability in the public sector produce a robust structure that tends to manage these risks. For example, the development of public e-services in London (UK) maintains public sector control whilst working in partnership with the private sector (ibid.). Despite constraints on institutional change, a growing number of government agencies are employing ICTs to change the way services are delivered and how citizens interact with services.

One recent example that addresses the above discussions is an implementation of local eGovernment in England (2002) that sought to use ICT to modernize local government through a diverse and complex change programme. This programme has three main narratives that link ideas about the relations of production and participation in e-services in public policy terms. The three narratives themes of eGovernment are

1. Transforming services – making them more accessible, more convenient, more responsive and more cost-effective. EGovernment can make it easier to link local services (within councils, between councils and between councils and other public, voluntary and private agencies). It can improve customers' experience of dealing with local public services, whoever provides them.
2. Renewing local democracy – making councils more open, more accountable, more inclusive and better able to lead their communities. EGovernment can enhance the opportunities for citizens to debate with each other, to engage with their local services and councils, to access their political representatives and hold them to account. It can also support councillors in their executive, scrutiny and representative roles.
3. Promoting local economic vitality – a modern communications infrastructure, a skilled workforce and the active promotion of e-business can help local councils and regions promote employment in their areas and improve the employability of their citizens. (The National Strategy for Local e-Government, 2002, Office of Deputy Prime Minister and UK Online and the Local Government Association; see Figure 6.1).

In addressing the three aspects of eGovernment as a socio-cultural form, research by Cornford et al. (2004) found that the relations of production of eGovernment involve a range of public services including social services,

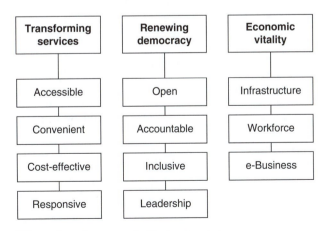

Figure 6.1   Narrative themes of eGovernment
Source: 'Objectives of e-government (National Strategy)' Cornford et al., (2004) p. 7.

housing and education as well as every department of local government. It involves local health care trusts, the police and various charitable and voluntary bodies and commercial ICT suppliers. As a programme of transformation, it changes structures, processes, working practices and corporate cultures of local government as well the way citizens and local businesses interact with local authorities. With regard to participation, eGovernment increases flexible working for council staff and the number of ways in which the public can access information and services (helping to meet the goals of accessibility, convenience, openness and accountability) (ibid.). EGovernment also increases the take-up of e-enabled information and services and public participation in decision-making processes (ibid.). Service providers, however, did not achieve any significant cost savings through e-government (ibid.).[3] For instance, the cost increases or stays the same in relation to requirements for office space and office running costs; the costs of providing information; the time spent providing information and the total cost of processing transactions. The only decrease in cost is in the time spent processing transactions, which also improves the responsiveness of services (ibid.).

The details of the above example are replicated in differing ways across Europe, United States, Canada, Australia, as well as in developing countries. The Canadian New Brunswick eGovernment programme from the mid-1990s onwards is seen as an international leader in the field with many national governments looking to its work as an exemplar service. The European Commissions' push to European eGovernment by 2010 illustrates how generic issues of the production, design and use of ICT enabled services are shaped through national, regional and local cultures. For example, the KZC (Konekta Zaitez Ciudadan) project in the Basque Country in Spain is a regional public broadband network that delivers a range of training programmes across the population including migrants, retired people and those unemployed. It delivers the training in physical community centres using ICT. In Poland, however, inclusive eGovernment is focusing on Internet access and ICT training in schools, local government institutions and public access points. Whereas the Czech Republic's National Programme for Computer Literacy operates through 6000 teaching centres across the country underpins the development of eGovernment there (Millard, 2007).

The focus on services varies too, for instance in Slovenia the Ministry of Labour, Family and Social Affairs has developed the Social Work Information System (SWCIS), which has a 'family helper' module. This module protects personal data, increases control over the payment system and analyses data to aid service providers in their decision-making, planning and monitoring and implementation of social policy programmes. From an end-user citizen perspective Greece has developed multi-channel citizen services (CSC) to support social integration. CSC provides public services via the Internet and telephone as well as through a 1000 local one-stop-shops. As mentioned in the English case, efficiency is also a factor and despite problems of evaluation different countries and regions are seeking to gain efficiencies, which are gauged in various ways. For example, Latvia has a national museum catalogue that has been digitized. It contains 5 million artefacts from the 110 national museums and its rationale is that it will reduce the distance between local eGovernment and its citizens through cultural engagement and build trust between government and citizens. The service providers of the Belgium 'My File' initiative provide every Belgian inhabitant with a tool so that each person can access his or her personal data that is stored on the National Register. The purpose of the scheme is that it will help ensure that online services are transparent and accountable and thus diminishing risks of data fraud as well as guarding against the development of a surveillance state (ibid.).

Key areas in the development of eGovernment also include the issues of interoperability, identity and authentication. This means ensuring that data can be exchanged across different systems and that communication is facilitated between ICT systems too. The development of remote access also means that the system needs to be able to identify people using it as well as ensuring that citizens can access eGovernment in a secure and reliable way. To this end, governments are developing services that have these factors built into them. For example, Finland and Estonia have OpenXAdes, which is a free software development project that aims to profile advanced electronic signatures based on European Telecommunications Standards Institute (ETSI). The aim of this programme is to introduce legally binding signatures into everyday life and business practices. In Estonia the 'Having your say:iVote' programme launched in 2007 is a nationwide e-voting service. The system is built on a national identity card for electronic authentication. The smart card technology facilitates secure electronic signatures that link into a national infrastructure that is interoperable. These examples show the complexity of developing eGovernment and how services are being developed in different ways in relation to cultural mores (ibid.).

Another aspect of public policy is education. The role and character of education is changing in informational capitalism. Education has to foster the use of ICT in ways that equip students to learn how to use information in ways that produce knowledge for the new economy (Castells, 2001). Furthermore, education needs to provide students with the life skills for survival in the new economy (Sennett, 1998, 2001). This relates to inclusion because students require the necessary skills to become 'flexible' to participate in the new economy, which also involves life skills of adaptability, reskilling and mobility (ibid.). Castells argues that the networked society requires a

> new pedagogy based on interactivity, personalization and the development
> of autonomous capacity of learning and thinking. While, at the same time,
> strengthening the character and securing the personality, and this is uncharted
> terrain. (Castells, 2001, p. 278)

There are some innovative pilot projects that seek to address how education may change.[4] One example of innovation in education is based on a
regional regeneration strategy in the East End of London (UK) (Wessels,
2000a; Harrison and Wessels, 2005). The relations of production are based on
a partnership approach at regional level, which addresses education in relation to developments in an ICT related economy as well as that of a multicultural society. The narrative focus is that the Internet both requires and
facilitates participative learning. This narrative supported by the regional
relations of production generates new forms of participation in education.
For example, the 'Infinity Story' project involves 300 primary pupils creating a 40,000-word story told and illustrated on a website. On one level it is
a school portrait, on another an exercise in the making of communal culture and a creative means to address social exclusion. The dimensions of the
project combine through the interaction of technology and imagination to
open doors to new styles and modes of learning. Within the same regional
partnership, the Young People Online project shows that education need
not be constrained by the same spatial assumptions that the UK national
curriculum makes and enforces on group size, age banding, timetabling,
classrooms and so on. Its members run their own websites and mailing lists
as well as creating online animations and music. The regional partnership
reasons that the young and ethnically diverse population of its region can be
a major advantage in terms of developing online content and services with
international appeal. The way the region is able to build these types of educational forms and activities is through a broad-based ICT strategy which
incorporates an understanding of the technological and social aspects of
developing an inclusive e-learning environment situated in regional regeneration. This involves the development of a portal in the region, a local Intranet
and access to ICT across the region, with the fostering of a local creative
industry involving new media companies. The regional partnership situates
education within these broader e-developments thus integrating education
into social, economic and cultural trends.

A different approach to the issues of ICTs and exclusion in education involves 'reshaping the school'. There are four dimensions to this
development:

1. The provision of laptops for teachers, which aims to encourage teachers
   to develop content for online resource.

2. Laptops for pupils, primarily for low-income families to enable them to have their own laptop.
3. The school Intranet, which not only seeks to facilitate an online resource within the school but also starts to develop links between home and school.
4. Redesign of spaces within the school, such as cyber cafés and ILIAD centres (Independent Learning, Information and Design) enabling ICT access all day and in the evening.

The rationale for supplying pupils with laptops is to give them greater flexibility in managing their own learning. Providing teachers with laptops enables them to choose when and where they work, as well as developing their ICT skills. Laptops, therefore, become the front-end interface and the Intranet the infrastructure to support it, with flexibility added by wireless technology. This adds another layer of communication between pupils and teachers and allows greater flexibility and a more individual approach to pupils managing their own learning. Within the school's narrative, these activities are producing a 'connected learning community'.

However, Stephonone et al. (2000) argue that it is inadequate to just provide access to ICT because schools also need to foster a positive and appropriate social environment for learning. This is particularly problematic in de-industrialized areas that have high levels of socio-economic deprivation, characterized by long-term unemployment, poor housing and lack of opportunity with concomitant low aspirations. Important aspects in the take-up of ICT skills are social networks and support that have the relevant knowledge and skill sets, which may not be available in areas of high deprivation (ibid.). One strategy to overcome this particular issue involves

1. The development of an e-learning foundation – a scheme for low-income families to provide laptops at low cost.
2. Access to skill development for parents and pupils through, for example, adult education courses and links with local further education bodies.
3. Provision of a network of support so that pupils and parents learn about ICT together.
4. Access to mentors in industry for pupils with little family history of formal employment.

This strategy shows that the development of ICT in education involves not just implementing the technology, but embedding ICT within a broad learning environment. This environment extends beyond the school to the socio-economic and cultural contexts of pupils and their families and aims to support people in learning at school age and beyond, to lifelong learning. Lifelong learning is a key aspect of contemporary society because workers constantly have to upgrade their skills to meet the demands of a constantly innovating labour market.

The above strategies are examples of the development of ICT in advanced Western economies. However, ICT in education is also being used in developing countries. Very often in these contexts the flexibility of the Internet and in particular Web 2.0 is harnessed to meet specific educational needs. One example is the educational and health issues surrounding the HIV/ AIDS pandemic, which also interacts with developmental strategies of some third world countries. Health practitioners in India argue that the disease is a cross-cutting issue for India that involves streamlining systems and fine-tuning governance in health care. Education and awareness is an important part of health care surrounding AIDS. There are a range of initiatives across the regions of India that address the disease, however, the use of Web 2.0, especially YouTube is emerging as a key aspect in AIDS education. The YouTube Non-profit Programme seeks to let organizations connect with their volunteers, donors and supporters without having to undertake expensive outreach campaigns. Many Non-Governmental Organizations (NGOs) are using YouTube in seeking to spread education about AIDS. For example, 'UNAIDS' has a series of short films to generate awareness about issues such as women's fight against stigma, discrimination and ignorance that surround AIDS. 'NoHIV, NoAIDS' uses YouTube to disseminate information about the early stages of the disease. YouTube is also being implemented in South Africa, Malawai and Cambodia. For example 'The FacetoFaceAIDS' project's channel carries information about AIDS and supports local agencies in their fight against HIV and poverty through Web based campaigns linked by YouTube.

These innovative pilot projects are some examples of the ways in which the character of education is being shaped to meet the needs of informational capitalism. They also seek to address the dynamics of inclusion and exclusion and try to ensure opportunities are there to enable people to participate in multicultural and de-industrialized contexts. However, they are pilot projects and as yet just serve as examples of how education could change more generally. This means that education more broadly is negotiating organizational and pedagogical change surrounding the use of ICT and outcomes of any change are still unproven in terms of educational practices and achievements.

The Internet in Health and Social Care

The complexity of e-enabling public services is seen especially in health and social care services. Healthcare is an information-intensive activity that is centered on communication between professionals and patients. The implementation of ICT in healthcare has been, and continues to be, difficult (National Audit Office, 1996). Keen et al. (1998) explore the complexity of ICT in healthcare in General Practice (GP) in the United Kingdom. This case illustrates the tendencies to a post-Fordist organization of welfare as well as highlighting the complexity of information flows in General Practice.

In relation to post-Fordist organization of welfare, the UK National Health Service underwent structural reform in which there is a separation of the purchasing roles from service provider roles. However, the organization of GP practices covers both of these roles because they are key providers of healthcare in the community and they also purchase a limited range of services (such as minor surgical procedures) (ibid.). To manage this dual role, groups of GP practices in a locality are forming networks with health authorities to coordinate the purchasing of services. In the context of the purchasing and service provider roles, Keen at al. argue that there are advantages for GPs to join networks (as long as basic assumptions such as security and compatible systems are met) with gains in administrative efficiency and improved patient access to health information. One form that might work is if local networks for GP area-related work were linked to public information on a national network. Debates as to whether an NHS net is better than the Internet relate to key issues such as network security and confidentiality, which as yet are not fully resolved.[5]

In relation to the complexity of information flows in GP practice, Keene et al. identify six types of interactions and networks. These are

1. Information provided by patients about their problems during consultation and the advice and instructions given by professionals to patients.
2. A subset of the information generated in a consultation, which involves sending a message to another provider of health services.
3. Administrative information, which is generally aggregated from individual contacts and used by general practices themselves and sent to local purchasers. It also provides details about variables such as waiting times, treatment processes and so on. This information is in the form of a 'one-to-some' interaction.
4. Information about effective and cost-effective treatments, which is collated by government-funded centres, in a 'one-to-many' interaction.
5. Information in various forms about changes in drug licensing, guidelines from the Department of Health, Royal Colleges and other agencies – a 'one-to-many' interaction.
6. The role of charities and pressure groups, where patients and others can exchange information about specific conditions, either with or without the support of health professionals. Information is also carried by newspapers, magazines, and the Internet, in both 'some-to-some' interactions and 'some-to-many' interactions. (pp. 218–219 *numbering added*)

These categories are different from each other in both form and content, but they define the role of the GP in relation to patients and others. Thus, 'one-to-one' interactions address the area of private data that relates to individual patients. The most clinical information is confidential and is recorded in traditional medical notes or on computers in the consulting room. The 'one-to-some' information is generated within a practice or by a health-care trust, and then sent to a specific and limited number of other parties. The 'one-to-many' information is collated in a single place and distributed widely, for example, performance data published by the Department of Health. Keene at al.'s research shows that information in and around GP practices is a mix of public and private data. In general terms, this research shows that flows of information are central for GPs' work at the level of purchasing services and in patient and practice interactions. The information flows have different provinces, which make designing an information system difficult. This context illustrates the complexity of the health environment and indicates the intricacies of implementing ICT within this environment.

Change is therefore complex and slow in this sector, however, there are services emerging that are supported by well managed and secure ICT networks. For example, work by a regional partnership in South Yorkshire (UK) has created a service that enables patients to make doctors' appointments online. This service uses a variety of platforms such as Internet access via personal computers, public multimedia kiosks, mobile phones and interactive digital television. In this context GP practice managers provide secure access to the GP system for the public, they make sure that patient e-records are confidential and that their own online purchasing is secure (Wessels, 2008b). This has been a learning experience for those working in GP surgeries in the region (c.f. Williams et al., 2005). Nonetheless, the service is proving to be popular with patients. It is also saving the GP surgeries money by reducing transaction costs and is improving efficiency as it is reducing the level of missed appointments (Wessels, 2008b). However, achieving these types of changes require levels of knowledge and experience that accrue over time through innovation projects. In the context of South Yorkshire, the doctors' online appointments service is the result of eight years of regional innovation in ICT projects and organizational change.

The case of joined-up services for children with disability in the United Kingdom brings together many of the issues of agency, equality and use of ICT in care networks. Activities by groups such as the Disability Action Network and the British Council of Disabled People promote the needs of disabled people, including supporting the use of the 'social model' of disability in inclusion policies. In policy terms, the New Labour government's (1997 to present time) agenda of modernizing public services focuses on investing in technology, putting the citizen at the centre of the process and providing more transparent, open and accountable services. Changes in health and social care policy and the renaissance of childcare policy placing specific focus on the child have been influential in the move to multi-agency welfare provision in the 'community'.[6] For example, the Children's National Service Framework[7] proposes that children and their families should be involved in shaping their services. In this context, 'key workers'[8] and ICT are, respectively, emergent actors and systems whose role is that of mediator and mediation between the needs of the child and family and broader systems of health and welfare. This move blurs traditional boundaries between ICT designers and users by situating the design and development of ICT with welfare practitioners and service users in the community, as well as ICT suppliers and technologists (Wessels et al., 2008).

Wessels et al.'s research shows that key workers are the developers of new services. They have to manage organizational and related technological change at the same time as delivering care services. The development of networked services places the agency of key workers within several roles and competing priorities – as practitioners, managers, developers and designers (ibid.). Key workers work with children and families in their homes, in various community centres, hospitals, schools and hospices. They provide care and coordinate care plans with an array of health and social care agencies. Communication is central in generating a network of care around each child in ways that facilitate participation and inclusion in each child's social life. Private sector ICT suppliers often do not have the knowledge to design information and communication systems to meet the needs of complex multi-agency community care services. This problematic is fostering the use of participant design[9] in the development of services, which involves key workers working with researchers to formulate the ICT requirements of services. (ibid.). A characteristic of this practitioner-led development is a 'hands-off' approach from senior managers, which is couched in terms of 'empowering' key workers but it denotes 'management without responsibility', typical of work in flexible organizations (Sennett, 2001). This often leaves key workers feeling vulnerable (Wessels et al., 2008). Nonetheless, key workers work hard to deliver high quality care for disabled children and actively build networks to do so. Their agency and dedication moves definitions of welfare provision beyond lean networks narrowly understood in economic terms of quasi-markets. In this context, the agency of key workers is therefore important in ensuring that networked welfare meets the needs of disabled children and their families (Wessels et al., 2008).

These case studies illustrate different aspects of the restructuring of services, such as developing networks of services in e-government and in health and social care. They also demonstrate new forms of participation, seen in the innovative education projects (c.f. Allen and Seaman, 2003).

However, technological change is complex and all of the organizations involved in change have to address both organizational and cultural change. The overall narrative of change is one of flexibility and efficiency in meeting new demands on services that are in line with changing perceptions of welfare and the needs of a diverse range of individuals and groups in the twenty-first century society.

Conclusion

The logic of the Internet in public policy is shaped by changing narratives and ideologies of welfare and citizenship and the Internet's flexibility to underpin networks of communication, information flows and services. Public services are changing to address the vagrancies of exclusive society, the demands of a flexible labour market and individual choice. The requirement to meet an array of welfare, educational and democratic needs in an equable and comprehensive way with limited resources means that organizational and technological change is difficult. Actors in the social relations of public sector production negotiate a fading ethos of public service rooted in the classic welfare state with emerging neo-liberal market-oriented approaches using partnerships and networks to provide services for citizens who are also perceived as consumers. Nonetheless, as the case studies show, actors are creatively rethinking service provision to meet new demands, including non-class-based priorities such as the needs of children with disability, to foster inclusion and participation. Of primary importance in these dynamics of change is the agency of those working in the public sector, which is managing to counter risks of welfare becoming 'too lean a network'. In conclusion, use of the Internet in developing networks has the potential to underpin some of the changes in public services and, if political culture becomes more vibrant, it could support a more informed and participative public that could push to ensure high quality and inclusive services. These dimensions are important because equality and inclusion is not a given and communication and participation are vital in the struggles for inclusion and equality.

7

Exclusion, Inclusion and the Internet

Introduction

The discussion of exclusion and the Internet links with issues in public policy and identifies contemporary forms of inequality. In terms of the Internet in the dynamics of inclusion and exclusion, the focus of the debate is often on the concept of a digital divide or divides. However, to fully appreciate the complexity that underpins a digital divide means addressing the relationship between the social materialization of the Internet and the dynamics of exclusion. In general terms, the digital divide can be understood as the differentiation between the Internet-haves and Internet-have-nots, which adds a fundamental cleavage to existing sources of inequality and social exclusion (Castells, 2001). This understanding requires an analysis that moves beyond a definition of the digital divide that focuses on those who have access to ICT and those who do not, to understanding the characteristics of participation within open societies. Digital divides are multidimensional and include the dynamics of socio-economic position, geographic location, ethnicity and language, as well as educational capacities and digital literacy. These dynamics are further complicated in the global digital divide, where lower Internet penetration in developing countries (although this can be uneven within these countries), combined with the rapid change of the Internet-based technological paradigm, requires that the less-developed countries have to outperform advanced economies just to stay where they are, thus fostering and reproducing global inequalities (ibid.). The chapter concludes that under the current social and institutional conditions of transnational-networked capitalism there is an uneven development that is putting many at risk of poverty and social exclusion.

General Context of Inclusion and Exclusion

The problem of inclusion and exclusion requires consideration of the dynamics of the restructuring of the capitalist economy, its networked

103

logic underpinned by ICT and trends towards post-Fordist welfare. The dynamics of transnational, informational capitalism within an ethos of neo-liberalism is interacting with social and economic life at the local, regional, national and global level (Room (ed.), 1995). Situations of exclusion are experienced at the local level, which link to regional and national economic conditions and policy, while also relating to trends in the global economy (Steinert and Pilgram (eds), 2007). Steinert (2007) suggests that innovation phases in economic cycles tend to undermine security within labour markets. The heightened competitive environment in innovation phases means that a proportion of labour is at risk of becoming excluded from the labour market – either through lack of relevant skills and attitudes or through the structural reorganization of labour. This has reverberations for the way in which individuals can participate economically in society and therefore also their capabilities to secure their well-being. The current phase of capitalism is resulting in a horizontal model of exclusionary risk because its restructuring is altering work patterns and skill-sets across the socio-economic spectrum (p. 44). A further factor in these dynamics is a relative loss of state power to protect national economies, which undermines the possible scope of national welfare policy.

Although there is a debate about the rigour of the term 'social exclusion', it does represent the experience of insecurity, marginalization and poverty in the current innovative phase of capitalism (Bryne, 1999; Young, 2000). A phenomenology of exclusion points to different dimensions such as political exclusion (via citizenship), economic exclusion (through lack of means), social exclusion (through isolation) and cultural exclusion (through deficits in education). Steinert's (2007) definition captures the dynamics of exclusion, arguing that social exclusion is a

> dynamic and multi-dimensional process rather than as an all-or-nothing event and status. The process and the variety of dimensions can be broken down into an array of situations of (possible) exclusion ('sectoral exclusions') to be described in their mutual relations of positive or negative feedback. Social exclusion can thus be understood as the continuous and gradual exclusion from full participation in the social, including material as well as symbolic, resources produced, supplied and exploited in a society for making a living, organizing a life and taking part in the development of a (hopefully better) future. (Steinert, 2007, p. 5)

The dynamics of exclusion are embedded in post–Fordist relations of production and the processes of globalization (Bauman, 1998; Hutton and Giddens, 2001; Steinert, 2007). There is a lack of employment security, with actors having to be flexible to survive in the labour market (Sennett, 1998, 2001). There is need for labour with skills to work as symbolic analysts

(Robins and Webster, 1999) and as knowledge workers with appropriate skills and education to use the technology to turn information into know-ledge and knowledge into action (Castells, 2001; Dutton, 2001). There are others who are on the 'outside' of these developments, who do not have the necessary skills and resources, including that of geographical mobility to compete successfully in the market (Bauman, 1998; Steinert and Pilgram, 2007). Very often, these dynamics produce geographical spaces of exclu-sion in the form of ghettos, run-down estates, few local services and a gen-eral lack of opportunity (Madanipour, 1998).[1]

The role of the Internet as a tool in the new economy of informational capitalism, which underpins the flexibility of networks (as an organiza-tional form) of global capital means that it interacts in material ways with the dynamics of social and cultural life. It does so at an abstract level in eco-nomic modelling, *in situ* in the movement of capital globally, in the location of firms,[2] in the shaping of employment opportunities and in the require-ments of educational ability and skill sets. The way in which the Internet is embedded in the social relations of production influences narratives of the forms it manifests in and, crucially, the characteristics of participation in society. Robins and Webster (1999) describe this relationship as a 'technoc-ulture', in which technologies are understood as

> articulating the social relations of the societies in which they are mobilized – and, of course, that must mean power relations. Within our own society, then, we need to be concerned with the way in which technologies mediate capital-ist social relations. On this basis, our account has a strong political-economy orientation, critically exploring the capitalist mobilization of social and human resources, and the ways in which technologies have been implicated in this process. (Robins and Webster, 1999, p. 2)[3]

The state is a key institution bridging the economy and individuals (through citizenship), and its role is influential in managing exclusion. The role of the state in social control is integral to the management of exclusion and, thus, in facilitating a framework for participation. When post-Fordist trends in welfare are combined with lightly regulated market economies, it triggers remote forms of control that reinforce social exclusion, managed, in part, through various technologies of surveillance. The Internet as a technology in the relations of production is part of these dynamics. First, its network-ing logic makes it a perfect tool for post-Fordist and global production processes. Second, its use within bureaucracies and by the state means it can be used to as a tool of surveillance over the populace. Baggulay (1994) draws these aspects together to state that advanced nations are grouped by the ways their traditional social welfare policies are constructed and how these influence employment and social structure. He draws on Esping

Andersen's (1990) term 'regime' to illustrate that the relation between the state and the economy is systematically woven from a complex of legal and organizational features. The way in which situations of exclusion emerge and are managed is, therefore, a result of how the economy and the state interact to produce either opportunities for participation in open societies or fosters increasing levels of surveillance in society.

In this context Steinert and Pilgram (eds, 2007) argue that, rather than discussing 'exclusion', the focus should be on 'participation'. They posit that individuals as members of social formations have differential access to resources. The levels of access and the quality of resources are key to enabling individuals and groups to participate in the life of society (Pelikan et al., 2007, p. 256). The question therefore involves ensuring that individuals and groups have access to the relevant resources to enable them to participate. When the Internet is seen as a resource then it can be seen as part of a virtuous circle, where those with access to (fast) Internet, good education and socio-economic background are in good positions to take advantage of economic development. However, those who lack access to any of these resources are at a disadvantage and at risk of exclusion. The allocation of resources is related to positions of power, with those with the least resources having less power in determining their futures, securities and freedoms to participate. Theories of the way power operates in society vary (Lukes, 2005) from ideas regarding oppression (c.f. Freire, 2000), hegemony (c.f. Gramsci, 1971) and technologies of power and discipline (c.f. Foucault, 1977); however, with regard to the Internet there are two main dimensions of power and exclusion. First, access to the Internet as it materializes in the relations of production provides the economic opportunity to participate in the labour market and economy and thus for individuals to have some power over their life chances. Second, the Internet gives states and commercial organizations the potential to control individuals through the information they can electronically gather about them. Any lack of transparency in the workings of the state and the commercial sector is a form of power that can either be used to incorporate or exclude. In this context individuals need access to the data held on them and the skills, education and power to protect their rights and identity (with the state having the responsibility to ensure freedoms are maintained through proper legislation). Given the ways in which the Internet is becoming embedded in the relations of production, in working life, in public policy and in everyday life (see Chapters 5, 6 and 8), it becomes a resource for participation – social, economic, political and cultural. This does not, however, reduce exclusion merely to access to the Internet, rather Internet-related resources become one aspect embedded within the multidimensionality of exclusion.

This argument enriches debates on the digital divide, which can reduce complex issues of exclusion to divides in digital capacities of various kinds, rather than tracing the social relations of exclusionary situations and the role of the Internet within those relations. It starts to elucidate what an individual or group is excluded *from*, and what resources are needed for him/her and/or groups to participate. The meaningfulness of what one is excluded from and included in is understood through culture. This is significant across the dimensions of social life because the character of inequality varies across cultures, as does the meaningfulness of technologies (Wyatt et al., 2000). Therefore, understanding the digital divide means addressing the relations of production which underpin participation in social and cultural life (ibid.).[4] By understanding the Internet as comprising socio-cultural forms one can start to understand the dynamics of exclusion. This is because these forms represent *what* people are excluded from in terms of social and cultural capital and *how* they are excluded by not being able to participate in socio-cultural forms such as not being connected in networked individualism. Therefore, one can readdress digital divides through the lens of participation and so address the constraints on participation, thus making the link between exclusions and socio-economic trends within types of information society developments.

Exclusion and Digital Divides: The Global Dimension

Any analysis of the character and significance of digital divide(s) requires placing its concerns within broader debates about the changes and continuities of an informational and intermediated society. The diffusion of the Internet is uneven across societies and within specific societies. To assess the significance of exclusion from, and inclusion in, Internet-based networks means considering the significance of Internet-related activity (Wyatt et al., 2000). Castells (2001) argues that 'the centrality of the Internet in many areas of social, economic and political activity is tantamount to marginality for those without, or with only limited, access to the Internet, as well as for those unable to use it effectively' (p. 247). From this view, the digital divide is

> [t]he differentiation between Internet-haves and have-nots [that] adds a fundamental cleavage to existing sources of inequality and social exclusion in a complex interaction that appears to increase the gap between the promise of the information age and its bleak reality for many people around the world. (ibid.)

Nonetheless, Castells questions if it really is the case that people and countries are excluded by being disconnected from Internet-based networks. He argues that it is the character of social relations of the connection to the Internet-based networks that produces the inequality (ibid.). Part of the analysis of the global digital divide, therefore, requires addressing the ways in which connections to global networks produce situations of dependency on more powerful economies and cultures by less-developed economies. This includes addressing how this reduces the possibilities and abilities of those countries with less-developed economies to generate their own material well-being and cultural identity (ibid.). To a degree, this follows an underdevelopment of development argument, in which less-developed countries are locked into dependency with wealthy nations (Frank, 1966). The diffusion of the Internet has been uneven across the globe and has followed these histories, with Westernized advanced economies far out-reaching less-developed nations in terms of access, infrastructure and Internet-based knowledge. For example, in 2000 there were 378 million Internet users, which is roughly 6.2% of the world's population. When this figure is broken down by country, the divides between global regions becomes apparent: North America's share is 43%; Western Europe's 24%; Asia including Japan has a 21% share. Compare this to Latin America's share of 4%; Eastern Europe's 4.7%; the Middle East a mere 1.3% share and Africa's 0.6% share (mostly South Africa) (Castells, 2001).

Locked into histories of dependencies, from colonialism through imperialism to the current politics of globalization, the digital divide question involves considering what are the conditions that define levels of connectivity to Internet-based networks to produce either better opportunities or, conversely, greater inequality. Castells argues that 'under current social and institutional conditions...the new techno economic system seems to induce uneven development, simultaneously increasing wealth and poverty, productivity and social exclusion, with its effects being differentially distributed in various areas of the world and in various social groups' (p. 265). The social unevenness of the development process is linked to the networking logic and global reach of the transnational informational economy, facilitated by the Internet, and which enables companies to network and be flexible in a global market. In this context, education, information and science and technology become critical sources for value creation in an Internet-based economy. These resources are unequally distributed across the globe with capacity concentrated in the advanced economies. Economies, which due to their historical past of capital exploitation and scientific and technological capability, have the intellectual property to take advantage of the current economic and technological paradigm. However, countries and regions without this type of legacy lack the capacity to compete in a fast-moving global market. A further risk factor that hampers less developed counties is that the development of Internet-based connections in the global economy is vulnerable to global financial flows. This leaves them vulnerable to the inbuilt crisis of capitalism. In the less-developed countries when these crises occur there are only limited, and often inadequate, resources for coping. This is because these countries can only provide weak state support for people and their poor economies leave little flexibly to counter the ravages of recession. These conditions put people at risk of exclusion (Wessels and Miedema, 2007) and without adequate resource to devise coping strategies for exclusion that are at risk of further exclusion by falling back on the informal economy (Castells, 2001).

In more specific terms, the speed of change in the ICT technological paradigm means that the later-developing countries have to outperform advanced economies just to stay where they are, otherwise they will get left even further behind (ibid.). Given the existing gap between them, it is extremely difficult for less-developed countries to outperform the leading nations and therefore get ahead of them. To compete, countries need to be able to respond efficiently to the movement of global capital, which requires an up-to-date communications infrastructure. The outdated communication systems of less-developed countries put them at a disadvantage and it is a disadvantage that is not quickly remedied because it takes time to build an ICT infrastructure. Another factor is that Internet service providers tend to be dependent on United States or European Internet backbones, which increases cost and complexity for those in developing countries, as well as creating problems in the design and maintenance of the network (ibid.).

These types of issues are reflected in the geography of the Internet. In mapping Internet domains at the global level, Zook (2001a) shows that Internet content providers are concentrated in a few large metropolitan areas in the developed world. For example, London has more domains than the whole of Africa. Another consequence of this concentration is that this reinforces the language of the Internet as being English, generating patterns of inclusion and exclusion through language. It also means that large metropolitan centres have more influence over the form and content of Web-based traffic, accessibility and intuitive 'look and feel' of the interface and its usability. The geographic logic of the Internet is producing nodes in a global network that links key economic centres across the world. This is resulting in the establishment of key urban centres for globalized activities in which higher-educated social groups are being included in the Internet-based global networks. It is leaving those in the peripheral regions and places which lack ICT infrastructure as well as production and consumption resources outside of the global economic network, in effect 'switching people off' (Castells, 2001, p. 264).

These dynamics of exclusion in the networked logic of Internet-based capitalism is undermining agriculture and is resulting in a rural exodus (especially in Asia). There are high levels of migration to overcrowded metropolitan areas – the global nodes of the networked economy (ibid.). Exacerbating these dynamics is the fact that networked globalization limits governments' capabilities to act, because they are increasingly constrained by global flows of capital and information, which weaken their power in economic policy and generates defensive strategies to survive globalization. The logic of global capitalism and its consequences means that global digital divide permeates and penetrates national and regional economies and societies and global nodes; thus generating risks of exclusion in regions and global nodes. Concretely, this is seen in the in way in which neo-liberal conditions with flexible work patterns creates labour that is individualized and workers are left unprotected. This creates a new social cleavage between a few protected workers and mass of unorganized workers who form a casualized workforce (ibid.). Casualized workers are part of a reserve army of labour, which means they can be used by the economy in times of growth and discarded in times of recession. This dynamic affects global nodes and world regions, and although there is a particularity to each context, there is a risk across all societies that economic crisis can lead to a break down of regulations in which the social contract becomes challenged. The global dynamics of the capitalist economy means that governments are subjected to pressures from above and below and may suffer a crisis of legitimacy in the eyes of their citizens. There is a risk in some extreme cases of a crisis of legitimacy leading to political disintegration (ibid.).

The dynamics of global digital divide materialize at local, regional, national as well as global levels, affecting different individuals and groups. In local contexts it interacts with existing conditions of inequality to produce situations of exclusion. The specific characteristics of the digital divide in situations of exclusion involve a social divide between the 'information-rich' and 'information poor' and the democratic divide between those who use and those who not use digital resources to participate in public life (Norris, 2000). These dimensions interact with local conditions in particular ways in the context of regional and national frameworks. A phenomenology of exclusion that incorporates ideas of a digital divide therefore needs to unpack the meaning the forms the digital divide can take by addressing several dimensions, such as access, skills, knowledge and people's capacity to engage in the knowledge economy as well as in their political and socio-cultural environments.

Access and Knowledge

A straightforward analysis of a digital divide might focus on the issue of inequality of access to the Internet – however, access alone does not address the way in which Internet-related activity interacts with the dynamics of exclusion. Other factors include the acquisition of skills and knowledge to work with ICT and participate in socio-economic, political and cultural activities. Nonetheless, access is a prerequisite for overcoming inequality in contemporary society whose dominant functions and social groups are increasingly organized around the Internet.

Access varies across countries and within them. For instance, in the United States (an advanced economy and early adopter) in 2005, 68% of American adults had access to the Internet. However, within this figure there are inequalities in access and in levels of use in America. The inequalities are related to income, education, age and ethnicity. These inequalities are seen in the following figures of gradations of use:

- 26% of Americans aged 65 and older go online, compared with 67% of those aged 50–64, 80% of those aged 30–49, and 84% of those aged 18–29.
- 57% of African-Americans go online, compared with 70% of whites.
- 29% of those who have not graduated from high school have access, compared to 61% of high school graduates and 89% of college graduates.
- 60% of American adults who do not have a child living at home go online, compared with 83% of parents of minor children. (Fox, 2005, p. 2)

Social groups less likely to have access are those with disabilities and non-English speakers (ibid.). In 2002, only 38% of Americans living with disabilities had access to the Internet (Fox, 2005, citing 2002 Pew Internet & American Life Project survey). US Census data shows that access to the Internet for Hispanics (age three years and older) in 2003 was only 37%, compared to Internet access for 65% of non-Hispanic whites (age three years and older) (US Department of Commerce, September 2004). The gender divide has, in most cases, disappeared with men and women accessing ICT in equal measure across groups. Although most gaps in Internet access are closing, the exception is the ethnicity gap – certainly figures from the United States show how racial inequality continues and is at risk of being reproduced in the age of the Internet (Castells, 2001).

The emerging picture of use of Web 2.0 and mobile applications is complex and indicates the ways in which socio-economic position, education, age, gender and ethnicity are interacting to produce differences in the quality of ICT access and use. Addressing Web 2.0, mobile devices and wireless technologies as well as user-generated content, Horrigan (2007) constructed a typology of ICT users. His ten distinct groups[5] form three main categories of users are as follows: elite users (31% of American adults); middle-of-the-road tech users (20% of above); and few tech assets (49%). The demographics of these groups in part reinforce some of the patterns of access and use, but they also cut across groups. For example, 'ominovores',[6] who are extensive and informed users, form 8% of the population. They are young (median age is 28 years), ethnically diverse and mostly male (70%), 64% are white, 11% are black and 18% of this group is

English-speaking Hispanics (ibid.). Forty-two per cent are students who have access to high-speed and wireless Internet connections at university. Just below this group in the elite user category are the connectors,[7] who are 7% of the population, median age of 38 with a similar ethnic profile. However, unlike the above group, most of these users (55%) are women who are, however, above average in educational attainment and income (ibid.). In the 'middle-of-the-road' category, the 'mobile centrics'[8] include a relatively sizable percentage of African Americans (21%) and Hispanics (14%). Within the 'few tech assets' group, the 'off-the-network group' have a median age of 64 and lowest levels of household income, and are more likely to be women (57%). This group is more ethnically diverse than some of the other groups, with an 18% proportion of African Americans (ibid.).

These figures suggest that inequalities based on income, education and ethnicity are still influential in shaping the quality of access and use of the Internet across a range of platforms and devices. Another key aspect of ensuring access, and the quality of that access, is the widespread availability of high-speed broadband. Although some rural areas in the United States are not fully connected to broadband provision, that gap is closing – in 2005, 24% of rural Americans had high-speed connections at home compared to 39% of suburban dwellers (Horrigan, 2006). Together, these factors suggest that access is widening but still needs to improve in terms of reach and quality. In relation to participation, elite users have high levels of the required skills, education and access to Internet-based technology to engage in knowledge generating communication across economic, social, political and cultural domains. The levels identified by Horrigan (2006) indicate that, although many people are 'connected' in one form or another, distinctions are emerging which suggest that the quality of that 'connectedness' is varied between those with high quality access and those with lower quality or no access. The quality of access is a factor in people's ability to participate in economic and social life; therefore differentials in quality of access are part of inequality in a digital age.

Similar profiles of access and use exist in Europe but research shows that take-up of the Internet in Europe is differentiated with overall lower levels of use than in the United States (European Commission, DG Information Society and Media, 2007). The European Commission's (EC) interest in developing a competitive European ICT sector and a vibrant European information economy produces a series of ICT policy initiatives that in overall terms aim to mobilize a European Information Society[9] (Mansell and Steinmuller, 2000; Wessels, 2009). The EC identifies that there is a risk of producing a society divided by the Internet 'haves' and 'have nots' (Bangemann Report, 1994) and argues that policy interventions are needed to overcome digital exclusions (ibid.). The 2006 Riga Ministerial Declaration[10] set policy targets for the EU to achieve 'e-inclusion'. E-inclusion is defined as 'both inclusive

Information and Communication Technologies (ICT) and the use of ICT to achieve wider inclusion objectives and policies aiming at both reducing gaps in ICT and promoting the use of ICT to overcome exclusion' (Riga Dashboard Study, 2007, p. 3). The rationale underpinning this aim is that ICT can drive growth and employment, improve the quality of life of Europeans and foster social participation (ibid.).

The Riga Ministerial Declaration notes that 57% of individuals living in the EU do not regularly use ICT and that this gap in usage means many Europeans are not gaining any benefits from ICT (Riga Ministerial Declaration, 2006, p. 1). Divisions in ICT usage are clearly seen in relation to age, educational levels and employment status. For example,

- 10% of people over 65 use the Internet, compared to 68% of those aged 16–24.
- 24% of people with low education use the Internet, compared to 73% of those with high education.
- 32% of unemployed people use the Internet compared to 54% of employed people.
- In relation to accessibility levels to ICT for those with disability (15% of the EU population), only 3% of public websites complied with the minimum Web accessibility standards. (Riga Ministerial Declaration, 2006, p. 1)

These statistics show how levels of ICT usage can link to situations of exclusion, such as unemployment and lack of opportunities due to factors like low education, disability and ageing. The Riga Dashboard (2007) study also identifies regional differences in trends of social exclusion and low ICT usage. One example is the context of de-industrialization in South Yorkshire (UK) where access to ICT is low which combines with high levels of unemployment and low levels of educational attainment to produce situations of exclusion (Wessels, 2008b, p. 2). Deviations in gaps in Internet usage are shaped through

- Age: with 73% of those aged 16–24 using the Internet compared to only 10% of those aged over 64.
- Level of education: with 77% of people with high education using the Internet compared to only 25% of those with low education level.
- Employment status: with only 38% of unemployed and 17% of economically-inactive people using the Internet compared to 60% of those employed and 84% of students. (Riga Dashboard, 2007, p. 4)

A further dimension of differential take-up is geographical divides resulting from a lack of broadband penetration in some regions. This also has a rural–urban dimension in that broadband provision in rural areas has lagged behind urban provision. However, in 2006, broadband coverage reached 89% of the EU population. The lack of digital literacy is also identified as a barrier to e-inclusion, addressing a lack of Internet, computing and general literacy skills. Groups at risk include the unemployed, immigrants, people with low educational levels, people with disabilities, the elderly and marginalized young people (p. 5).

Language is a particular issue in relation to exclusion and the Internet because the language of the Internet is English – 87% of global websites use only English (Castells, 2001). In Europe there is a diversity of cultures and many languages are spoken. In the United States, the issue of language is particularly relevant to Hispanics and African Americans whose first language is not English. In analysing Internet access generally, and also in relation to language and Internet access, one needs to consider what use and purpose the Internet has for different groups. Therefore to understand the way in which the Internet and its language, English, interacts with different language-speaking groups requires addressing their broader social condition. In general terms, ethnic minorities use the Internet for practical purposes (Silverstone, 2005). They use it to search for information, support and advice. However, for those whose first language is not English, the predominantly English websites restrict the benefits of the Internet for them and may feed into exclusionary dynamics of ethnicity. A similar issue arises with the situation of immigrants, who often need to access information in their new host country before knowing its language and the Internet is therefore of no use to them if they cannot read English. There is, however, some evidence of the growth of bi-lingual websites, especially within Europe (ibid.).

The lack of access to the Internet in the dynamics of exclusion goes beyond access to a concept of a knowledge gap (Castells, 2001). This gap is important because, in a knowledge economy and information society, it is the capacity to generate knowledge that enables people to engage in social and economic life. This particular online communicative knowledge-ability is also influential for generating participation in political and cultural life because one characteristic of knowledge in an information age is the capacity to create knowledge from a range of sources and to be innovative in developing forms of communication and networking (social and technological). This means that education and life-long learning become essential resources for work achievement and personal development (ibid.). Access to innovative schooling, university and ongoing development is a key resource for inclusion in contemporary society. It is not just the extension of education over the life course but also concerns the quality and character of education. Castells points out that schools are differentiated territorially and institutionally through class and race (including the divide between public and private schooling). Better-resourced schools can invest more heavily in ICT and teacher training as well as having the advantage of pupils equipped with the cultural capital to engage in education. In contrast, schools in poorer areas have less resource in real terms to meet the intensive demands of overcoming poverty and in consequence, they have less to invest in ICT-related activities. Schools in more deprived areas often have pupils with lower cultural capital than pupils from more affluent areas, which makes teaching more difficult and limits innovation within schools, whether in ICT-related areas or the arts and sciences.

This aspect is significant in the information age because forms of pedagogy need to change to produce pupils who can work in an environment that requires creativity and versatility. Pedagogy has moved towards focusing on opening minds and fostering creativity, which is very different from the industrial model of learning facts and prescribed skills. Schools with more resource and pupils with high levels of cultural capital often have a more open and creative approach to teaching. The demands on schools with less resource and with pupils with greater needs often means they have to operate in more authoritarian way due to these conditions (ibid.). In these contexts, responsibility for supplementing their child's education gets passed onto parents, which is precisely where the issue of home background and educational achievement is played out. One of the consequences of this is that children from poorer backgrounds fall farther behind in their education than their more affluent peers, which puts them at a disadvantage in further education and in the labour market. This severely limits these young people's capacity to evade situations of exclusion and reproduces situations of poverty.

The discussion in this section of the chapter shows how access and the quality of access are important in the dynamics of inclusion and exclusion. The inequalities of access place restrictions on people being able to participate in the societies in which they live. Thus good quality access in the United States is important due to its generally high levels of use and for many it is a tool that facilitates social participation. In Europe access is important because the EC is seeking to develop economies based on ICT and to use it as a tool for participation. In developing countries the focus is on building a fast broadband infrastructure, improving education and digital literacy, facilitating commercial activity as well as addressing poverty. In broad terms to ensure inclusion in digital related communication and work means addressing the knowledge gap so that everyone has the skills and education to be able to use ICT in a productive and fulfilling way and so participate openly in the society in which they live.

Case Studies: The Dynamics of Inclusion and Internet Socio-Cultural Forms

Access to ICT and levels of knowledge in using it within networked digital environments interact in a multidimensional way with situations of exclusion. Combinations of factors configure in particular ways to form conditions for inclusion and participation or, alternately, they configure to induce situations that are exclusionary at varying levels. The following case studies illustrate just some of the ways in which various factors combine in different situations.

In London, the divide is not simply between the Internet 'haves' and 'have-nots'. Rather, divides exist between high, medium and low users, with disadvantaged users always having to play 'catch up' with higher level users in the city. These divides are linked to household connectivity patterns – in 2001, 45% of London households were connected to the Internet, a higher percentage than other regions in the United Kingdom. However, there is a great deal of variation in levels of connectivity within London, for example, the least connected London boroughs of Barking & Dagenham, Hackney and Islington have less than 25% of households connected to the Internet, whereas the three most connected boroughs of Kingston upon Thames, Richmond upon Thames and the City of London have more than 50% connectivity. This pattern mirrors existing inequalities, as these two clusters of boroughs represent the poorest and richest boroughs respectively.

Another layer in the divide are the barriers to adoption and use amongst the more socially excluded groups that correlate with socio-economic factors, such as unemployment, poorer housing and local facilities and low levels of education. For example, ICT use by socially excluded groups living on council estates where the level of unemployment is high is only 16% of the estate population (Association of London Government (ALG), 2002). The ALG argue that the most important factors for enhancing ICT adoption is not access *per se*, but training coupled with a reduction in access costs. ALG researchers question the assumption that the Internet has the potential to counter exclusion by considering the way in which the Internet may actually improve people's life chances. Once this question is asked then the focus becomes a more insightful one of – how can the Internet be shaped to counter exclusion? In other words, what would make the Internet more valuable for groups at risk of exclusion? From this perspective, initiatives need to explore how socially excluded groups could benefit from ICT and then ensure that content and services are designed to meet those needs. This approach is one in which development takes a user focus rather than a service provider focus.

Overall, the ALG research shows that a holistic policy approach is needed to counter the divisions in Internet access and use. ALG recommends that policy should address levels of awareness, access to the Internet, the provision of skills and training and the use and impact of Internet related activity for local communities. From a development point of view this means creating leadership in e-domains with the knowledge to develop strategy for digital inclusion, to foster research and resources and people and partnerships to address the complexity of the issue of digital divides within the dynamics of inclusion and exclusion. The London example shows how aspects of digital divides interact with situations of exclusion in multidimensional ways.

The German context provides a different slant on the dynamics of inclusion and exclusion, in that data from there highlights inequalities in private access to the Internet and sheds light on whether Internet usage discourages other leisure activities which form part of an individual's social capital within a specific society (Wagner et al., 2002). In Germany, the private use of the Internet is spread across all social strata. There are, however, substantial differences in levels and quality of privately accessible ICT access and knowledge that relate to different levels of income and education. Thus when higher levels of education are correlated with higher incomes, wealthy parents are more likely to provide a computer for their children than parents from lower-income families. In particular, single-parent households, with mainly low incomes, have less access to the Internet and children in this category do not have private access to computers at home (ibid.).

In countering these private divisions in Internet usage, all German schools have Internet access for all children. The quality of this access extends beyond the supply of hardware and software to ensuring that teachers are well trained in skills for Web-based learning. The rationale behind this policy is the belief that a lack of computer skills puts low-skilled people who are already in the workplace at a disadvantage and that it also forms barriers that stop low-skilled people such as young people with only the minimum school-leaving certificate from getting into the labour market. From within the German policy-making community and in popular discourse, German people see 'getting computer-trained' as vital before engaging with the job market (ibid.).

In relation to social capital and leisure time, Wagner et al. found that teenagers who use the Internet do not do so at the expense of other leisure activities such as reading and playing sport. In fact, young people who use the Internet are less likely just to 'hang around' and 'do nothing', with many using the Internet to organize other cultural activities as well as for educational and networking purposes. The Internet is therefore seen as contributing to a young person's social and cultural capital. In the German context the use of the Internet is viewed positively in that it facilitates participation in social and economic life. In Germany, policy seeks to address exclusion in employment terms by providing training and education in ICT skills. However, policy does not *directly* address inequalities based on household incomes. This is despite the fact that use of the Internet is seen in Germany as part of a person's social capital which enables him/her to participate in social and cultural life.

Another context of digital inequalities is found in the positions of low-skilled migrants, which are exclusionary across many dimensions. The situations of migrants tend to be exclusionary because they often have low-paid casual jobs, they lack access to state-provided social services and either have to build ties, or only have weak ties, with networks of support in their host country (Steinert and Pilgram, 2007; Wessels et al., 2007; Karazman-Morawetz and Ronneling, 2007). A further dimension of the migrant experience, and that of minorities, is the loss of everyday use of their own language and engagement in culture. In this context, being 'connected' has a different meaning. In the first instance, migrants seek access to basic information that will help them to settle into a new country. Second, they seek to find ways to connect to their relatives and friends from the places left behind, which in some cases form diasporic communities. Very often, accessing local information is hampered by a lack of online access including access to online information in their mother tongue. In response to this, migrants and minorities construct a media space from national, local and transnational media, and their use and appropriation of media is complex and layered (Silverstone, 2005). Within these contexts, the local is of primary importance; for example, access to media and communication for minorities in cities is through neighbourhood phones, Internet or video hire centres, Internet cafés and local authority centres. These sites are important as they provide access to media and communication systems for those who otherwise may not have the resources to obtain individualized and privatized access. Although some sites may generate specific user groups based on ethnicity due to their location within migration patterns, they nonetheless form open and inclusive sites of communication that can be appropriated by locally placed and transient communities (pp. 90–95). Thus, the Internet is part of a configuration of media technologies that migrant groups can appropriate to construct connectedness in ways that are meaningful and useful to them.

Another area of work is in the developing countries, which in some cases also address the dimension of women and exclusion. For instance, in Zambia the problem of gender inequalities, inequities and the empowerment of women is a concern. Many of the women there are poor, do not have access to education and are illiterate. This leads to low levels of awareness about issues that affect them and their development. They also suffer many injustices and have many of their rights violated. Although there are many women's organizations working in the country they tend to be fragmented because they cannot share information, knowledge and experience easily. Women in Zambia tend to be the heads of households holding responsibility for children, household expenditure and other essential livelihood activities. However, they lack the opportunities to generate or receive income that curtails their ability to overcome poverty and to sustain their families.

The Zambia Association of Research and Development (ZARD) is a nongovernmental organization that seeks to support and empower women in Zambia. ZARD identified the issue that sharing information and knowledge was a barrier in the empowerment of women. They developed the programme 'Women's Information for Development Network' (WIDNet, launched in 2007). WIDNet is an Internet portal for information on the status of women and it aims to promote the use of ICT4D (ICT for development) among women. The project seeks to empower women from the informal sector by providing them with information and contacts with which to improve their livelihoods. It raises awareness of women's issues amongst the women themselves and enables them to share information. This has invigorated collective action involving the Zambia's women's movement, civil society organizations, government departments, the media, learning institutions and communities as well parliamentarians. The programme has developed a strong strategic partnership that enables it to lobby for national reform through engaging with parliament, and research and publishing to enhance capacity and awareness. Some of the barriers to participation are digital literacy and basic literacy amongst the women. To address this issue WIDNet has IT literacy training for women, which included learning ICT skills to access new knowledge and educational material as well as seeking job opportunities, business contacts and further training. The training, support and advocacy combined with access to information are proving to be successful in enabling women to participate in local economies and in lobbying for improved health and social care. This programme is providing a support for women from poorer backgrounds to participate in social and economic life and it fits with Zambia's development strategy of knowledge society by 2030 (Zambia Information and Communication Technology Policy (2007), launched under the theme of 'ICT-For accelerated wealth and job creation').

Another dimension to inclusion is in relation to rural areas in developing countries. Many of these areas experience a rural exodus and those who remain often live in conditions of poverty. Developing and sustaining a good rural economy is part of development strategy. Although in some parts of rural India e-agriculture is helping farmers there are rural areas where there are high levels of poverty. One area is in the North East of India, called Arunachal Pradesh. The situation of the rural tribal farmers is that of low and uncertain agricultural productivity and frequent natural disasters. The region is remote, its terrain is difficult to farm and there is a lack of farm workers. All these combine to hinder socio-economic development in the region. A project funded by Technology Information

Facilitation Programme (TIFP) called e-Arik seeks to examine the application of ICT in agricultural services and any socio-economic outcomes among rural tribal communities. From research to ascertain the information needs of the farmers the project developed a single window system for information using computers, phone, radio and television. The single window service provides expert consultation on agricultural production, protection and marketing through the portal. This service supported by field visits of farm scientists is helping to improve the management of crop pests, as well as diseases and nutritional deficiencies in crop production. Regular training and ICT awareness lectures support the development of ICT in agriculture alongside farmer-to-farmer communication, local leadership and self-help approaches. The village advisory committee regularly reviews the progress of the project. The early experience of the e-Arik project shows improvements in farm technology dissemination, in digital literacy and e-awareness. The access to information and expertise within village learning is supporting and improving agricultural productivity in this area that may in the longer term support development and improve standards of living there.

These examples of a range of exclusionary situations help to elucidate the ways in which different people experience varying levels of access to the Internet. The case studies demonstrate that the Internet as a technology, or simply access to it, is insufficient in overcoming the dynamics of exclusion because skills and knowledge are important in utilizing the benefits of Internet connection. Furthermore, these connections need to be located within social and economic opportunities that enable people to participate in social life. However, once the Internet is understood as a socio-cultural form then the links between the dynamics of inclusion/exclusion, information and communication tools and ways of life can be elucidated (Wessels, 2000b). One example is the case of community telematics developed in the East End of London (UK). Its 'relations of production' is based on local government, business and voluntary organizations. The narratives of the form are ones of participation, creativity and diversity and it fosters innovative and inclusive forms of participation. In this instance, the social shaping of the Internet as a telematics cultural form is informed by the needs and desires of the East End of London's multicultural population. Very often the richness of the language and culture of the area's people fails to reach its potential due to a severe lack of material and symbolic resource. Given this situation, the developers and users of community telematics shape it through a range of digital, social and cultural resource centres and networks. Through these networks and resources they create community interactive digital television and user-generated content, online storytelling, ethnic language and information services, local advice and service centres, political fora and blogs and a vibrant new media sector (Harrison and Wessels, 2005). These cultural forms generate participation and inclusion in social life – in economic, political and cultural terms to counter exclusion.

A similar process can also be seen in the ex-coalfield areas of South Yorkshire. The dynamics of exclusion include de-industrialization. The distinctiveness of ways of life is based on culture built around coal mining (Gilbert et al., 1992; Warwick and Littlejohn, 1992). It is also a predominantly a white-working-class culture. The profile of the population indicates that there are risks of exclusion interacting with a digital divide, such as an ageing population, low levels of education, high levels of unemployment and a significant number of people with disabilities (Wessels, 2008b). The way in which the Internet is being shaped in this context is through a regional public sector e-forum. The forum links production of e-services with narratives and strategies for inclusion in relation to the ways in which local people participate in education, employment and cultural and everyday life (ibid.). This is resulting in diverse forms of communication and services such as an e-campus and Digital Media Centre, local interactive digital television, young people's e-fora and a wide range of online services via e@syconnects (which joins up services and uses various digital platforms for access and communications). Nonetheless, the e-forum recognizes that it needs to move beyond these forms because, as the ICT Director says

> The technology exists. The services are online. The community vehicles are in place. The missing element is people. Rather than introducing new 'gizmos', we believe the real digital challenge is to empower people to shape their own lives. (in Wessels, 2008b, p. 6)

This vision is resulting in the development of digital outreach teams and a digital directory that aims to work with local people of all ages, with local business and social and cultural centres across the region. The goal is to empower local people through education in e-skills and e-learning so that they can participate in shaping a regional knowledge economy and inclusive society.

These examples show that the Internet develops in different socio-cultural forms by being crafted out of specific sets of relations of production, narratives and forms of participation. By being sensitive to the interdependency of these three dimensions of the socio-cultural form, inclusion is more likely to be fostered because the Internet will be shaped to meet the needs and potential of local people to enable them to participate in the richness of social life – economic, political and cultural – in a genuine and vibrant civil society.

It is necessary for such an ideal, inclusive, civil society to be open and democratic, with freedom of expression and movement.[11] The focus of this chapter has therefore been on the importance of ensuring participation and the conditions for participation for all so that the Internet can be harnessed for the purposes of inclusion and not used solely as a tool of control and surveillance.[12] However, as discussed earlier in the book, the increasing use of ICT not only has the potential for new freedoms but is also making surveillance pervasive in society (Lyon, 2001a, b). The character of this surveillance is ambiguous in that it has a 'care and control' dynamic to it (ibid.) in which individuals exchange aspects of their privacy for security and convenience in most domains of contemporary life. A key part of participation in Internet-related communication and services involves using some methods of identification and authentication. To access systems and services, users need to provide information such as social security numbers, passport details, bank details or work information, depending on the context of use. This virtual identity is shaped through an individual's ability to have the right credentials and status to warrant online access – thus inclusion is based on a range of eligibility criteria, which others in situations of exclusion may lack. Access is therefore being controlled via a range of authentication criteria, which may reinforce social exclusion.[13] Digital inclusion therefore has both care and control aspects to it, since it has the capacity to empower individuals, regions or countries or exclude them and lock them into dependencies. The use of the Internet in relation to the dynamics of inclusion has to be carefully monitored. If it is used as a tool of control and incorporation then it can generate exclusionary situations in which individuals are curtailed from freedom of expression and movement by being heavily policed through their electronic profile. However, if access to the Internet is supported by transparent and accountable services in which individuals have access to their own data (see Chapter 6) then it can be a tool that might serve in policies for inclusion into information based economies and societies.

Conclusion

The dynamics of inclusion and exclusion in contemporary society are related to the innovation stage of the socio-economic paradigm, which is currently that of globalization underpinned by the Internet and the networked organization of capital. These relations of production are supported by neoliberal narratives that posit the market as the most efficient mechanism for the distribution of resources and one of ensuring individual freedom. However, in relation to participation, globalization and the development of flexible production processes are undermining the capacity of national states to develop and maintain social welfare programmes to support people in situations of exclusion. Situations of exclusion are multidimensional and the way in which the Internet, as a socio-cultural form, plays out in varying situations shows that the digital divide is located within existing inequalities. The ways in which the Internet is becoming embedded in social life (to varying degrees across the globe) means that the lack of access and the knowledge to utilize it curtails participation in society. A key aspect for fostering inclusion is building capacities in individuals, communities, regions and nations to utilize ICT and 'knowledge' for economic and social purposes. The aspects of access and knowledge, as they interact in existing situations of inequality, are played out at the global level whereby developing countries are locked into existing patterns of inequality in relation to advanced economies. Therefore, transnational, informational capitalism and its current institutional arrangements are inducing uneven development across the globe and within nations that puts people at risk of poverty and exclusion (Castells, 2001).

8

Culture, Everyday Life and the Internet

Introduction

This chapter discusses how the Internet is becoming embedded in everyday life, highlighting the ways in which social actors are negotiating their lived realities and cultural sensibilities in shaping the Internet through its use. Everyday life is seen in terms of the 'parts of life outside of the formal worlds of work and education' (Haddon, 2004, p. 1) although, of course, the more formal worlds are integrated into the everydayness of getting on with one's life. There are two interrelated dimensions to this: first, how the flexibility and interactivity of the technology is adapted for multiple everyday purposes. Second, how the culture of everyday life shapes the Internet to produce socio-cultural forms that give the Internet its meaningfulness. In the early twenty-first century, ICT was reaching a 'second age' in which it was becoming embedded in everyday life. The social form of the network is underpinning changes in everyday life, but institutions of culture of the everyday continue to shape communication and communication technologies. The concept of 'domestication' is introduced to address the ways in which ICT is taken up in everyday life and shows how the Internet becomes embedded in households' social relations. The discussion extends to look at differentiated usage of the Internet by addressing participation in socio-cultural forms, such as diaspora hubs, remote mothering and communication in cosmopolitan conditions. Very often, socio-cultural forms of the Internet and their attendant forms of networked sociability and networked individualism are a combination of old and new forms of participation. The use and ongoing adaptation of the Internet by social actors are shaped through contemporary cultural trends that are, in turn, shaping culture (see Chapter 9).

The exploration of the Internet, culture and everyday life needs to be undertaken in relation to the characteristics of the Internet's relations of production and its narratives; however, the emphasis is now on user-participation (as consumers and as producers) in various everyday contexts of use. Earlier chapters considered the production and narratives of the Internet and modes of participation within those dimensions, this chapter and the following chapters will focus on understanding the ways in which the Internet[1] is taken-up, adapted and appropriated in everyday life.

Cultural Change and Everyday Life

Before considering the Internet in everyday life, it is necessary to identify the 'everyday' and to understand changes within everyday life. One way to understand everyday life is to consider the social and cultural forms through which everyday life is shaped and which, in turn, gives shape and meaning to the everyday. These forms are located in and in many ways structure the situations of daily interaction in meaningful ways. The framework of the cultural form is applicable in the context of everyday life in that 'social and cultural forms which make sense of everyday life do so practically for their inhabitants and as representations to be observed, enjoyed and interpreted as cultural performances' (Chaney, 2002, p. 3). Part of understanding the Internet and society involves gaining a grasp of how social life is changing, or not, in relation to communication practices, and the organization of everyday life in forms of entertainment and in ways of representation. In general, the social sciences and humanities started to address everyday life as a distinct category in its own right when it became identified as a site for political and social engagement in the 1960s.[2] Radical and counter-cultural movements during the 1960s not only affected campus life as noted in Chapter 2, but they were also located and played out within society more broadly. At that time, some cultural genres were questioning established conventions, social and gender orders. From these activities, the notion of everyday life became a focus for social theory as well as a theme of cultural representation (Crook, 1994). Crook suggests that, from the early identification of the importance of everyday life for social thought, it remains a significant domain when analysing the cultural changes of late modernity.

If, as mentioned before, one takes Dewey's (1939) assertion that social life is made in and through communication, then the ways in which we communicate become a significant aspect of everyday life and its study. As Silverstone (1994, 1996, 2005, 2006) argues, technologies including ICT and media are located and given meaning through the dynamics of the everyday. This does not, however, just include the take-up and use of these technologies but also the way in which they are vehicles in forming meaning that shapes contemporary culture and the way it is experienced. These technologies are both a communicative medium and a source of representation and cultural content. Silverstone (1994) calls this their 'double articulation' because they comprise both a media artefact and a sphere of the production and interpretation of cultural content. Thus, if one follows the idea of a 'communicative turn' (Silverstone, 2005) within late modernity, then new forms of communication are embedded within the social relations of everyday life, and they are both implicitly and explicitly part of changes in everyday life. The dynamics of the everyday can be both progressive and reactive, with some forms of communication being taken up within new ways of living everyday life whilst, in other cases, everyday life can prove to be resistant to some of the opportunities, or threats, that the new technologies may bring. Deciding whether change and the resistances to change prove progressive and positive for different groups in society, or whether they represent a reactionary and conservative stance, involves value judgements that are, in part, constructed from within broad cultural frameworks.

Within contemporary change and everyday life there is a rise of what can be termed popular democratization, in which populism is dominant in public discourse but which may not entail any substantial popular emancipation (Chaney, 2002). Second, in relation to increased social fragmentation (Castells, 1996) there is a pervasive sense of cultural fragmentation (Chaney, 2002). Chaney uses the term 'fragmentation' not to imply that culture is becoming less important but that the authority of a dominant culture is increasingly contested from a variety of perspectives (ibid.). Together, these processes are seen as part of a wider process of 'informalization' in which there is a blurring of many of the authority structures dominant in earlier phases of modernity (ibid.). As a result of undermining of culture understood in modernist terms through informalization, 'the everyday' has become a focus for cultural criticism and is a source of cultural production and representation that now holds a dominant position in cultural discourse (ibid.). However, this does not mean that everyday life is more 'transparent' or that it ceases to be the context for social action (Silverstone, 2005).

In relation to cultural change,[3] society has become more diverse and multicultural, thus destabilizing any cultural homogeneity of conventional experience. There has also been an expansion in the means of entertainment for everyone through, for example, the development of television as a mass cultural form, the transformation of popular music using new means of recording and distribution, the development of web-based cultures and a proliferation of types of performance (Chaney, 2002). There has been some expansion of notions of leisure time – however, with the development of flexible work patterns, contract-based employment and new forms of parenting practices, this assumption of additional leisure time cannot be adopted without further consideration. Negotiations over the control of time and space have, on the one hand, changed the structure and rhythms of daily time and place and, on the other hand, introduced a new range of consumer goods and services for the management of time and location in everyday life.

These dimensions of social and cultural life interact with the shaping and use of the Internet in the experience of the everyday. Chaney argues that individuals gain understanding and aptitudes for a variety of activities through culture. Culture gives forms of life their distinctive characteristics, which are meaningful to the social group in which particular activities are created and embedded.[4] Cultural activity addresses the variety found within social life as well as indicating that there is a level of collective, or at least intersubjective, experience that shapes our everyday lives. As previously noted, the Internet was designed as a democratic medium of communication to enable people to communicate with each other and was shaped through the countercultural movements of the 1960s. The ongoing popularization and commercialization of the Internet is continuing to shape its form and use. In fact, how users shape the Internet (as producers or consumers) is adding to the forms of participation available to people in the twenty-first century.

By focusing on socio-cultural forms we can address the way that cultural change materializes in practices and artefacts, which also provides some understanding into the meaningfulness of these forms for social actors within their respective forms of life. Thus, social actors accomplish cultural change as they engage with the world around them, which is manifested through ordinary and extraordinary experience and ordered through routines. Cultural change is not only evident in the changing character of routines but also how these routines (whether changing or static) are talked about and mediated (to include representation and articulation) in public discourse within modes of performance including the 'factual', the 'fictional' and the 'staged' (ibid.). The disruption to routines is a significant part of change, seen, for example, in the concept of 'disruptive technologies' in which the use of technologies may break established routines as part of the social constitution of change.

This dynamic character of cultural change means that any analysis of change must address both the substantive aspects of change, for instance lifestyles and levels of engagement in types of entertainment, as well as the forms of that change (ibid.). An exploration of the content of change is necessary because it provides a snapshot of the process of change but it is insufficient in that it cannot produce an interpretation of the significance of those changes (ibid.). To explore the significance of change, form must be considered as well as the content of change. Form includes structures of change framed by members of a community or culture, their sense of identity and selves, their characteristic discourses, representations and artefacts as well as their actions, habits and accomplishments (ibid.). Thus, as described in Chapter 3, technologies themselves do not determine how they are to be used in different social settings. On the contrary, the meaning of technology is shaped by the context of competing expectations, interests and powers (ibid.). As technologies become shaped meaningfully by the activity of everyday life through different cultural constellations, they constitute the cultural forms of everyday life. These cultural forms then become the catalysts and frameworks in which contemporary social life is negotiated (Wessels, 2000b, 2007).

The concerns of everyday life in the second half of the twentieth century and in the early twenty-first century have been, and continue to be, articulated and thus constituted through what Dorothy Smith (1988) calls the 'materiality of consciousness'. She argues that consciousness is realized through artefacts, technologies and symbolic forms, which provide the means for overlapping physical and virtual environments, asserting that 'the simple social acts of tuning in, ringing up, and logging on can therefore have complex meanings for subjects' (p. 86). She is referring to the way these practices constantly overlay and interlace both the situated and the mediated worlds of late modernity (Moores, 2000, p. 9). Chaney argues that this means 'that through adopting, using, rejecting – that is selecting amongst the performances, services and artefacts of mass culture industries – practical understandings are institutionalized' (Chaney, 2002, p. 53). For example, the media have not determined people's core expectations but have, nonetheless, been a key resource in the embodiment or materialization of cultural expectations and mores. Given this, it is more productive to think of the 'products' of mass cultural industries as environments rather than texts, performances or services (ibid.). This is because when these products are used and brought together within cultural frameworks, they help to shape and constitute the everyday world. In similar vein, Silverstone (2005, 2007) points out that the media are best understood as an environment that is made up of different media platforms, channels and audience participation. The media environment is intimately linked with everyday life and its elements are mutually constitutive of the mediated and situated life that is characteristic of late modern everyday life. However, as Silverstone (ibid.) shows, this does not mean that media and its cultural content are straightforwardly adopted; rather the process by which both the forms of media and its content are interpreted and embedded in social life constitutes its form within broader media and cultural frameworks and environments.

The use of Internet-related technology in everyday life is part of a broader change in general institutional frameworks – disembedding time and space within modernity (Giddens, 1984). The development of mobility in everyday life (Urry, 2000) is also contributing to the way the everyday acts as a framework in which social identities are established and re-established. The different ways in which individuals play with and display their identity is a characteristic feature of the taken-for-granted-ness of everyday life, which is not only accomplished at the local level but also draws on individuals' respective interaction with the cultural and creative industries.[5] As Kellner (1995) argues that if everyday life appears local, then the borders of locality have been diffused or extended by engagements with cultural industries that have global reach.

The expansion in telecommunications through mobile phones and the development of digital networks enable people to create new spaces and sites for engaging in communicative and media practices. This means that traditional spaces for communication, entertainment and cultural performance such as theatre, cinema and television, radio and phone are no longer the only places for communicative cultural work. These spaces are still key sites but they are expanded within environments in distinctive ways, such as digital video installations in built environments, user-produced content on blogs and wiki-based media, user-produced videos on YouTube and social networking around music on MySpace and so on. Equally and conversely, of course, the performance arts and traditional rituals have appropriated, used and created sites for performance from space and place using these new technologies. The development of mobile media means that individuals can stay connected whilst on the move, becoming – in effect – the 'primary unit of connectivity' (Wellman and Haythornthwaite, 2002). This means that individuals have to learn to manage a network of people and places in different contexts. The late modern individual, who is connected via these technologies, therefore manages the local and the global, work and domestic life through technology, as well as using the Web for entertainment or cultural activity.

The Second Age of the Internet and Everyday Life

Wellman and Haythornthwaite (2002) assert that the Internet is in its 'second age' (*c.* 2000)[6] because it is now being used routinely within the everyday lives of many people. The research they report on shows that the Internet is embedded in everyday life, with almost all Internet users routinely communicating via email (which is used more than the phone), and many web surf and shop online. Another example of take-up is participation in Usenet groups, whose members participated in more than 80,000 topic-oriented collective discussion groups in 2001 (ibid.). Although a smaller percentage of Internet users play online games, their numbers are enough to sustain a sizeable industry. Internet telephone accounted for 5.5% of international telephony traffic in 2001 (ibid.). The recent phenomenon of social networking has gained significant numbers of users, with MySpace logging 110 million unique users and Facebook logging over 100 million in January 2008 worldwide. The ten most popular Internet activities in the United States in 2000 were web-surfing/ browsing, email, finding hobby information, reading news, finding entertainment information, shopping online, finding travel information, using instant messaging, finding medical information and playing games (ibid.). The use of the Internet is integrated into the everyday life, for example, online commerce is integrated with physical stores to produce a 'clicks and mortar' form of shopping. A similar pattern of on and off-line everyday life routines are seen in the way actors use online communities alongside face-to-face, phone and postal contacts to keep in touch with friends and family. Wellman and Haythornthwaite stress that the Internet is used in both old, familiar ways and new, innovative ones. They suggest that the Internet is starting to be taken for granted because it is now an accepted part of everyday life.[7]

Given that the Internet is integrated into much of everyday life, Wellman and Haythornthwaite raise critical issues about earlier approaches that address the Internet in dichotomous terms – such as: Is the Internet providing new means of connectivity in domestic relations or is it sucking people away from husbands, wives and children? In relation to community, this type of approach leads to questions such as: Is the lure of the Internet keeping people indoors so that their 'in-person' (and even telephonic) relationships with friends, neighbours, and kinfolk wither – or is it enhancing connectivity so much that there is more than ever before? A similar theme is enacted out with regard to civic involvement, with questions such as: does the Internet disconnect people from collective, civic enterprises so that they are connecting alone – or is it leading people to new organizations and to the increase in organizations? In general questions of alienation run along the lines of: Is the Internet so stressful or disconnecting from daily life that people feel alienated – or does their sense of community increase because of the interactions they have online? As far as daily activities are concerned, this framework of analysis asks questions such as: Is the Internet replacing or enhancing everyday pursuits, be it shopping or finding companionship and social support?

Wellman and Haythornthwaite argue that although these questions raise issues about the Internet in everyday life, they fail to touch on how the Internet is integrated into ongoing daily life, actions and practices.[8] Research, therefore, they argue, needs to take an integrative approach to computer mediated communication (CMC) to address and understand how online activities fit with and complement other aspects of an individual's everyday life as well as examining how convergence has materialized into socio-cultural forms such as vlogs and so on. Factors that influence how the Internet is being taken up in everyday life include the increasing access, commitment and domestication of ICT, longer working hours, the use of ICT in schoolwork, 'keeping up' with trends in technology and media use and the pervasive development of a networked society (ibid.).

Routines and Practices in Daily Life

In the second age of the Internet, Wellman and Haythornthwaite define the Internet as a complex landscape of applications, purposes and users that interact with the entirety of people's lives, including interaction with their friends, the technologies they have around them, their life-stage and life-style and their offline community. They argue that people's Internet usage is related to their non-Internet attributes and behaviour. The patterns of behaviour include the observation that Internet users in the United States are more media connected than non-users: in the United States, books are used by 12% more Internet users that non-users; video games are used by 15% more Internet users than non-users; recorded music is used by 22% more Internet users than non-users; and Internet users use newspapers (6% more), radio (9% more), phone (3% more) more than non-users (ibid.). The only exception is television, which is viewed less by Internet users than non-users. These patterns of media use may be a reflection of the higher education and income of Internet users. It may also indicate characteristics of early adopters whose pre-existing inclination to use all types of media, combined with familiarity and ease with media, may have made it easier and less complex for them to adopt computing and the Internet (Rogers, 1995). It is not, therefore, surprising that people with higher incomes and education levels were the early adopters of the Internet, and that their lifestyles set some of the norms (netiquette) for online behaviour. However, although there are early shaping factors, the Internet is nonetheless adapted and located within multiple interactions and responsibilities, both online and off-line that are comprised of people's activities, relationships and community.

Time weaves through everyday life and the increasing mobility and flexible schedules of everyday life means that time is something that individuals negotiate and manage daily; adding another activity into everyday life means making adjustments to the shape of daily life. As Wellman and Haythornthwaite (2002) note, people cannot add 16 hours spent on Internet activities a week to their daily lives without changing some patterns of their existing behaviour.[9] One key area for time transference is from television viewing to Internet activity, with Internet users spending 28% less time watching television than non-users.[10] Nie et al. (2002) show that heavy Internet users cut back on use of all traditional media, as well as shopping in stores and commuting in traffic. Anderson and Tracey (2002), however, find that average use of the Internet only marginally reduces time spent gardening, reading newspapers, magazines and books, shopping, telephoning, going to the pub, doing nothing, writing letters and sleeping. Thus average time spent using the Internet tends to involve some rescheduling of activity with changes in television viewing being the most affected. Only heavy users of the Internet cut back on the usual activities of everyday life.

In relation to young people, Wagner et al. (2002) note that teenagers' use of the Internet does not reduce their more socially acceptable activities of reading or playing sport. Instead, they find that 'computer kids' are less likely to engage in the less-socially accepted activities of just 'hanging around' or doing nothing. Robinson et al. (2002) identify a similar in that Internet users in general tend to have a more active lifestyle than non-users, including having less sleep and more social contact with friends and co-workers. A different pattern of behaviour emerges when the Internet is used at home for a major undertaking such as studying or working online, with online learners dropping some activities first, while preserving others.[11] The first activities to go are relatively solitary experiences such as watching TV, reading for pleasure, needlework and gardening; the next activities that are curtailed are leisure activities with friends and work for volunteer groups; in the last instance work, sleep and food are compromised. Time with family (especially children) is maintained until the end, as well as work on the educational programme itself (Wellman and Haythornthwaite, 2002). This discussion shows that the Internet has become integrated into the routines of everyday life. It indicates that people adapt time and existing activities in ways that integrate the Internet into their daily lives. The types of changes they make relate to their interests and priorities through which they not only take up ICT but they shape it too. The next section considers the form in which the Internet is appropriated in everyday life, which is followed by a consideration of how people shape ICT.

Networks and Networked Individuals as Social Forms

Late modern lifestyles that involve varying levels of mobility and the micro-management of time is influential in shaping how people maintain contact with each other. Overall, the use of the Internet neither increases nor decreases contact in person or on the telephone. Very often staying in touch with people using the Internet results in people being in more contact with friends and relatives than when without Internet communication. The very act of communication is part of organizing and sustaining relationships. For example, in North America, being wired has local benefits: Blacksburg Internet users report increased communication with both formal groups and friends. In Netville, those with high-speed Internet connections had more informal contact with neighbours than the non-wired did and wired residents knew the names of 24 neighbours compared to 8 for non-wired individuals (Wellman and Haythornthwaite, 2002). Some of this is attributable to the Internet, although a key factor is how well connected people are in that some people might make new friends via the Internet but usually online connectivity starts with pre-established ties with friends and relatives in whom the Internet is utilized for communication purposes. Strong ties between friends and relatives often go beyond the local neighbourhood, especially if people move away for work or study, and in these contexts Internet communication builds on existing relationships, ensuring the maintenance of the relationship across distance. Furthermore, adding a new medium to communication repertoires is more likely if the relationship is already strong. Frequent contact via the Internet is associated with contact via other means and people use more media in closer relationships (ibid.). Relationships and their character are therefore influential in shaping the take-up and use of ICT for communication purposes and it is proving to be useful in maintaining relationships at distances of both local and beyond the local levels.

Research in the United States shows that connectivity goes with those who are online and well connected via ICT, and that people who are already well situated socially with good incomes and education derive the greatest social benefits from the Internet (Nie, 2001). Existing connectivity levels may also interact with the success of community-wide Internet initiatives, with civic engagement via the Internet being positively associated with higher levels of other forms of civic involvement. Community networks may succeed because they are established in environments that already have high levels of connectivity, suggesting that social capital is a prerequisite, rather than a consequence of, effective CMC (ibid.). Overall, communication and connectivity reinforce each other with those already with vibrant networks of friends and relations and those active in civic life exploiting ICT to enhance communications underpinning relationships and socio-cultural life.

Wellman and Haythornthwaite argue that changes to communication practices in everyday routines are located in a social trend signifying a different relationship between the individual and society, which they call 'networked individualism'. They show how an individual within a range of social networks has become the node of connectivity: it is through the individual that connections are made and the individual manages those connections. This transition is seen as being one from 'groups' with 'each in their place' to 'networks' involving the 'mobility of people and goods'.

Examples of these trends include shifts

- From a united family to serial marriage, mixed custody.
- From shared community to multiple partial networks.
- From neighbourhoods to dispersed networks.
- From voluntary organizations to informal leisure. (p. 33)

Wellman and Haythornthwaite argue that the Internet facilitates changes that were already in process towards a networked society. They suggest that society was changing from one of bounded communities to numerous individualized, fragmented, personal communities. Many people's close friends and family are not geographically close – transport systems and modern communications sustain the ties. This pattern is identified as being 'glocalized' (Hampton and Wellman, 2002; Graham and Marvin, 1996), which means 'the combining of long-distance ties with continuing involvements in households, neighbourhoods, and worksites' (Fischer, 1982 cited by Wellman and Haythornthwaite, 2002, p. 32). Furthermore, they assert that the Internet has supported the move to networks, which are characterized by more permeable boundaries – interactions with a greater diversity of others, as well as engagement in multiple networks (p. 33).

The personalization, portability, ubiquitous connectivity and wireless mobility of the Internet facilitate networked individualism as a basis for community. In this way, it is the individual who is becoming the primary unit of connectivity. The characteristics of these changes point to the emergence of new social forms – first, the network as a communicative community which links different aspects of an individual's life. This social form emerges from, and is located in, the needs and desires of individuals to coordinate the fragmentation of social life. The network facilitates them to construct the everyday meaningfully by crafting time, space and a range of resources through ICT and a myriad of communication practices. Second, networked individualism is the form through which individuals select significant others and cultural products in creating their own lifestyles in their everyday life. Underpinning these forms are communication systems configured from human, as well as old and new communication technologies. However, the role of the Internet and ICT is influential in facilitating late modern networks and the communicative agency of the individual within those networks.

Placing the Internet in the Meaningfulness of Everyday Life

Although there is some evidence that the network is emerging as a social form, social life and changes in social life require change in institutional terms. The routines, practices and meanings of everyday life are performed in the institutions of everyday life. The household and the domestic sphere are important institutions and sites in the domain of the everyday and they interact with wider social and public life. Innovation occurs in the everyday, both in terms of a range of practices and products including innovation in forms of communication and their technologies. Very often the interpretation and appropriation of goods and services by the diversity of everyday users is a source of innovation. As Chaney (1994) argues, engagement with cultural products is social action and – in relation to the innovation of ICT – the processes of the ways in which these technologies are used (or not) and shaped shows that the innovation process does not stop once a product leaves suppliers' shelves (Silverstone and Hirsch, 1992).

ICT enters the everyday through the key institution of the household. The household is the site for the domestication process, which involves fitting and fixing the new ICT into the familiar and the secure, while moulding its novelty to the needs, desires and culture of the family or household (ibid.). The shaping of ICT is in the relations of the household through four non-discrete phases, which are the appropriation of ICT, its objectification and incorporation into the household through which it is meaningfully converted into domestic use (p. 16). Silverstone (with Hirsch) asserts that this process is one by which consumers incorporate new technologies and services into patterns of their everyday lives in ways that maintain both the structure of those lives and their capacity to control that structure. Domestication of ICT shows how changes around patterns of communication are contested within socio-cultural and institutional frameworks. Silverstone argues that consuming ICT is a struggle between the familiar and the new, the social and the technical. It is situated in the contested space between the revolutionary potential of the machine and the evolutionary demands of family and household. Furthermore, this concept addresses the struggle within households in the appropriation of ICT, seen, for instance, between parents and children, between male and female siblings, between male and female partners, between same sex partners and between levels of computer 'experts' and computer 'novices'. In all these relationships, individuals seek to manage space, time and technologies without losing position and identity within the complex and uncertain politics of age, gender and status in the home.

Silverstone (with Hirsch, 1992; also in Berker et al., 2006, pp. 229–247) posits that the domestic sphere is a 'moral economy', a distinct social and cultural space in which the evaluation of individuals, objects and processes which form the currency of public life is transformed and transcended once the move is made into private life.[12] In these domestic spaces, individuals are more or less free – depending on their available material and symbolic resources – to define their own relationships to each other and to the objects and meanings, the mediations, communications and information that cross their thresholds. Households are both economic and cultural units within which their members can define for themselves a private, personal and, more or less, distinct way of life. The materials and resources they have at their disposal come both from the inner world of family values, as well as the public world of commodities and objects. This moral economy is constantly changing, affected by the 'relentlessness of the human life cycle, as well as the buffetings of everyday life, historically specific yet uneven in their consequences' (p. 230).

The dynamics of the moral economy are defined through an eternal cycle of consumption and appropriation in which a commodity is accommodated into the spaces, times and functional requirements of the home. New hardware and software technologies and services are brought into the home to be placed, displayed and incorporated into the rituals of domestic and daily life to enhance efficiency or increase pleasure (ibid.). New skills may be developed, meanings generated and new conflicts are, or are not, resolved – all of which are expressions of the constant tensions between technological and social change within the household. The novelty and achievements, the significance created and sustained in the ownership and use of new machines, access to new computer software or TV channels then become part of the currency of everyday discourse – discussed, displayed and shared in the social gossip and talk in neighbourhoods, schools and workplaces. Silverstone's understanding of the consumption and domestication of ICT is a significant contribution to understanding the Internet and everyday life. In particular he shows how institutions and institutional change is part of technological change. Therefore, although networks might be gaining greater and a particular relevance in late modernity, the social relations of households and the moral economy of the domestic sphere remain significant institutions in shaping ICT and the characteristics of communication in late modern everyday life. Furthermore, these processes are intrinsically cultural and therefore, the everyday and the shaping of the Internet are informed by the culture of everyday life in its routines and in its engagement with cultural activities whether that of networks of friends, public culture or cyber culture (see Chapter 9).

The significance of the institution of the household is often neglected in conventional discussions of the diffusion of ICT. These discussions fail to acknowledge the work that households and the public at large do in 'domesticating' ICT to serve their own particular values and interests. This work also includes people's patterns of consumption and their everyday choices in consuming ICT (Silverstone and Hirsch, 1992). The producers of ICT, however, have significant power and influence in creating and managing the use of ICT through the way they shape and frame consumer choice (Mansell and Silverstone, 1996). Nonetheless, despite their power, the rejection of some ICT, such as the videophone, demonstrates that consumers also play a pivotal role in ICT developments. Woolgar (2001) explains that the degree of influence exerted by producers depends on their ability to 'configure the user'. Producers can position ICT in relation to users long before they reach the marketplace; however, as research by Silverstone (2005) shows, the 'everyday is not biddable to the desires of technology' (p. 13) or that of its producers.

Contexts of the ways in which members of households shape technologies and their cultural usage includes how TV audiences and PC users actively engage in consuming technologies by deciding how to use them and how to interpret the messages they convey. These decisions are various and include the ways households consciously regulate access to communication technologies and media other than TV: such as books, answering machines and services that screen and return phone calls. Parents regulate the use of ICT by installing software that allows children to use their parents' PC while preventing them from destroying electronic files or accessing pornographic sites on the web. Another example of parental shaping of technology and its use is the taking out subscriptions to cable or pay-TV services that are suitable for children.[13] The gendering of space is another aspect of ICT use in the home. For instance, putting a PC in the male partner's office restricts privacy of the female partner, which might constrain her use of ICT (Haddon and Skinner, 1991). The design of the home is also changing as more homes are being built to accommodate PCs and other ICT equipment, in contrast to previous homes being designed to accommodate print technologies by installing bookshelves.[14] Culturally accepted beliefs and attitudes about the organization of the household structure these choices.[15] In so doing, households actively shape access, sometimes by design, but often inadvertently, in the pursuit of other values and interests. However, the choices for households are not open-ended, being constrained by prevailing attitudes to the arrangements of the home, which varies across cultures, socio-economic groups and time. Consumers' choices are also constrained by the influence of producers as well as by the larger social, economic and political ecology outside the household.

The culture of everyday life extends out into numerous forms of households and patterns of living the everyday. In a culture of everyday life influenced by neo-liberalism – whether embraced, managed or resisted – individuals negotiate the socio-technical environment creatively in relation to the specificity of their lives. These negotiations are diverse and produce distinctive fabrics and flows to the everyday. For example, different patterns emerge in diverse studies of a small seaside town in North County Dublin (Ireland) in an established community (Ward, 2005); in Trondheim (Norway) amongst mobile cosmopolitan scientific researchers (Berker et al., 2005); and in the management of travel in everyday life and mothering

(Haddon, 2004). Another pattern of everyday life is that of those living in diasporic communities where communication is intrinsically linked with the dynamics of inclusion and exclusion. These transnational communities have always been reliant on networking to communicate with, and maintain their relationships with, dispersed friends and relatives from around the globe (Georgiou, 2005). Apart from the Irish example, these contexts, in differing ways, show how communication extends domestic space, traditionally understood, to a range of public and semi-public spaces and publicly accessible media outlets.

The study in Ireland shows how the residents of the town[16] are learning to integrate the Internet into existing routines and media consumption mainly by using it in a structured and targeted way (Ward, 2005, p. 107). Households appropriate the affordance of ICTs and shape them into local and private cultures, which are also reshaping the relationship and interactions between their private and public spheres. Principally, this means that the Internet is incorporated into family cultures, especially those families with children. Although parents recognize that part of the pressure to engage with ICT is ideological, they nonetheless say that take-up of ICT in the family home is triggered through the demands of education, with many parents feeling that they need to be Internet literate to support their children's schooling. Parents also feel that lacking access to ICT and not being ICT literate is increasingly restricting their capacity to participate in public life. This is because access and information about public events are increasingly being made available via ICT such as the provision email addresses on the radio for public events for booking tickets and getting details of an event. However, the use of ICT, in this established community, is largely privatized, in that the influence of family cultures extend in shaping ICT use through many of the families wanting to maintain communication with friends and family who live in Australia, South Africa, America and Canada. Family cultures in this community setting are influential in shaping the Internet, and they temper any rapid, and potentially disruptive, innovation of ICT in the patterns of the everyday.

A rather different pattern of use emerges in Trondheim amongst geographically mobile researchers living within a condition of cosmopolitanism (Roche, 2007). Their condition in particular highlights the dynamics of public and private spheres, and how the blurring of these spheres is managed in contexts of internationally situated work (Silverstone, 2005). The life of scientific researchers can involve time working in foreign universities because international and transnational networks are common in the production of knowledge (Berker, 2005). In this situation, workers who are away from 'home' configure ways to use the Internet to mitigate senses of displacement, to keep in touch with family and friends as well as maintaining their professional links with researchers worldwide. The researchers' use of the Internet as a research tool in their work setting is relatively unproblematic. In contrast, however, researchers experience difficulties in negotiating personal and work based ICT for their own private communication. Researchers learn how to utilize ICT within the personal sphere and work spheres by manoeuvring social spaces and time boundaries to carve out time and communicative resource to contact distant friends and relatives. They combine personal and work technologies such as mobiles, PCs and wireless technologies to communicate and bracket pockets of time in the day when they know they can contact their relatives and friends.

The context for this is that these researchers are living their personal lives in internationally dispersed households (with partners and family in other countries) and networks of local and international researchers, but have little contact with local people in their geographical place of residence. This means that notions of a daily routine in which activities that can be conventionally done 'in work' times and 'in home' times are blurred. However, to secure their senses of self in these contexts, they reflexively construct routines of communication with their families using ICT, whilst keeping their research networks alive through the same online communication tools. The separation between non-work communication and networks and work-related networks and communication means that the researchers have to negotiate and mediate different lifeworlds in trans-local and local spaces. Most researchers hope that one day they will find a secure job and place and, in the meantime, ICT is a resource they manage to live an everyday life of extreme flexibility (ibid.).

A key part of everyday contemporary life is travel, in its many diverse forms. The recent rise of travel is often termed 'hypermobility' (Adams, 2000), which marks the increase in journeys, including linking journeys taken in everyday life as well as global travel. This increase occurs despite the earlier belief that ICT would enable people to engage in local everyday life by working from home with tele-access in configurations of tele-cottages and in so doing reduce travel (Richardson and Gillespie, 2003). Other dimensions to this trend include the rise of mothers working and commuting and also the ways in which young people increasingly organize their own leisure activities. This aspect of travel illustrates the extension of the domestic space into public space and highlights the relationship between the two, namely how the use of communication technologies is important in managing travel. For instance, children use fixed-line phones to organize meetings with peers (Buchner, 1990), a practice also undertaken by young adult friends in France (Manceron, 1997). Adults use email to plan events at relatively short notice, such as arranging to meet up after work – although delayed or lost emails can be problematic (Haddon, 2000). Mobile phones and mobile devices such as Blackberries are a popular technology whilst travelling because they enable users to communicate whilst mobile, and thus micro-coordinate travel (Ling, 2004). Examples include arranging to pick up or drop off children whilst travelling between work and home and teenagers confirming meeting times and places when out enjoying leisure time. Another example is that of women using mobiles to be available to their children even when they are not physically present, which is referred to as 'remote mothering' (Rakow and Navaro, 1993). Mobiles therefore enable individuals to manage their private affairs whilst away from home and extend the meaning of the domestic sphere, shaping ICT to fit into late modern lifestyles (Haddon, 2004).

For diasporic communities, the everyday has distinctive characteristics. In particular, the fabric of the everyday is weaved from the dynamics of inclusion and participation in highly mediated society (Georgiou, 2005). One defining characteristic of the experience of a diaspora is that the perspectives within it recognize the ways in which identities are transformed through relocation and cross-cultural exchange and interaction (Gillespie, 1995). These populations rely on, and benefit from, communication technologies to maintain links with their networks across the globe. A key aspect that these communities face in their everyday lives is that, on the one hand, they actively participate in distinct communities (across local, national and transnational contexts) whilst, on the other hand, they face constraints in their efforts to participate (Georgiou, 2005). The use of the Internet in this context is located within the broad range of media used by members of diasporic communities (see Chapters 7 and 10).

However, the Internet plays a particular role in the communication ensembles in diasporic experience and sensibilities. This is because communication via the Internet helps to sustain cultural identity through the exchange of the ordinariness of culture shared across the everyday, as well as cultural distinctiveness shared through language and politics. The availability of online communication, primarily email, has increased communication between members of communities across transnational, local and national networks. Members of diasporic communities report that they regularly share everyday experiences and mundane news with those in other positions in the diaspora network (Georgiou, 2005). In sharing news, they also exchange intimate email attachments, such as family photographs. This sharing of the mundane, the intimate and the common routines and practices of everyday life (De Certeau, 1984) foster feelings of belonging to a community and extend the possibilities of imagined sharing (Georgiou, 2005). A further element that sustains the culture of everyday life is the development of diasporic cultural projects (ibid.), which utilize the web to sustain language and dialects and to exchange music and cultural knowledge. The sites for these activities tend not to be in domestic spaces, because many diaspora members do not have the resource to access the Internet privately. Instead, they use Internet cafés, community centres, local shops and minority media centres. Therefore, the intermediation of the everyday for diasporic communities is across public and private spaces, interweaving the richness of cultures in the exchange of everyday news via online communication. In this way, these groups participate in local and transnational everyday life, but need public access to the Internet to do so.

The above examples show how ICT is appropriated into a range of routines and cultures of everyday life. They also show how the culture of everyday life – whether of established communities in coastal towns or that of transnational diasporic communities – shapes the ways in which the Internet becomes a communicative tool in the expression of shared experience, whether ordinary or extraordinary. The examples show the ways in which individuals, each with his or her own role and identity, actively engage with the Internet to configure forms of communication to manage the flexibility of their everyday lives, which they do reflexively. A key characteristic of communication and the everyday is the idea and form of the network and networking, which is embedded within each example; even amongst settled residents in Ireland who use the Internet to communicate with networks of relatives. What is significant, however, is that each of these networks is institutionally shaped – and their distinctiveness is shaped through the cultural engagement of actors within those institutions. These engagements and negotiations are performed creatively in the ongoing flow and fabric of everyday life – it is through the everyday that the Internet finds its forms and its meaning.

Conclusion

This chapter has shown that it is through everyday life and communication that the shape of social experience is formed, performed and expressed. The culture of everyday life is interacting with changing social forms, such as the emergence of networks and networked individualism. Although the Internet can underpin and facilitate social networks, the institutions of everyday life give such networks and networked communication meaning. Distinctive characteristics of the contemporary culture of everyday life such as its populism, fragmentation, informalization and multiculturalism inform the ways in which actors engage with the Internet as a communicative and media technology. Through popular understanding of parenting practices, of cultural performances of diasporic communities and of flexible work patterns in the cosmopolitan condition, social actors appropriate

ICT, shaping it, as well as the fabric of the everyday. The distinctiveness of everyday engagement in social life means that networks are made meaningful through the institutions that constitute them.

One important process in the ways in which ICT gets taken up, or not, is domestication. This shows how the social relations of the household and narratives of family life shape the participation in communication, including through the Internet. However, given the mobility of contemporary everyday life, whether via journeys, communities or work, the relations of households extend into public spaces in which actors integrate the public and the private in communicative forms such as remote mothering. All of these practices show that actors in late modern everyday life are reflexive in the ways they integrate ICT into their lives. Although producers can try to configure the user, real life continues to fight back, with cultural and social forms questioning a simplified reading of networked individualism – rather, we are situated in webs of meaning which shape our communication and its tools.

9

Cyber Cultures and the Internet

Introduction

This chapter discusses cyber culture to address the specific characteristics of the Internet by addressing virtuality, identity and community. It shows how social actors play with, and negotiate, their mediated worlds in relation to their situated lives, illustrating how people are creative with the Internet, producing cultures of Internet in its 'second age'. Although 'the virtual' is a distinctive feature of cyber culture, this culture is crafted out of the materiality of machines and wires, it is engaged symbolically through popular culture, fiction, film and people's imaginations, and it is lived in the experiences of its participants. Nonetheless, the notion of the 'virtual' is central in understanding cyber cultures and must be considered in relation to the ways in which, and to what degree, social actors play with virtual identities, virtual communities and subcultures and virtual sexualities. It is, however, the ways that the virtual is given meaning through culture that gives cyber culture its resonance and shape – the way it is experienced and materialized in cultural forms. These forms, which vary in content, give the Internet its salience in the ongoing performances of ways of life.

Considering Culture, Mediated Communication and Practice

Culture, as Geertz (1973) argues, relates to the ways in which humans interpret, understand and act within particular social contexts. These contexts vary but, prior to the development of mass media, they were often experienced locally with immediacy in relation to customs, rituals and idioms understood *in situ*. To understand and analyse cyber culture requires building on the discussion of contemporary culture discussed in

Chapters 3, 4 and 8. A key aspect of modern and late modern culture is the media (see Chapter 10). The development of mass media produced a communicative environment that mediated events, experience and meaning remotely. Thompson (1996)[1] argues that the media in modernity disembedded time and space, expanded access to other cultures and places and became a source through which people re-imagine the local, the global and cultural specificity and exchange. The character of the communication through which this cultural activity is achieved was one of 'one to many', that is producer to audiences. The audience is influential to some degree in its interpretation of the content (Hobson, 1982; Ang, 1985; Radway, 1987; Scannell et al., 1992; Morley, 1980, 1986), and through feedback in the form of viewing figures and market research. A key process in media communication is mediation that – although complementary to communication – is also different from it, as its dialectical character requires communication to be seen as both institutionally and technically achieved and embedded (Silverstone, 2005b). The institutionalization of mass media within the media industries and public service broadcasters has, in part, defined the form and content of cultural exchange and the relations embedded within that exchange. As discussed in previous chapters, the design of the Internet and WWW is informed by a democratic and egalitarian ethos and is a many-to-many network of communication. It is, therefore, interesting to see how culture is weaved in relation to that form of communication and mediation (both disintermediation and re-intermediation) in the spaces it constructs for cultural content, representation and performance. Some observers have named this environment 'cyber culture', a term grounded in the genre of science fiction writing.

The early rhetoric surrounding cyber culture emphasizes the possibilities of liberation from traditional forms of identity, community and sexuality. However, although, there is some playfulness and self-expression, many of these hopes have not reached their envisaged potential. For example, some of the early utopian feminist arguments posited that cyberspace could liberate women from traditional gender roles and from their gender embodiment. However, Internet practices such as online dating, chat-rooms and MUDS show that these practices often reproduce stereotypical notions of sexual and gender identity. A similar process can be seen in relation to the early rhetoric suggesting that the Internet could be used to form 'virtual' communities in response to a perceived loss of 'real' community. Although virtual communities provide some sense of participation and belonging, they tend to be interest-based and transient. The developments of community type spaces on the WWW tend to form through an interaction of on and off-line associations, thus not reaching the early visions of entirely online communities. Another dimension of online interaction is the way people 'tame' total free-play in virtual worlds because of their human values such as trust, reciprocity and honesty that maintain their importance in Internet-based communication. Examples of these are seen in chat-room sanctioning and in the general management of risks and threats in the Internet environment. Therefore, the virtual as practiced in cyber cultures is a negotiated reality mediated between imaginations, on and off-line experiences and social mores – facilitated by machines, wires and websites.

Defining and Working with Cyber Culture

It is proving difficult to find ways to define cyber culture in any definitive sense. Without any specific and tightly defined character, social scientists view it as a series of ideas, issues and questions about what happens when one conjoins the word 'cyber' with 'culture'. The starting point for exploring this is the notion of 'cyberspace' – a word created by the science fiction writer William Gibson (1984), discussed below. Sterling (1990) provides a working definition of cyberspace as being a cluster of different technologies, which have the ability to simulate environments within which humans can interact. Featherstone and Burrows (1995) clarify and unpack Sterling's definition. They start by drawing on Barlow's[2] idea of a Barlovian cyberspace, which refers to international networks of computers. However, they argue that interaction within this space, although varied and potentially rich, does not involve the full range of human senses that make up communication. This is because full co-presence in human interaction involves sensory, visual and auditory cues (ibid.), something the Barlovian definition does not adequately cover. To address the richness of human senses in communication, Featherstone and Burrows draw on the term 'virtual reality', which refers to 'a real or simulated environment in which the perceiver experiences telepresence' (Steuer, 1992, pp. 76–77). Virtual reality which involves a computer-generated multi-media visual, audible and tactile experience provides a richer communicative experience (Featherstone and Burrows, 1995). These types of discussions contribute to understanding Jones's (1995a) idea of computer-mediated communication that seeks to address the ways people communicate via configurations of new and evolving ICT.

These definitions infer a sense of communicative-presence through technology; however, neither refers explicitly to the realm of the imagination and culture. Writing from within the popular science fiction genre, Gibson coined the term 'cyberspace' and defined the cyberpunk genre (see *Neuromancer*).[3] Gibson said that he

assembled [the] word cyberspace from small and readily available components of language. Neologic spasm: the primal act of pop poetics. Preceded any concept whatever. Slick and hollow – awaiting received meanings. All I did: folded words as taught. Now other words accrete in the interstices. (Gibson, 1991, p. 28)

He points out that cyberspace is constituted through 'a consensual hallucination experienced daily by billions of legitimate operators, in every nation, by children taught mathematical concepts ... A graphical representation of data abstracted from the banks of every computer in the human system. Unthinkable complexity. Lines of light in the nonspace of the mind, clusters and constellations of data ... like city lights, receding' (Gibson, 1984, p. 67). What Gibson is describing is the fact that cyberspace is the sum of the world's data accessible through computer consoles. This activity, known as 'jacking in', means uploading a user's consciousness into cyberspace, leaving the corporality of the body behind, allowing a user, once inside, to 'fly' through the data. The cyberpunk genre opened up imaginations to the possibilities of such a space, and triggered ideas of how it could imaginatively be lived and inhabited, in other words, enriching it culturally.

To ground some of these ideas around cyberspace, Bell (2001) argues that it is made up of three dimensions, which are the material, the symbolic and the experiential. Materially, cyberspace involves machines, wires, electricity, programs, screens and connections, and it comprises modes of information and communication: email, websites, chat-rooms and MUDs (p. 2). Symbolically, it has images and ideas: cyberspace exists on film, in fiction and in our imaginations as much as on our desktops or in the space between our screens. Experientially, social agents encounter and engage in cyberspace (in all its spectacular and mundane manifestations) by mediating the material and the symbolic (ibid.). For Bell the meaning of cyberspace involves considering the way in which it is shaped and experienced as a lived environment.

Considering cyberspace as culture emphasizes the point that it is a lived experience, made from people, machines, imagination and social life. Hine (2000) advocates a similar approach to Bell, asserting that cyberspace is both culture and cultural artefact. She argues that the Internet is represented through a place – cyberspace – in which culture is formed and reformed (p. 9). Although early CMC studies tended to posit a restricted sphere of communication, ideas regarding extending the uses of the Internet into, for example, online communities, pushed CMC research into richer communicative environments. The making of these environments, both the more restricted and the potential rich, is as cultural as the interactions that sustain them. Hine links this with Woolgar's (1996) concept of cultural artefact, which sees technology as a product of culture. Woolgar argues that a technology such as the Internet is produced by specific social actors with contextually driven goals and priorities and is shaped by the way it is marketed, taught and used. These discussions all point to an understanding of the Internet as a cultural entity – with its various forms, genres and performances (c.f. Chaney, 1983, 1990). Cyberspace can be viewed as cultural in much the same way that any and every thing around us is the product of culture. For example, the particular shape of computers and their design history, including how computers arrived on desktops and how they connect people with each other is a cultural tale (Edwards, 1996; Castells, 2001). Bell (2001) argues that cyberspace is both a product and a producer of culture simultaneously and that both these perspectives need to be kept in mind to avoid the slide into either technophilia or technophobia.

A distinctive characteristic of cyber culture is the idea of the virtual. The 'virtual' most often refers to that which appears to be, but is not, real or proper, although it may have the same effects as its real counterparts. It attests to the possibility that 'seeming' and 'being' can be confused, and that the confusion might not, in fact, matter. This sense of a virtual arises from a complex history of relations between reality, appearance and goodness. The roots of virtuality are in virtue and therefore in power and morality (Bell, 2001). The virtual also refers to optics, which involves a sense of re-viewing – via reflection, refraction, magnification, remote viewing or simulation. The growth of a secular understanding of virtue begins by assigning it more physical powers, so that virtue is equated with health, strength and sexual purity (ibid.).[4] The blurring between 'fact and fantasy' is an integral aspect of cyberspace, with some theorists such as Virilio (1995, 1997) suggesting that technologies of the virtual will not only simulate the real as Baudrillard (1983) suggests but will replace it. However, as discussed throughout this book, the 'real fights back' (Turkle, 1997), or at least the on and off-line worlds interact to produce experiences of cyberspace in which the virtual is a resource for questioning cultural values and mores. The social dynamic around the virtual produces distinctive cultural forms that give shape to participative cultures in the domains of identity, community, entertainment, (sub) cultural activity and the body.

The above debates point to a consensus amongst many social scientists (of technology and culture) that any distinction between cyberspace and cyber culture is a false dichotomy. This is because cyber culture constitutes cyberspace, and cyberspace is culturally produced. Cavallaro (2000) writes of cyber culture as 'an environment saturated by electronic technology', which is cultural and requires looking at ideas, experiences and metaphors in their interaction with machines and material change. The use of metaphors plays a distinct role in cyberspace, giving immateriality some sort of visible and material form (Hartmann, 2004). In relation to culture, computers do not just give shape to metaphors – in fact, metaphors shape the Internet and related technologies that spillover into everyday life in many different ways (ibid.). Miller and Slater (2000) argue that addressing cyberspace means looking at a 'range of practices, software and hardware technologies, modes of representation and interaction that may or may not be interrelated by participants, machines and programs' (p. 14). They move beyond the online and off-line relationship debate by suggesting that the interactions and practices of cyberspace need not occur at a computer as they are made and re-made in the various spaces of cultural activity by people.

Living Cyber Culture: Narratives of the Form

A key narrative shaping cyber culture is based in cyberpunk fiction,[5] which focuses on 'the intensities, possibilities, and effects of new modes of technologically mediated experience' (Kellner, 1995, p. 23).[6] The writers of cyberpunk imagine

> a future dominated by libertarian capitalism, where global wealth and power are the preserve of multinationals and nation-states are weak or gone: where a dual economy flourishes and is enforced through corporate modes of governance and surveillance; where society is increasingly urbanised within fragmented, divided, simulcra cities; where the body is enhanced through the use of genetic engineering and technical implants. (Dodge and Kitchin, 2001, p. 206)

Against this backdrop, the genre's heroes are often ambivalently located as working within and against the system, trading their machine skill across both legal and illegal markets. In part, this genre opens up the cultural shaping of a datascape and enables a reworking of bodies, identities and communities. Burrows (1997a) also observes social criticism within cyberpunk fiction because it presents a sociologically coherent vision of a very near future that may soon materialize in reality. However, as with all cultural products, audience and participants play a role through their interpretations, and aspects of social criticism and imagined worlds are picked up and acted on in varying ways. Kneale (1999), for example, argues that readers 'flesh out' some of the vagueness in Gibson's Neuromancer through their own experiences of cyberspace and, in turn, they extend their reading of cyberpunk into the development of cyberpunk online and in other cultural forms and practices.

The relationship between cyberspace and popular culture is not limited to cyberpunk. For instance, popular culture stories are another genre, which include cyber-thrillers as well as popular romantic novels (Bell, 2001). Cultural commentators often interpret the mainstream cyber fictions as unsophisticated and conservative indicators of technophobia and social anxiety (Kuhn, 1990). Bell (2001), however, argues that these stories are interpreted and engaged with by readers, who in turn may feed their interpretations back into cyber culture. It is important to acknowledge the role that is played by the diversity of representations in cyberspace because they provide a portfolio of meanings that audiences can piece together in meaningful ways. Thus, for example, as Bell argues, 'you've got mail' romances can provide particular insights into cyber culture, and they can be used as a symbolic resource in the ongoing interpretations of culture. In whichever genre, and however audiences interpret texts, representation nonetheless remains a complex issue and process. A defining feature of cyber culture is intertextuality and hypertextuality, by which producers and users of texts make links and connections between the meanings, referents and codes in texts of various kinds. Those who participate in cyber culture therefore obtain access to ways of thinking about cyberspace from a range of cultural resources and there is an ongoing relationship between popular culture and cyberspace including the representations of cyberspace in popular culture (ibid.). The production, circulation and consumption of popular culture are influential in how social actors come to envision and experience cyberspace.

Bell argues that narratives of the 'experiential story' situate the physical aspects of the Internet, its use and its imaginative sphere inside the realms of popular experience. The way into cyberspace is through the software of a computer's interface. The metaphor of windows (Windows interface) is indicative of the character of that interaction, in that

> windows have become the potent metaphor for thinking about the self as a multiple and distributed system ... The life practice of windows is of a distributed self that exists in many worlds and plays many roles at the same time. (Turkle, 1997, p. 547)

These characteristics point to the way in which the late modern or the networked individual engages in the communicative worlds of the real and the virtual. In many ways, this metaphor summarizes the ways in which individuals manage their communication in everyday life, as discussed in the previous chapter. However, the question remains about how these communication practices give specific form and meaning in culture involving cyber sensibilities.

Two main aspects of the culture of the human–computer interface are immersion and interactivity. These aspects of CMC reached the popular market through computer games. These games, developed by hobbyists, hackers and amusement arcade enthusiasts, brought the earliest forms of interactive software to the mass market and in so doing they introduced interactivity to the general population (Haddon, 1993). The early games were playful adaptations of computers and their 'arcade' look gave them family entertainment appeal. At the time of their introduction in the early to mid-1990s there was moral panic about online games due to fears around a gaming culture of violence and delinquency. There were also generational based concerns regarding 'growing up' and a ludic to work and place based adaptations of moving gaming from the arcade to home. However, researches since then have shown that these panics are largely unfounded. The social contexts in which games are played, such as within the family, mitigate against the development of such feared behaviours (Haddon, 1993; Miller and Slater, 2000; Wakeford, 1999).[7] Games, however, are important in shaping the human–machine interface because they demand players' intimate involvement, morphing the interface via immersion and interactivity of the gaming activity (Bolter and Grusin, 1999). Rushkoff classifies computer games into narratives such as dual, quest, apocalypse and simulation and argues that

> fully evolved video game play, then, is total immersion in a world from within a participant's point of view, where the world itself reflects the values and actions of the player and his [sic] community members. (Rushkoff, 1997, pp. 180–181)

Some interactions in cyberspace are more mundane, for example Miller and Slater (2000) comment that objects circulating in cyberspace have cultural effects, such as 'egreetings cards' and 'egifts'. They argue that these types of virtual objects reshape computer use through communication and are forms of expressing relationships such as friendships in remote and virtual interactions. Other objects fulfil different sorts of needs such as that of a family pet: for example, the virtual pet Tamagotchi originated in the desire of a Japanese child growing up in a small flat to have a pet. The Tamagotchi pet emerged from a particular situation within a specific culture and they have now extended to a craze amongst pre-teens in many countries.[8] Virtual objects, therefore, like any object, relate to forms of life through which they hold their meaning and they are part of people's culture (Turkle, 1997).

Experiences of (Cyber) Cultural Activity: Hopes, Dreams and Actualities

One of the most prominent and controversial aspects affecting the meaning of cyber culture is the question of community. Rheingold (1993), an early optimist, argues that 'words on the screen are quite capable of ... creating a community from a collection of strangers' (p. 7).[9] The desire to find a sense of community is popularly understood as a common response to the increasing global flows of information and peoples, which is creating a heightened reflexivity amongst individuals in advanced, disorganized (Lash and Urry, 1987) or transnational informational capitalist (Fuchs, 2007a) societies. This, combined with greater geographical mobility, generally and in everyday life, generates contexts in which individuals need to find ways to be connected and located within more fluid sets of social relations. Although these more dynamic relations can be experienced as chaotic, they are also embedded within systems of flows and communication and are grounded in social institutions. Various configurations emerge such as fandoms (on and off-line) (Hills, 2001), protest groups (Smith and Kollock, 2000), (sub) cultural constellations (Bell, 2001) and bunds[10] (Hetherington, 1998). Across this diversity of socio-cultural formations, Bromberg (1996) argues that 'people make use of this technology to combat the symptoms that are characteristic of ... the postmodern condition' (p. 147) – or, at least, late modernity.

Given the varying degrees to which individuals experience these trends in social life, they create spaces and time for cultural work. Rheingold (1993) suggests that virtual communities are a natural response to the hunger for community. He says

> think of cyberspace as a social petri dish, the Net as the agar medium, and virtual communities, in all their diversity, as colonies of microorganisms that grow in petri dishes. (Rheingold, 1993, p. 6)

He argues that virtual communities are like local pubs or cafés and that everything people do off-line could also be done online – they talk, undertake commercial transactions, support each other, make friends, make plans, create art and so on (p. 414). However, this is all done through 'words on computer screens', which 'leaves bodies behind' (ibid.). Rheingold continues to state that many people have created a virtual community in which their 'identities commingle and interact electronically, independent of local time or location' (ibid.). An example of a virtual community, from Rheingold's perspective, is that of the 'Whole Earth 'Lectronic Link' (WELL). WELL grew out of the Bay Area in San Francisco and its countercultural, hacking and hobbyists' cultures, and it generates 'customized neighbourhoods' which individuals configure to their personal mosaic of interests (ibid.).[11] WELL exhibits the feature Rheingold discusses in relation to virtual community in that it enables people to form community through the computer screen.

The kinds of intersubjectivity these communities of interest engender (or not) are seen in the ambiguities of their forms of participation. For example, these types of communities have different ways of visualizing the configuration of their identity. In early experiments these were text-based and coded in various ways, whereas more recent developments utilize visual and audio web-capacities. Thus, in the immaterial world of cyber culture, there are material traces seen in the texts and graphics that constitute shared spaces of interaction. Discursive patterns also emerge that give shape to the interactions, while social codes develop with participants establishing group norms that reveal implicit assumptions about senses of community. In design terms, 'groupware' signifies senses of online culture and communication: it embodies it in software and expresses the hearts and minds of cultures of collaboration. Examples of communication that seek to evoke common cultures include 'Systers' made up of female computer scientists and 'Seniornet' created by older people (Wellman and Gulia, 2001).

Another aspect of community is cooperation – an oft-quoted characteristic of online communities is their gift-economy (ibid.). This exchange materializes in online interactions and is often based on public goods,[12] which require an ethic of contribution from everyone in the community network to sustain the economy of exchange.[13] Examples of this type of exchange include the development of the operating system Linux by voluntary workers working in a collaborative and open source way, and another example is the collaboratively community and developer produced wiring of California's elementary schools in 1996 (Kolloch, 2001). The development of the online encyclopedia, Wikipedia is another such example. Online cooperation can positively facilitate the production of public goods in general terms, but this cooperation depends on the attitudes of those participating and, although it may benefit the group or community in question, it does not mean that the cooperation will automatically benefit wider social concerns.

Further dimensions of community are collective action and social protest, which link clearly with off-line activities. The role of the Internet in expressing social protest is most commonly related networked social movements and citizen networks (Castells, 2001). However, although online communication is useful in organizing collective action, it is the way in which groups and movements interact with political processes that influences their significance. Protest is closely linked to collective action and three distinct and possibly contradictory characteristics emerge regarding online communication in this context. First, in a positive sense, information can be cheaply, widely and quickly disseminated to relevant groups of people who are interested and seek to protest. Second and negatively, the very speed and reach of the medium creates a risk of inaccurate information being circulated. Third, another risk, is that the focus on exclusivity of targeted protest groups may inadvertently foreclose greater, and more diverse, participation in particular social causes (Gurak, 2001). This dynamic illustrates some of the issues of Internet-related activity, which include the fact that although online communication may provide space for the expression of more voices, it may also spread mis-information. It may also subsume informed citizen decisions to group manufactured beliefs. Furthermore, it is very often outside any organized democratic process informing social change, thus may prove to be ineffective in producing change although it may be influential in mobilizing opinions.

Robins (1999), however, asserts that the way the senses of community are described in accounts like Rheingold's freeze history, which in so doing and turn attention away from broader questions of society and politics. He argues that techno-sociality is seen as a basis for developing new and compensatory forms of community and conviviality. And in, as he says, 'this world gone wrong – community has become a lost object, nostalgized and looked for in cyberspace' (p. 87). He argues that this serves to preserve old forms of solidarity and community through simulation, which is not an alternative society, but is an alternative *to* society (p. 89). In similar vein, Davis (1990) points out that, online interaction can foster 'fortress communities' despite the rhetoric that cyberspace is inclusive and open to heterogeneity. Kroker and Kroker (2000) support this view by positing that the space online is a 'domain of order, refuge and withdrawal', a form of 'bunkering in' (ibid., in Bell and Kennedy, 2000, p. 96). And, as suggested in Chapter 4, seeking to escape others indicates that the culture of community in cyberspace is self-selecting, contingent and transitory and dependant on shared interests. It shows how presences in cyberspace can be imagined but may not ultimately be about social engagement as understood in traditional and industrial society. However, care needs to be taken that a traditional community is not regarded as an ideal. Bell (2001) supports this, arguing that the sense of a close-knit community can be repressive and stifling, in which 'strong ties matched with small minds, community spirit matched with oppressive regulation, safety matched with surveillance; [are] very uncomfortable if you don't fit in' (p. 106). Thus, the use of the Internet may provide spaces for people to connect and form variants of community, but its use may also generate new forms of ghettos and disconnection. As Slevin (2000) argues 'while Internet use may hold out the possibility of emancipation, we must at the same time be aware of how it might create new mechanism of suppression' (p. 109).

Even if the meaning of community is a highly debated, people do engage in online communication and so associate with others on the WWW. Part of online interaction and online formations are 'patterns of social meanings' that are 'manifested through a group's ongoing discourse' (Baym, 1998, p. 62). These communicative patterns allow participants to join online worlds, and, importantly, these patterns allow them to *imagine* themselves as part of a community' (ibid., emphasis added). This raises the question of what these imaginative belongings signify, satisfy and produce. If one thinks about community (on and off-line) through the usage of online communication by a configuration of individuals and groups then one can start to link perceptions of community (however understood) with identity and cultural activity. Therefore, senses of belonging can be understood differentially, which may or may not provide individuals and groups with feelings of community either in some authentic sense or as an illusionary one. These spaces have the potential to be either emancipatory or oppressive, relating to cultural change in late modernity. Individuals and collectives of various sorts negotiate on and off-line worlds from within a variety of positions and levels of mobility, which requires addressing questions of identity in culture and in cyber culture.

The fabric of identity is woven and rewoven through culture and communication – it is partly ascribed but it is also achieved and negotiated through interaction. The late modern individual constructs self-identity from imagined selves in relation to socio-cultural categories of gender, ethnicity, class, sexuality and age. The move from essentialist theories of identity to the deconstructed reflexive self is part of the discourse of modernity and late modernity. Slater (1998) argues that cyberspace extends the possibilities of deconstructing identity but with this deconstruction is the process of reconstructing identities. The virtual characteristic of cyberspace and the imaginative possibilities of culture have the potential for rethinking identity and its representation. Early optimists of the Internet saw cyberspace as emancipatory, through which individuals could escape and re-represent aspects of identity, their gender, their bodies, their sexualities and so on. This potential can be realized through the means of cyber-worlds and through the reflexivity of modern subjects. A cyber cultural artefact, the personal homepage, is an example of the reflexive presentation of self (Bell, 2001). Bell, drawing on Cheung (2000),[14] argues that homepages encourage a reflexive narration and presentation of the self, framed by the medium and perceptions of imagined audiences – in short, identity is being performed[15] (Bauman, 1977; Chaney, 1994; Schechner and Appel, 1990; Schechner, 1977; Turner, 1974, 1987). The performance of identity in cyberspace is cultural – it is a social activity in which scripts of author and audience, integrity and deception, fluidity and authenticity are rehearsed and played out.

As seen from the above discussion, the culture of cyberworlds is developing through complex webs of meaning (c.f. Geertz, 1973) and is often expressed through metaphors (Wakeford, 2000; Hartmann, 2004). An early, iconic metaphor, which exemplifies many themes of cyber culture, is that of the 'cyborg' (Haraway, 1985, 1991). Writing from a socialist–feminist position, Haraway develops a manifesto for feminists to engage with technology. She focuses on the shifting boundaries between human beings and technologies and constructs the cyborg. She uses the concept of the cyborg ironically to deconstruct and play with traditional dualisms between organism and machine and between social reality and fiction

(Haraway, 1991, p. 149). In this context 'the relationship between human and machine, authorship is questioned and made irrelevant because it becomes unclear who 'makes' and who is made' (Hartmann, 2004, p. 52). Hartmann points out that Haraway (1985) fuses communication and bio-technologies with the body in rephrasing gendered identities, in that the cyborg crosses borders of race, class and gender. The hybrid character of the cyborg is important because it signifies that there are possible pleasures in the confusion of boundaries, which imaginatively creates worlds without public–private distinctions (because everyone exists in networks) and without gender. Haraway's deconstructive turn aims to free women to rewrite their histories and themselves in language that is de-constitutive and capable of multiple and diverse re-representations.[16] The metaphor of the cyborg is representative of the debates regarding cyber culture and the relations between bodies and machines as well as those about feminism and technology.

Turkle (1985, 1997) engages with this debate more empirically in focusing on identity play surrounding CMC and cyberspace. Her attention is on identity shifts and the fragmentation of identity, and her ideas regarding self, space, the body and desire play a key role in approaches to cyber culture. Turkle argues that the production of the self in CMC is 'multiple, fluid, and constituted in interaction with machine connections' (Turkle, 1997, p. 15). Furthermore, the self is made through language and transformed through language (ibid.). Given this activity in language, the self can be re-imagined and reconstructed with CMC providing spaces to think about the 'I', life, intelligence and intentions. This is achieved through 'role play', which involves playing out life-like scenarios in environments that allow scope for experimentation in exploring possible outcomes of a range of actions. Turkle argues that online this type of play is continuous, anonymous and invisible, which opens up possibilities for role play. For instance, it is easier to change gender identity online than off-line because actors use textual descriptors to represent gender, whereas off-line experimentation needs a range of material resources such as dress, make-up and styling products as well as the knowledge of how to use them. This is not to deny, as Hartmann (2004) points out 'that changing gender identity over time requires more in-depth markers and is difficult to maintain over time' (p. 54). However, what Turkle offers is the suggestion that virtual identities are evocative objects for thinking about the self in worlds that are open to negotiation of self and identity.

These imaginative worlds are cultural and their ideas are not free floating – they occur in life worlds and sensibilities and have material outcomes (Geertz, 1973, p. 314). Wakeford (2000) and Hartmann (2004) focus on links between imaginative playful worlds and material worlds, focusing particularly on the use of metaphors as mediators between imaginative and material worlds. Taking a more sociological approach, these writers politicize metaphors, arguing that the work they do, what they attend to and evoke, is part of wider identity creation that makes an online presence public or at least semi-public, as well generating frameworks for online participation. They therefore point to the relationship between metaphor and user – imagination and identity. This takes us beyond metaphors to address the actualities of engaging in cyborg-like play in various cultural contexts of use and performance – in integrated cultural forms.

As discussed above, the cultures of engagement in cyber-related activities occur at the intersection of material, symbolic and experiential worlds (Bell, 2001). The character of their gestation and negotiation is, like any other cultural work, 'contested, temporal and emergent' (Clifford, 1984, p. 19). The work involved in playing, attesting and challenging cultural frameworks of gender (its performance and embodiment, c.f. Butler, 1990) shows how flexible, fluid, resilient and resistant culture is. For instance, representations of gender in cyberpunk and the metaphor forwarded by Haraway have room for counter-intuitive outcomes. Thus, the imaginary of cyberpunk reinstates gender strongly by exaggerated representations of bodies as highly feminine or masculine (Squires in Bell and Kennedy 2000, p. 364). This is pervasive across gender representation in cyberspace, in which there is a re-gendering of disembodied subjects (Bell, 2001, p. 124). For example, the techno-erotic body in popular cyber culture powerfully reinstates gender stereotypes in both physical and behavioural terms (c.f. Bell (2001) and O'Riorden and Phillips (2007)). However, given the diversity of cultural genres, those engaging in multi-user-domains are playing with gender identity. LambdaMOO,[17] for instance, offers ten gender types to its participants[18] so that participants have the freedom to choose alternative genders from their real-life gender. They can experiment with virtual cross-dressing, which Bell (2001) argues holds resemblances to the earlier Dungeons and Dragons MUD that emphasized fantasy and play.

However, even in this play, established culturally inscribed and lived gender and sexuality proves to be resilient and enduring. For instance, Kaloski (1999) soon discovered this in the limitations of Lamba during her search for the bisexual cyborg. She cruised the MOO's sex rooms as a tall, down-covered spivak (one of the ten choices of gender offered on Lambda); however, after having little success, she said that she 'received the clear message' that 'if you want sex, change your gender to female' (p. 125). A further dimension is that, in experimenting with gender, players are also located in off-line gender identities that are emotionally intrinsic to their senses of self. Given this factor, managing online play is not always easy and off-line sensibilities can act as a brake to free gendering, whether post- or hyper-gendering (Bassett, 1997). This is especially the case in feelings of betrayal that are experienced once real-life gender identity is discovered. In one example, Kendall (1996) recounts her sense of betrayal when she fell in love with a female character in MUDs, only to later find out that the 'she' was in fact a 'he'. This prompted her to never get personally involved with anyone in MUDs in future. Cases are even more problematic where fantasy is not foregrounded and where switching gender is not overtly playful. In these contexts, cross-dressing can be deemed as 'dishonest', bringing to the fore issues of trust and deception (Bell, 2001). A well known example of this is that of the 'cross-dressing psychiatrist', where a male psychiatrist posed as a disabled woman and built up a network of close friends. When he could no longer keep up the deception, he killed off his false persona, 'Julia', and disclosed his true identity. Once those who had befriended 'Julia' found out, they felt bitterly betrayed, confused and hurt. The idea of playing with boundaries surrounding identity, and the anticipated pleasure of doing so, is proving to be complex. This suggests that human liberation from binary dualisms requires dialogue and situated social change as well as experimentation in virtual worlds.

These issues also involve an understanding of sexual identity and feed into understandings regarding sexuality online. There was, as with other digital forms, an early excitement about virtual sex with the possibilities of technology-simulated sex being mooted by some (Dery, 1996). This was partly a response to the HIV and Aids panic at that time (1980s to early 1990s). Visions included sex in the form of 'teledildonics' in virtual reality and sex based on telepresence through sensory body-suits and virtual reality helmets. Apart from compu-sex,[19] however, this remains largely a fantasy. One area of sexuality in which groups have engaged with in cyber culture is that regarding non-heterosexuality, often termed 'queer culture'. Potentially, cyberspace allows for experimentation with identity and senses of the body, which may lend itself to cultural developments from queer cultures. However, Wakeford (2000) and O'Riordan and Phillips (2007) point out that joining queer theory and cyber theory is not straightforward. They, like Gauntlett (2000), explore one of the central themes of this chapter by questioning the ways in which fictionalizing identity, queer or otherwise, through notions of the virtual does not necessarily lead to emancipation. The 'performativity' (Butler, 1990) of sexuality is proving to be as complex online as off-line, including combinations of both. The culture of cyberspace itself (framed through its socio-economic context) produces a bias towards 'straightness', and its commercialization and appropriation by consumer culture are influencing the rise of individualized lifestyles. Both of these trends are part of 'new edge' and 'post political' cyber culture in which queer culture is also negotiated. Rather than ushering in liberation, the culture of the Internet in late capitalism is fostering new forms of bourgeois individualism including 'post-gay queerity' and 'post-left political cyberpunk' (Morton, 1999, p. 306). This can delimit the possibilities of queer culture online thus undermining the potential of using the Internet as a tool of emancipation within progressive cultural activity.

Similar themes occur in relation to ethnicity and cyber culture.[20] For example, the contributors of Kolko et al.'s (2000) volume ask does race disappear in cyberspace? They cover the question of race in the context of embodiment and disembodiment in cyber culture, focus on how race is visually represented in popular film and advertisements about cyberspace and explore whether narratives surrounding racial and ethnic minorities in cyberspace reproduce existing racist stereotypes or challenge them (p. 11). Gonzalez (2000) focuses on two websites which both use avatars to deal with issues of racial difference. The UNDINA site[21] is a virtual version of the Surrealist parlour game and 'exquisite corpse and the Bodies INC'[22] site invites participants to select body shape, surfacing and gender to build their own avatars. In researching these sites Gonzalez identifies contradictory tendencies in these virtual worlds. She argues that, on one level, there is a new 'freedom' – the freedom to choose body shape, surfacing and so on. However, this freedom is limited and reproduces existing racial preconceptions because it is based on existing stereotypes in which the appendages that users select from are racialized in shape, form, colour and so on. Gonzalez points out that this practice marks a new form of colonization, which is realized on the level of symbolic exchange. Other examples of racial difference in cyberspace include the deployment of stereotypes in video games (Ow, 2000) and in adverts by computer companies (Nakamura in Bell and Kennedy, 2000), some of which reaffirm current racial stereotypes. However, there are also examples that illustrate the possibility of 'jamming the ideological machine' (p. 719). For example, jamming in the context of MOOScape; this is a MUD that emphasizes the marking of race by getting its participants to use '@race' to signify their online self-description (their 'desc'). MOOScape is an ongoing social experiment that makes the impact of constructing race visible in MUD interactions and in so doing makes visible the construction of race online that may spill out into the off-line world.

The body and its representation is a significant part of the way individuals (and groups) create identities (Synnott, 1993) and in cyberspace the body occupies an ambivalent and virtual location, which is played out in a number of ways across identity, ethnicity, sexuality and community. The idea of leaving one's physical body behind in cyber culture is a significant aspiration in that it offers the promise of liberation from off-line embodiment. However, this aspiration and promise is set alongside the reality of embodied experiences of computer use. Taking the liberation from bodily experience to its logical extreme points to a post-human condition

(Haraway, 1985; Hayles, 1999), which raises questions about what makes people human and whether they want to retain or transcend their humanness. There are similar ambivalences around the idea of a cyborg and how it functions as an ironic metaphor and disruptive boundary figure in gender politics. The attributes of identity as lived in patterns of association are areas that actors work with as they seek to engage in socio-cultural life. They use and adapt cultural resources to find ways of expressing themselves – ways that may, however, prove to be contradictory. Expressions of self and group affiliations are performed in circles of participants and audiences using an array of available props. Some of these may provide forms of communication in frameworks of action that seek emancipation, while others, in contrast, prove to be conservative, maintaining forms of oppression and still others are contradictory and ambiguous.

The expectations of audiences and the affordance of props act as referees to any experiments with socio-cultural mores. Part of cultural expression, therefore, involves competing perspectives of socio-cultural life and, in this context, the diversity of culture is finding expression in cyberspace. Within cyber culture, users are finding ways to express themselves and their views on existing social and cultural orders. Some of this activity is often understood in terms of subcultures, in which groups form cultural responses to an established cultural order and/or themes within that order.[23] In some instances the Internet is used in activity that challenges existing socio-economic and political order with many anti-capitalist activists using it to organize agendas and protest. For example, popular protest and radical dissent surrounding the World Trade Organization (WTO) meeting at Seattle (1999) was organized in this way. Other types of groups seeking to critique established order and promote alternatives can be subsumed under lifestyle politics, which aim to democratize everyday life. These groups use the Internet to communicate and organize around topics such as green politics, post-materialism and so on. These groups (often forming elites) use techno-bricolage in rendering cultural order problematic. Techno-bricolage involves reinvesting technology with subversive meaning and intent, liberating it from the grasp of the powerful and reinstating it for their own use (Bell, 2001, p. 166).

Another type of cultural activity that plays with late modern cultural order in the production and reception process of consumerism is fan cultures. Fan cultures interact with consumer culture through the ways in which fans engage in the interpretive work of a cultural product's meaning-making process. In broad terms, fan cultures develop packages of stylistic dress, look, products and rituals to express their phenomenon of interest and these often become integrated into a person's identity and their patterns of association. Cyberspace has extended and added another platform to these off-line bricolage practices of fans. In the first instance, net fandom is an extension of off-line fan practice – fans have always engaged in long-distance communication and the Internet supplements the circulation of fanzines and letters (Clerc in Bell and Kennedy 2000 p. 217) but the Internet expands this by generating global meeting and marketplaces. Second, the Internet has extended fan culture by opening up its boundaries to encompass a wider selection of cultural products available for fan activity, incorporating more television programmes, web postings and blogs, celebrities and films.

This opening up of fan cultures is not, however, necessarily progressive as it is reversing some of the gains made off-line by fans in the area of gender politics. The dominance of masculine influences in cyberspace is re-introducing gender norms into fan-worlds that are oppressing woman. Nonetheless, in committed circles of fandom, women fans are countering this trend by forming mailing lists such as the ironically named[24] 'Star Fleet Ladies Auxiliary' and 'Embroidery/Baking Society' within 'Trekkie' *Star Trek* fandom. Despite there being some strong female fandoms such as *Xena: Warrior Princess*, the use of the Internet has tended to produce fan-like engagement with many mainstream television programmes. Therefore, although fan culture is not necessarily engaged with oppositional cultural politics, the opening up of fandom via the Internet is resulting in it losing some of its distinctiveness. This is because the Internet is interacting in the dynamics of fan culture by simultaneously opening it up and dispersing it so that 'everyone can be a fan' (Pullen in Bell and Kennedy, 2000, p. 56). Moreover, within this dynamic the conservative tendencies of popular culture are resurging, requiring the re-negotiation of identity and cultural politics with these types of texts, products and audiences.

Conclusion

The importance of culture in understanding the meanings of the Internet is seen in how those meanings are contested and mythologized in the narratives and practices of cyber cultures. The cultural work in and surrounding cyberspace is crafted out of material, symbolic and experiential resources, practices and meanings. A key characteristic of this cultural work is the way in which the 'virtual' is narrated, utilized and embellished. The potential and affordance of a technologically induced virtuality offers scope for imaginative experiments and provides a conceptual space for challenging established socio-cultural mores. Key areas of social life that give shape and content to forms of life – namely cultures – are infused into cyber culture, rarely however, without problems. Thus, ideas regarding community, identity, ethnicity, gender and sexuality as well as culturally engaged groupings are communicated and given presence and shape in cyberspace. However, this cultural activity and communication is firmly located in socio-cultural mores and trends of contemporary culture, including its consumer culture. The social relations of informational capitalism is the context of popular cultural activity, its narratives are both conservative and oppositional and its forms of participation offer scope for resistant and progressive practices but this is countered with popular participation. Therefore, despite early hopes that cyber culture could radically challenge and alter existing social and cultural order, these hopes have been tempered by the way the 'real' fights back.

The combination and integration of on and off-line communication and formation of culture militates against any straightforward notion that cultural change can be invented outside of established cultural boundaries, values and practices. Cultural change in progressive terms involves critically engaging with the cultural dynamics of late capitalism, its practices of consumerism and modes of production. Cultural change in regressive terms is something to be constantly guarded against, negotiated with and fought against. Culture, including cyber culture, is rooted in lived social conditions and provides resources for actors to engage in the struggles of meaning for progressive society. The way in which the Internet is utilized in these struggles is one element of culture with its flexibility giving rise to a range of socio-cultural forms that express both the freedom of the imagination and the contradictions of social life.

10

The Communications Environment and the Internet

Introduction

The aim of this chapter is to show how the Internet is being shaped, and is shaping, the media. The main aspect of the argument is that the media and new media are part of a new communications environment, which is also a mediapolis – a political and cultural media space. The social relations of the technological means for communication create opportunities for public communication, institutional arrangements frame the character and narratives of the communication and the forms of participation influence the openness of that space and its cultural ethos. The media play a significant role in the public sphere, forging a space for debate in civil society. The notion of the public sphere is a contested one but it points to a more or less autonomous and open arena for public debate in civil society and it involves the use of various forms of media including pamphlets, the mass media and the Internet. Traditionally, public spheres are national in scope; however, Internet-related communication with its networked global reach is interacting in the notion and practice of public communication through political and economic as well as cultural dynamics.

Another defining feature of Internet usage is that it blurs the public and private spheres of social life, producing interaction and culture that has varying levels of public-ness. The rise in the use of interactive and mobile communications technology interacts with changing experiences of the public and the private spheres in a physical sense of production and reception too. A further dimension of this trend is the growth of social networking sites and user-produced content in cyberspace, which is appropriated by mass media outlets (for example, for news items), and blurs private and public senses of communication. These dimensions are bringing a different dynamic into public communication by destabilizing the existing institutional understanding of private and public, of producer and consumer, of the rituals of reception in terms of place, time (daily, weekly and yearly) and audiences. These factors are reshaping the communication environments of late modernity and its socio-cultural forms.

This chapter first covers key themes in the shaping of a communications environment, which is followed by a discussion of the key aspects regarding understanding new media. To contextualize and explore these aspects the chapter discusses the new communication environment. This considers the spaces, identities and characteristics of its social relations, which define the integration of new media into the global, national and local media spheres. The chapter then discusses the culture and ethics of the interactions in this environment and in the mediapolis in the twenty-first century before its concluding section.

Shaping a Communications Environment: Continuity and Change

The ways in which people use media, including ICT, within various domains of social life are influential in shaping the communications environment. Culture is meaningful in domestic and public life, bridging both dimensions with each informing the other. As the previous chapter shows, individuals and groups engage with cultural goods and, in so doing, produce meaning to social life, that is they are cultural producers as well as consumers. These activities feed into the shaping of the public sphere. Particular patterns of using, sharing and debating 'private troubles and public issues' (Mills, 1959) illustrate the way in which information and its communication is used to develop public sensibilities within particular historical social orders, influencing the character of participation in a public realm. For instance, the emergence of the bourgeoisie in European nation states saw the development of a reading public that generated practices of debate. This literary public sphere created and sustained the practice of debate through engagement with cultural forms such as the novel as well as letters, pamphlets and the press. Using these forms, the bourgeoisie reflected both on themselves and on the role of the state in the formation of a good society (Wessels, 2009).

The sphere for public dialogue has changed from early capitalism, through organized and disorganized capitalism, to the present networked system of global capitalism. The communication environment for public dialogue is changing both in terms of the technologies and institutions of communication and the characteristics of participation in public communication. The role of the Fourth Estate as critique and in framing political and cultural commentary is part of print journalism and public service broadcasting (PSB), with PSB regulated to varying degrees, depending on state frameworks within particular nations. However, the development of the

Internet in new media forms is challenging existing media such as audio-visual broadcasting, radio and print journalism as well as the character of the public sphere. Part of the challenge is to the institutional relationship between producers and consumers because networked new media offer consumers the potential to be more actively involved in the production of content, voicing their own concerns and in defining media agendas.

The development of new media reaffirms the ways social actors negotiate their mediated and situated worlds. It extends their activity into the realm of negotiating interactive communication, including user-generated content and varieties of alternative socio-political and cultural activity, in contrast to the mass media of commercial and PSB. There is an element within traditional media especially PSB that seeks to ensure quality programming stemming from the Reithian view that the media should educate and inform, as well as entertain its audiences. New media as a defining feature of late modern life reiterates the tension between the consumerization of the Internet on the one hand and its historical legacy of free and unregulated communication, on the other hand. It can therefore be considered a communication tool for open and free communication to be used for the public good, but it is also a tool appropriated by global capital for marketing and consumerist communication. Likewise, although Habermas (1989) recognizes the democratizing opportunities of the mass media, he argues that – with the commoditization of culture – the mass media are drawn towards populist programming in which publics are comprised less of debating publics and more of consuming publics. In this context, the commercialization of the media (both new and traditional) and the commodification of culture leads to private life being publicized and public life being privatized, and culture as a site of critical debate becoming emptied of meaning (ibid.).

Key Concepts in Analysing New Media

Two key characteristics of new media are digitization and convergence, which, in the communications environment, generally also adds to their recombinant characteristic. Recombinant refers to the way that

> new media systems are products of a continuous hybridization of both existing technologies and innovations in interconnected technologies and institutional networks. The recombinant and hybrid metaphor suggests that, although ICT are influenced by existing technological contexts, and may have unintended consequences, to a great extent they are the result of human actions and decisions. (Lievrouw and Livingstone, 2006, p. 23)

Digitization and convergence need to be seen in relation to interactivity in mediated forms of communication, the rise of a networks, virtual communities and identities in the context of political, economic and cultural globalization. The characteristics of institutional agency and the actions of people are central in the definition of new media. The case studies discussed below show that new media is actively configured at an institutional level and through the agency of people. This relates to the fact that new media involves 'artefacts or devices that enable or extend our abilities to communicate; the communication activities or practices we engage in to develop and use these devices; and the social arrangements or organizations that form around the devices and practices' (Lievrouw and Livingstone, 2006, p. 23). These aspects of ICT and their social contexts interweave within cultural forms and, in so doing, produce specific forms and content for media production and use.

Part of understanding new media involves addressing three interrelated social and technological processes:

- Digitization and convergence.
- Interactivity and networks.
- Virtuality and globalization. (Lievrouw and Livingstone, 2006)

The convergent approach addresses the way in which new media technologies arise out of the interaction between digitized content, convergent media forms and global communications networks (Flew, 2002). Convergence arises in the first instance out of the growing linkages between media, information technology and telecommunications. This approach posits that the consequences of digitization, convergence and networking include a shift in employment towards service and information in a new economy, away from agriculture and manufacturing (as discussed in Chapters 5 and 6). A further indicator is the rise in major corporate mergers and takeovers in media, telecoms and computing sectors and, finally, there is the growth in global Internet access and computer mediated communication. Digitization, convergence and networking manifest themselves in the growing significance of interactivity in all forms of mediated communication, in the rise of network society, in the rise of virtual communication as expressed by virtual communities and through the adoption of virtual identities, as well as political, economic and cultural globalization.

Part of the general debate regarding changes in the media environment includes the notion of virtual culture and the emergence of digital media. Gauntlett (2004), for example, argues that social relations have become increasingly 'virtualized' with the development of the Internet and CMC. As described in Chapters 4 and 9, this approach sees that virtual communities have the potential to provide a basis for new forms of community, a revival of democratic citizenship. From this perspective, extended online participation is made possible by developments in digital media, which includes all media that combine and integrate data, text, sounds and images stored in digital formats and distributed across networks. To understand the way in which these technologies have become integrated in a communications environment means considering digitization in relation to traditional media industries such as print media, radio, cinema and TV and in the hybrid forms that have emerged, for example networked games and short-message-services (SMS) delivered across platforms such as mobile phones. Another part of the dynamic is considering the ways in which digitization can promote the re-purposing of existing media forms. The development of new forms of communication and narrative include the use hypertext, for instance in linking sequencing of material. On an organizational level there is the development of industries based on new media production and consumption. As this book reveals, the stress is on the social relations that produce the virtual, which is something realized through character and narration of on and off-line relationships.

Some aspects of new media development are influential in transforming media industries, and one consequence of the changes is that they are leading to some level of disintermediation, or undercutting the middle-people between content creators and users. The potential of any such change is dependent on a range of legal, economic and policy related factors, seen, for example, in peer-to-peer developments such as Napster shareware as well as in developments of interactive digital television. The trend, however, is actually towards re-intermediation of information by new intermediaries (Verhulst, 2005). It is questionable whether these processes of re-intermediation in new media enable users to shape the media itself. However, some commentators maintain that new media has the potential to give users an unprecedented ability to modify and redistribute content. This capacity creates a situation of the *underdetermination* of new media in comparison to traditional media (Poster, in Lievrouw and Livinstone, 2006). In addition, the debate about user participation and influence leads commentators such Livingstone (ed., 2005) to stress the need for re-conceptualizing notions of 'the audience' and exploring the characteristics of audiences in the digital age. Finally, and related to the diversity of these examples, each shows the influence of an audience's role and character as well as their patterns of participation in shaping new media forms.

Robins (in Lievrouw and Livingstone, 2006) raises another aspect regarding new media, which is that new media has produced a new kind of 'knowledge space' or 'communication space' that is 'de-referentialized'. By this, Robins means these spaces are disconnected from local, situated knowledge and experience. Commenting on Levy, who sees this as an emancipatory break from older forms of knowledge that were linear, hierarchical and rigid, Robins argues that the 'new relation to knowledge' serves to further global corporate capitalism and the interests of a relatively small elite. In this environment, information and communication are valued not for their substance or meaning, but for their capacity to be processed, circulated or connected for their own sake: 'contemporary knowledge culture is regarded as essentially about the acquisition of generic information skills and competences' (ibid.). Evidence of both processes is apparent in the discussions made in this book.

In general terms, a point-to-point 'network' has become accepted as the main form of contemporary social and technical organization (Lievrouw and Livingstone, 2006). The network metaphor applies not just to new media technologies but also to patterns of social relations and organizing the institutional formations associated with them. It can be argued that the more traditional mass media technologies, as well as the organizations that employed them and the institutions that governed them, embodied industrial-era notions of social and work organization. This configuration was hierarchical in character, which supported large-scale production and distribution of messages directed from a few media centres to 'mass' audiences. It ensured the rapid diffusion of information from the 'top/centre' of the hierarchy to the bottom/periphery and provided little or no capacity for going the other way, meaning little feedback from below or the periphery travelled to the top or centre. As it is understood today, the network denotes a broad, multiplex interconnection in which many points or nodes are embedded. Links amongst nodes may be created or abandoned on an as-needed basis at any location in the system, and any node can be either a sender or a receiver of messages, or both. High-tech firms tend to cluster in geographic places, and network topographies of telecom, media and computing are unevenly distributed around the world. The London Connects Project (see below), for example, takes advantage of London's media base. However, these hubs and regions do not necessarily dominate new media content in the same way a few major cities did with traditional forms of mass media. New places and spaces for sociality and culture have been created as systems such as the Internet have been designed to allow any node to connect to any other with network access, as shown by the example from Ronneby in Sweden (see below).

Another dimension of new media is that it enables interactivity for and by its users. The switching technology of new media systems affords users more selectivity in their choices of information sources and interactions with other people. New media give users the means to generate, seek and share content selectively, and to interact with other individuals and groups on a scale that was impractical with traditional mass media, as the examples of SNS and new media projects show. This selectivity provides a sense of interactivity in niche services as well as social networking and peer-to-peer communication. In turn, the proliferation and diversity of content and sources now available through new media have raised concerns about the quality of the content (ibid.), namely, its authenticity or reliability, as well as questions about the nature of online experience and interaction, for example issues about anonymity or identity in particular online interactions in cyber culture and new media contexts.

The debates of new media developments point a relative underdetermination of new media when compared to traditional media, as users are able to participate more interactively in media forms and engage in various participant dialogues. New media within both situated- and cybercultural frameworks can de-referentialize knowledge from its respective frameworks and sources which can and does in some cases facilitate a more open communication space (Levy cited by Robins in Lievrouw and Livingstone, 2006). However, although these 'new relations to knowledge' offer possibilities for various forms of emancipation, they are also formed within the culture of global capitalism, which is reproducing media concentration as well as generating new media nodes in the communications environment. The ubiquity[1] of new media and its more individualized use involving interactivity and selectivity raises questions of the authentication and reliability of content as well as quality of online experience. These questions reflect some of the core themes of the social relations of the Internet and situates the Internet in broader social and cultural change by exploring the ways in which new media is materializing in cultural forms in everyday life and in broader institutional change.

These characteristics have been discussed in this book and they are evident in the context of new media and the communications environment. However, through their use and ongoing development these characteristics become shaped through their institutional contexts. This is seen in the organization of the media – including issues surrounding PSB – and in the variety of new media forms. It is also seen in the way new media is socially shaped and culturally informed resulting in a variety of forms which each has its own social relations, narratives and patterns of participation, seen in SNS and community-led projects. Within the broader communications environment, these diverse ways of engaging with the media illustrate how pervasive Internet-related activity is across society and how the way we communicate is intertwined within social relations. The dynamics and the way in which socio-technical change is contested can be seen in the new communications environment.

The Social Relations of a New Communications Environment: The New and the Established

Harrison and Wessels (2005)[2] address the social relations of a new communications environment populated by traditional and new media technologies and institutions. Part of this changing environment includes the ways in which the emerging multi-channel and multimedia environment is reshaping the traditional broadcasting sector. Programming in the traditional broadcasting offers set choices for audiences and frames pluralism within institutional frameworks. Furthermore, the increase in the concentration of media ownership is resulting in an increasing homogeneity of programmes and news services and is diminishing of the role of small programme suppliers, who can produce diversity into the overall broadcasting schedule. The development of niche channels may appear at one level to add choice within the broadcasting environment but these channels often form part of a themed strand within a homogenous media package. These aspects of broadcasting with the ongoing expansion of numbers of channels are fostering audience fragmentation with enhanced television and interactive digital television (iDTV) services also contributing to this process.

However, within the new public communication environment, research by Wessels (in Harrison and Wessels, 2005; Wessels, 2009) identifies some pilot developments within new media that are producing senses of audience cohesion, understood as communities of interest (see below). In this environment there is some evidence that non-media professionals and audiences-as-users are active in shaping the production and content of programmes and modes of participation in them. These forms show that pluralistic, engaging, associative and critical environments can foster audience engagement (Harrison and Wessels, 2005). This environment stimulates the expression of a pluralism defined by the activities of diverse individuals and groups within their different social, cultural and political experiences and settings (see case studies below).

Given these dynamics of, and developments in, a new public communications environment, the analytical framework in Table 10.1 shows how new social relations are mixing into a communication environment, which also consists of traditional media organizations. The basis of the analytical framework is generated by a need to situate changes in the relationship between media technologies and the social organization of the media (i.e. the media institutions) with the experiences of participants and audiences in everyday life.

Table 10.1 sketches out the characteristics of traditional, new and reconfiguring media. The reconfigured media point to various developments that use new media technologies in new forms of media organization as well as those that draw on the legacy systems of traditional media. The various types of media reconfiguration include the reintegration of public service values into new aspects of form and content. To identify the emerging characteristics of some of these reconfigured media, it is necessary to trace the social relations of particular media forms and outline their

Table 10.1   The Social Relations of a new Communication Environment

'TRADITIONAL MEDIA'	THE PROCESS OF 'RECONFIGURATION'		'NEW MEDIA'
Social relations	**Social relations**		**Social relations**
Mass and niche PSB	Networks		Individualization and choice
Origins: mid-modernity	Origins: late modernity		Origins: late modernity
National and regional broadcasting	Partnerships and nodes		Local, national and supra-national initiatives
FORMS	FORMS		FORMS
Broadcasting	Informate, e.g. iDTV		Internet and WWW
	Community networks		IS services
			Mobile phones
	Weblogs		Weblogs
	Automate		Social networking sites
	Niche channels		
	VOD		
	PVRs		
	Traditional media Online		
USAGE	USAGE	USAGE	USAGE
National unity	Indiv. use of mass media	Nodes of participation	Global networks of interests
Audience fragmentation	Self-selection	Community of interests	Networks of interests (various)

Source: Harrison and Wessels, 2005.

respective patterns of usage. Thus, for example, traditional media emerged within the ethos of mid-modernity and its focus on the nation state and national identity. Here, for example, PSB is couched in terms of reaching mass audiences whilst providing some niche programming to ensure that both majority and minority tastes and interests are served. In contrast, new media emerged in late modernity with an emphasis on individualization and choice within a culture of freedom (Castells, 2001, p. 17), which resists strong institutional structures to encourage communication initiatives at local, national and supra-national level. Also, as Table 10.1 shows, developments in the communication environment are reconfiguring either the traditional or new media in new ways that borrow aspects from each other. These reconfigurations are materializing as enhanced services for traditional forms of media, or transforming both traditional and new media into innovative media forms.

The use of new media within the communications environment can be viewed as either 'automating' or 'informating' established media products and services (c.f. Zuboff 1988). Automating refers to 'add ons' to linear programming and channels, such as online publishing or video-on-demand services. These developments extend an individual's engagement with a medium by introducing greater technical control and an extension of mechanically facilitated choice but maintain many of the characteristics of traditional media. Informating refers to the way the new media transforms traditional media by intellectual and non-mechanical means, through the innovatory use of new technologies which can be seen to be the pursuit of socially, politically constituted goals or in forms of cultural activities (Harrison and Wessels, 2005). As the case studies below show, various groups and alignments of groups are developing which illustrate ways of using new media that 'informate' media production and use: for example, the production of community iDTV by new types of networked organizations made up from community groups and local authorities. These distinctions illustrate the different patterns of emerging media usage that emanate from different sets of social relations of media production and use, as well as new rituals of participation. For instance, participants within audiences that are fragmented make use of automated reconfiguring media (e.g. personal video recorders, enhanced television services and so on, see Table 10.1) to make individualized selections from media programming. Whereas, participants who engage with the media in informated terms reveal a community of interests approach organized through diverse modes of participation (ibid.).

To contextualize the above dynamics means considering the ways audiences engage and participate in the media. In contemporary everyday life audience participation can be understood through the role the media play and by the audiences' own experiences which, in part, shape their understanding of the world. Mediation (Silverstone, 2005b) and mediated discourse (Smith, 1988) are both distinct features of contemporary societies.[3] These processes are part of the communicative and interpretive practices of individuals and groups who are differently positioned, socially and culturally, and in their relations with media institutions. It is through the interpretive practices of actors that various media intersect with, and structure, everyday life. The ways in which audiences interpret, engage with and participate in these processes are part of socio-cultural dynamics that relate to and feed into socio-economic and political processes (Smith, 1988). In this sense, audiences tend to form around particular interests, tastes and life experiences, with biographical and cultural factors as well as individual motivation and aspirations shaping participation in media forms (Wessels, 2000a). These cultural dynamics that are enacted out in everyday life demonstrate the ways in which audiences practice discretion in viewing, selecting and contributing within media environments (Chaney, 2002).

As mentioned in Chapter 8, contemporary processes of the fragmentation of culture and the undermining of cultural authority as traditionally understood provides a context in which the meanings of mediated views and their associated mediated discourses are interpreted and negotiated through the different cultural frameworks of diverse audiences. These diverse audiences are motivated by various social, cultural or political goals and facilitated by the extension of choice and intervention in the reconfiguring media, potentially creating a new dynamic in the communication environment. In new media projects audiences can voice particular views, foster new forms of local democracy through grass-root participation on the Internet and so on. Such media forms coexist within an environment dominated by commercial media companies. However, some of these reconfiguring forms show that a distinction can be made between populism informed by commercial imperatives and genuine cultural pluralism informed by the social, cultural and political experience of different individuals and groups. The dynamics of everyday life, the roles of various media and forms of audience participation all generate the social and cultural context for the institutionalization of traditional, new and reconfiguring media.

As noted in Chapter 3, an analysis of technological change involves addressing institutional change (Mansell and Silverstone, 1996). Two institutional facets of the new communication environment that require consideration are broadcasting and information society arrangements. The dynamics of these institutional facets vary across nations and provide an example of the institutional complexities of technological change in the media context. For instance, in the Europe Union, the plurality of services and diversity of content of traditional broadcast media are linked to their legacy of ownership and funding arrangements. It also relates to their PSB obligations, which seek to ensure that citizens have access to a diverse range of opinions and that the freedom of expression is responsibly upheld. The requirements and legacies of these frameworks of broadcasting will have to adapt as broadcasters enter into new media areas[4] (Harrison and Wessels, 2005; Sparks, 2007). In this environment the European Union continues to support for public funded programming because of the fear that if the private sector media market is left to its own devices it may not provide public services[5] (unless regulated) and produce solely commercialized output (Harrison and Wessels, 2005).

In parallel, EU Information Society strategy shows how some policy-makers are addressing new media technology in relation to visions of an inclusive information society (Mansell and Steinmueller, 2000). Policy-making instruments stem, to a degree, from some of the early ideas that drove the development of new media, namely free and democratic communication, as seen in Ted Nelson's 1965 Computer Lib manifesto, and in the ethos of Berners-Lee's development of the WWW. The early rhetoric surrounding new media variously suggested that the Internet has the potential to facilitate new political associations, a new libertarianism and new forms of economic production. More modestly, it spoke of an increase in democratic participation, the provision of free information and communication and support for freedom of speech (Castells, 2001; Negroponte, 1998; Rheingold, 1993). The current EU Information Society and Media portfolio extends and takes forward the understanding of economic competitiveness based on ICT into an information society by focusing on the underlying communications infrastructures and beyond to the content and services they deliver. It encompasses telecommunication networks, broadband internet access and satellite communications, new communications technologies such as '3G' mobile communications and internet telephony, and digital material as diverse as cinema releases as well as channel strategies and portal services. This Information Society and Media perspective is beginning to bring a more convergent view to communication within a European Information Society framework, albeit still within a perspective that sees ICT as a key enabler in facilitating a variety of cultural and political initiatives (Wessels, 2009).

The expansion of the media environment to include new media raises the question of access. Several commentators point to issues such as lack of access to technology, lack of skills and capacities, the knowledge gap and the domination of elites in online discussions (Jankowski and van Selm, 2000; Norris, 2000), which are relevant to a range of new media contexts. As discussed in Chapter 7, all of the above-mentioned issues have their own exclusionary dynamics but when taken together they point to divisive trends in accessing and participating in new media forms (Freeman and Soete, 1997). A constraint in ensuring universal access is that changes in economic activity, education and symbolic work stimulated by new media technologies occur 'within capitalist relations of production' (Papacharissi, 2002; Garnham, 1998), which means that the adoption of new media technologies is a function of price and market demand. In this context, policy-makers in the European Union have taken a stance that embraces the dynamics of commercialization, but which also aims to address issues of social justice. These dynamics raise the question of the character of emerging media as cultural forms, which also includes considering the respective roles these new forms take in relation to the public sphere. To explore this, this chapter first considers the dynamics of a social networking site called YouTube and, second, outlines some new media projects that engage with 'public issues and private troubles' in fostering public dialogue (c.f. Mills, 1959).

The development of social networking sites (SNS) raises many of the themes surrounding media, new media and public communication. SNS are websites that allow individuals to construct a public or semi-public profile[6] within a system and articulate their relationship visibly with other users through their profile (Boyd and Ellison, 2007). Users build networks by developing contacts with whom they interact, called 'friends', 'contacts' or 'fans', depending on the site. Users leave messages – often called 'comments' – on each other's profiles. Some sites have privacy settings and some have photo-sharing or video-sharing capabilities; others have built-in blogging and instant messaging technology; and others support mobile interactions such as Facebook. There are a variety of audiences in SNS (ibid.).[7] For instance, SNS can focus on targets from specific geographical regions or linguistic groups, although this does not necessarily determine who participates – for example, Portuguese-speaking Brazilians adopted Orkut – an English-only interface launched in the United States (ibid.).

In more general terms, some sites are designed in relation to ethnicity, religious affiliation, sexual orientation, political views or other identity-driven categories. Other SNS are designed to generate their own micro-social network using tools such as Ning.[8] Usage of SNS, however, is overwhelmingly characterized by nationality, age, educational level or other factors that segregate society (ibid.). The rise of mobile devices is another factor to consider in patterns of SNS usage. In the United Kingdom,[9] in 2008, for instance, 43% of Internet users with a mobile phone and/or handheld devices use them to access emails and websites, and 24% use them for accessing SNS (Haddon, 2008). Although social networking is not the main online use, the 24% uptake is significant nonetheless, given that SNS is relatively new in the mobile portfolio (ibid.). The predominant users are young adults between 18 and 24 years old, with use being partly construed through levels of mobility and accessibility of that user-group's life stage[10] but also through the design of the mobile interface. To explore SNS in more detail, the public video-sharing website YouTube demonstrates some key themes of the dynamics of SNS as new media.

Research by Lange (2007) shows that YouTube participants develop and maintain social networks by manipulating both the physical and interpretive access to videos. The different practices of circulating and sharing videos reflect different relations between users. For instance, a common practice is posting videos that friends and family can see and respond too (ibid.). Posting comments enables people to express their affinity for the video and/or video-makers. These practices reveal different levels of 'publicness' in sharing videos, with some video-makers revealing their identity – often while sharing more private content amongst a limited network, that is 'publicly private' behaviour (ibid.). In other cases, participants share content more widely with many viewers, providing only limited information about the video producers' identities, which Lange calls 'privately public' behaviour. It is through these practices that a media circuit is created in which memberships of social networks are negotiated. YouTube circumvents the traditional media's organizational structures and utilizes the technology and social networking sensibility to produce semi-public spaces of sharing user-generated content amongst self-selecting audiences with varying degrees of privacy and publicness. The character of this semi-public realm is one that foregrounds interaction and dialogue around affinities that are entertainment-based and individualistic. This places SNS such as YouTube away from a public sphere ethos and more towards networked individualism of taste friendships rather that taste publics.

There is evidence of some new media projects that challenge both mainstream media and the more individualized social networking. Pilot project and fledgling media start-up cooperatives are developing innovative media services based on new media within new relations of production and patterns of association that include producer-as-user groups. For instance, the Carpenters Connects Project in London developed an iDTV network. They did this by forming a partnership between Newham Council, the Carpenters Tenants Management Organization and tenants of Carpenters Estate, with other public, private and voluntary sector organizations. The tenants built on existing infrastructure, set-top boxes and skills and media training to provide their own content and produce their own television programmes and videos. They created 'Home2Home', a new company in the iDTV market, and continue to make their own films, documentaries and programmes. The manager of the Tenants Management Organization feels that new media organized at the local level can provide media services that are produced *by* the residents *for* the residents who are both the producers and consumers of the service. The manager says it is a steep learning curve, not only in organizational, technological and skill-related terms but also in understanding how programming is received by audiences. Most programmes, such as 'Meet the Neighbours', 'Down Carpenters Way' and a series of documentaries produced under the title 'Carpenters Shorts' are well received. However, 'Living the High Life' did raise controversy over its depiction of life in a tower-block in a deprived area. Nonetheless, the manager felt that the Carpenters Connects team could respond to the issues raised by their critics in a fair way, without losing their own voices and perspectives (Harrison and Wessels, 2005).

Another example shows how new media partnerships and patterns of association can empower people. The Dialogue project involved citizens and municipal councils from Bologna (Italy), Ronneby (Sweden) and Lewisham (England). Citizens were trained to use the Web, with 'use' understood through the metaphor of 'communication as a network, as a cyberspace, and as participative' (project worker, 1999). This is reflected in a phrase commonly used in Bologna: 'we teach you the techniques, you teach us the content to which they can be applied' (ibid.). In Ronneby, a group of feminist researchers based their project on Virginia Woolf's argument that women need their own space to write, viewing new media as a contemporary space for the development of self-expression. The women of the town and surrounding region developed four virtual rooms, each with its own function and representing different aspects of women's writing. Room one was for participants' personal presentations, room two contained a 'Virtual Cookbook' as an example of collaborative writing, the third room was for poems and short stories and the fourth room was a chat-room for discussions. The women mediated key political issues through new media by involving Bosnian women migrants in the project by sharing stories, experiences, political and historical debate and recipes. They also fostered active parental involvement in schools through an interactive site linking them with the school, and they encouraged mothers and daughters to work together and learn from each other using new media (ibid.).

In Lewisham (UK), the Dialogue project involved citizen-panels' use of online 'Live Chat' and video-conferencing to improve participation in local democratic processes. Online 'Live Chat' fed into formal council procedures and was relayed back to residents through the local authority's website. Residents find that politicians do listen to the 'Live Chat' sessions. For example, in one instance, John and a number of others took part in a chat-session on proposed changes to local government and they were subsequently asked to attend a council meeting to air their opinions further. The project also fostered participation from schoolchildren 'connecting on screen' (their terminology) via video-conferencing. The children from Lewisham, Bologna and Ronneby took part in discussions ranging from the character of their everyday lives, their hobbies and school-life to issues such as bullying, racism and migration, finding that they all had different ideas and experiences of these. Laura (Lewisham), for example, remembered that a migrant girl from Bologna had said: 'I have had no problem with the language so far, and nobody has made me feel unwelcome because of my culture'. The schoolchildren felt that the project gave them some understanding of what life was like in Bologna, Ronneby and Lewisham, which widened their understanding of other cultures in that they could see similarities as well as differences (ibid.).

These innovative projects informate new media and show how it can function in the public sphere in ways that give individuals and groups a voice and which link into political processes. This has the potential to include and empower people to be influential in public dialogue and debate, regarding private problems and public issues (Mills, 1959). The exploration of a new communications environment shows how complex change is in the media and how change interacts with notions of a public sphere. The development of the Internet within the media environment may be disruptive in that it challenges the existing status quo. In a positive way it can open communication and generate new fora for public debate and engagement. However, given the media's role in the democratic process in the public sphere, risks to the quality of media content needs to be monitored and regulated (c.f. Keane, 1991). Communication is central in society in public, semi-public and private terms and as noted by Dewey at the beginning of the book 'society is made through communication'. Given the centrality of communication in social and democratic life, there is a need to consider the normative aspects of this environment as a mediapolis.

Mediapolis and Proper Distance in Communication

To address the media and its role in late modernity, Silverstone (2007) develops the concept of a mediapolis. He defines it as

> [t]he mediated public space where contemporary public life increasingly finds its place, both at national and global levels, and where the materiality of the world is constructed through (principally) electronically communicated public speech and action. There is of course no integrity within the contemporary mediapolis. The public space which it constitutes is fractured by cultural difference and the absence of communication, as much as it is by the homogenization of global television and genuine, if only momentary collective attention to global events, crisis and catastrophes. (Silverstone, 2007, p. 31)

The development of a shareable mediapolis means that analysts need to address what can be termed the 'relations of communication'. This encompasses the values and mores of the media within the production and reception processes (including the processes themselves) as they combine to define media outputs and their interpretations (Wessels, 2008a). Many people who work in media institutions claim that their practices are objective, or that they express particular views overtly. However, the values of the media (from whichever camp) are expressed through the reporting and production practices of its workers. A key aspect of this is the respect that media workers practice in producing content and representations of people, events and places. This theme of respect for the 'other' extends to audiences and users in their interpretive practices of media content and in any user-produced content they themselves produce. This is equally applicable to the media, virtual communities and forms of cyber culture in which senses of identity and otherness are performed and played out.

Silverstone (2007) critically assesses the current media through the concept of 'proper distance' and addresses hospitality,[11] responsibility and trust in the mediation of public and everyday life. Proper distance means the degree of proximity required in mediated interrelationships to create and sustain a sense of 'other' sufficient for reciprocity and for the exercise of duty of care, obligation and responsibility, as well as understanding. If proper distance is achieved in mediated communication, it maintains a sense of other through difference as well as shared identity, and thus proper distance is a perquisite for, and part of, plurality. Silverstone argues that 'proper distance involves imagination, understanding and duty of care and involves an epistemological (Arendt) and an ontological (Levinas) commitment to finding the space to express what is experienced (Arendt) and essential (Levinas) in our relationships to the other' (p. 47).

Relationships and social knowledge amongst peoples are highly dependent on the media as a key communicator within late modern society. Silverstone asserts that the current organization of the media fails to value and to practice proper distance. In general, he argues, the media 'trade in otherness, in the spectacular and the visible' (p. 47), and in doing so they limit the possibility of connection and identification. Identity, in this context, is a commodity that is traded, which empties identity of its distinctiveness and connective-ness. It denies the validity of difference and the irreducibility of otherness in social relations. This approach to representation highlights the failure of the current media to hear different perspectives and to address the complexities of social life. This method of communication sustains modernity's inability to engage with plurality and the rights of the stranger (ibid.).

Silverstone gives examples of distances that are 'too close', 'too far' and distances that are neither 'too close nor too far'. For example, he cites journalists within the armies of occupying forces, media intrusion into public figures' private lives and exotic images in global advertising as all examples of incorporation and the denial or reduction of difference. These are instances of being 'too close' to foster respect of the other. In contrast, the way that Moslems, Iraqis and Palestinians are represented by Christians/secular society as beyond the pale of humanity, is in practice and convention a position that is 'too far' to create understanding of the other. An example of distance that it is neither 'too close nor too far' is found in the cult of celebrity, which destroys difference by exaggerating it (the ordinary made exceptional) and naturalizing it (the exceptional made ordinary) and thus, this dialectic negates the legitimacy of difference. Proper distance in mediation as being 'both close and far' where the other is acknowledged, understood and needs are respected, Silverstone argues, requires producers and audiences who have the imagination to understand and respect the other and otherness (pp. 47–48).

An important aspect in imagining and achieving proper distance is the virtue of hospitality, which is the first virtue of the mediapolis (ibid.). Hospitality is an obligation to welcome the stranger; it is a right to enjoy freedom of speech and an obligation to listen and to hear. It is universal, by which 'the right to visit, to associate, belongs to all men by virtue of their common ownership of the earth's surface; for since the earth is a globe, they cannot scatter themselves infinitely, but must, finally, tolerate living in close proximity, because originally no one had a greater right to any region of earth than anyone else' (Kant, 1983, p. 118). In relation to the media, Silverstone (2007) argues that hospitality must be seen as a culture rather than one ethic in an array of media ethics. This is because hospitality is about a sense of ethos which is about 'home, the familiar place of dwelling ... the manner in which we relate to ourselves and to others, as our own or as forgiveness ... ethics is so thoroughly coextensive with the experience of hospitality' (Derrida cited in Kant, 1983, p. 139).

From Silverstone's perspective, hospitality is the ethos in which 'the other' not only speaks but 'the stranger' is also heard. He also differentiates hospitality from tolerance or toleration, in that it is not a relation of sufferance or patronage of the powerful. In Derrida's terms, tolerance is 'scrutinized hospitality, always under surveillance, parsimonious, and protective of its sovereignty' (Derrida in Borradori, 2003, p. 128). Hospitality, however, is unconditional, entirely innocent and devoid of judgement and discrimination. For Silverstone (2007), hospitality is uniform and universal, and it is an obligation whatever anyone's position is in social or symbolic hierarchies. The culture of hospitality is therefore at the centre of a plural and just mediated world that informs and is constituted through a proper distance between selves and others (Wessels, 2008a). Culture and the spaces for critique are therefore important aspects in the processes that inform an emerging communicative environment, an environment constituted through an array of institutions, organizations, people and technologies.

Conclusion

The media are a key institution in society and an important aspect of the public sphere and civil society. They are a medium in which private troubles and public issues are articulated and debated. The development of new media spans both the public and private aspects of social and everyday life and is part of a broader communications environment. This environment is a complex arena of established media organizations, technologies and forms of audience participation, and new media is being shaped in – and is shaping – that environment. New media have the potential to undermine established practice and open up the possibility of a more pluralistic media and public sphere through their interactive capacities. It is, however, the activities of people who think creatively and find new forms of organization that are central in the development of new media as cultural forms. In some new media projects, this is working towards creating open spaces of dialogue and participation, whereas in other cases new media such as SNS are creating semi-public communications, forming privatized spaces of user-generated entertainment.

These cultural forms are part of a broader environment where there is an increasing tension between commercial media services and public service media provision due to the pervasive neoliberal ideology and deregulatory policies. The contest between commercially based populism and responsible and pluralist media production opens up a normative debate regarding the character of public communication in late modern culture. The call for a culture of hospitality within our media communication environment and polis is timely – the multiplicity and enhanced forms of Internet-based communication can provide opportunities for dialogue and cultural exchange that, if it is to be progressive, requires hospitality. This ideal is contested, especially in the current neoliberal environment and the commoditization of culture that run in parallel with multicultural, diverse and mobile experiences of late modern life. The founding spirit of the Internet made communication tools that have the potential to change the media but it is the way the media is socially shaped and culturally informed that will shape the way it frames public expression, culture and politics across localities within a global world.

11

Conclusion

Introduction

This book explores the dynamics of the Internet and contemporary society. To achieve this, an analytical and conceptual framework was developed to account for the way in which the Internet and its related technologies are socially shaped and culturally informed. Using the framework of the cultural form, the book considers and explores the history of the Internet, its social landscape and debates about an information society. It then addresses specific domains of social and cultural life such as work, public policy, inclusion and exclusion, everyday life, cyber culture and new media. The framework of analysis is the cultural form, which encompasses the social, political and symbolic meanings of technology as it is institutionalized in sets of social conventions.

Social and Technological Change in the Context of the Internet

The overarching framework for technological change is the cultural form. Cultural forms emerge from three interdependent elements:

1. The 'relations of production', encompassing the social organization of producing, including the specifics of any technology.
2. The characteristic modes of narration which include discourses of a range of economic and public policy, culture, media and everyday life.
3. The types of participation in the Internet's socio-cultural forms.

The use of concepts such as performance and transformational spaces, as well the metaphor of theatre, provides insights into the way the Internet is socially shaped and culturally informed. Performance is understood as the dialectic of spontaneous action and reflexivity in which artefacts, meanings and values are represented in dramatic form and become institutionalized as cultural forms. The innovative processes that shape technology are to be found not only in the technology's design and production but also in the contexts of technology in use. Within this broad theatre of innovation, change is achieved through an array of transformational spaces – some in the field of research and development – and others in user contexts. Innovations, therefore, do not simply enter economic systems, but are culturally constituted within socio-historical contexts. The shaping of the technology in use is embedded within the trends and ethos of contemporary society and therefore, together, social and technological change is producing the Internet as a socio-cultural form. By understanding the processes of innovation as the institutionalization of cultural forms, the social, political and cultural aspects of innovation are addressed, thereby elucidating the richness and complexity of the development of the Internet and society. The history of the Internet involves the way in which the materiality of the technology was developed and shaped by social actors within networks of institutions, giving the Internet its distinctive cultural characteristics.

The focus on the process of innovation in relation to the Internet is important because it encompasses the characteristics of socio-technical change, which Freeman (1994) argues is social and the result of human actions, decisions, expectations and institutions. This approach means addressing the 'awesome paradox' (Berger and Luckmann, 1967) of how human activity produces a world of things, such as the Internet as a socio-cultural form in relation to personal activity and experience, on the one hand and social organization as something that is continuously constructed in time, on the other hand. The social contexts and cultural ethos of each phase of the Internet's development have combined to form an open and networked communication system. The flexibility of the form within the dynamics of social change is generating scope for the formation of new socio-cultural forms. Its founding features of open communication within a philosophy of freedom continue to shape its development, albeit in combination with its more recent commercialization. The interaction of these values, features and processes are embedded in broader socio-cultural contexts of changing communication environments within the social relations of late modern society. In addition, the historical process of the innovation of the Internet produced characteristics that actors are currently engaging in and negotiating and, in so doing, their activity continues to shape it via the 'awesome paradox' of how human activity produces a world of things.

Internet as Socio-Cultural Form: The Communicative Turn

The Internet is pervasive and ubiquitous across society and it materializes in distinctive ways (and unevenly) within particular domains and dimensions of society. The specific characteristics of this materialization are constructed out of its relations of production, its narratives and its types of participative interaction in its form. There are broad characteristics of the form that give shape to particular adaptations of the technology within context specific socio-cultural conditions and situations.

The social landscape in which the Internet is materializing is one that is flexible, adaptable and communicative. The disembedding of time and space and the rise of mediated and remote communications in a more mobile society means that individuals actively generate forms of connectivity. In fostering connectivity, they reconfigure social and cultural forms, finding new ways to participate and express community as well as constructing and reconstructing forms and expressions of identity. The agency of individuals is important in generating networks of communication which cut across the many dimensions of late modern life – the economic and social patterns of work; civil society and democratic process; social movements and citizenship; and cultural and everyday life – as well as in the media. Networked individualism is a social form of late modernity that bridges many established social and cultural forms with evolving social and cultural forms – hence the dualism of the virtual and the real, the online and the off-line are mitigated through social agency.

The dynamics of these broad themes are also interpolated into socio-economic trends. The organization of capitalism is developed to adapt to a global economy in which information is a commodity in capitalist relations, resulting in the network itself becoming the primary organizational form. The flexibility of the network for capitalism interacts with the dynamics of inclusion and exclusion in that workers have to be entrepreneurs to enter and re-enter the labour market. Divisions between social strata remain, but are reconfiguring established class- or identity-based distinctions. New distinctions emerge from the interactions of education, socio-economic background and the social and individual capacity to use Internet technologies for communication and knowledge generation. Access to these resources follows existing patterns of inequalities found locally and globally amongst people experiencing varying levels of poverty and sets of discriminatory practices based on ethnicity, gender and age. All of this creates powerlessness for some people in the Internet age, in contrast to those who have access to resources and can therefore compete in the labour market and engage in the production of knowledge for capital accumulation.

Across the social landscape of contemporary society, communication and the ability to communicate is a significant resource in the dynamics of participation. Communication is deeply rooted in culture and culture is interwoven within the social life of late modernity through its forms of communication. Adding to established forms of communication, the

Internet and its related technologies are providing an extra dimension to the communicative environment. This added dimension is ushering in a communicative turn within the socio-cultural dynamics of society – the constitution of that environment and society is realized through its relations of production, its narratives and forms of participation.

Relations of Production

In the first instance, broad characteristics of the relations of production involve the social relations of late capitalism. The ability of capital to adapt and configure around new modes of production is clearly seen in the development of transnational, informational capitalism. The rise of knowledge as a key commodity in the late modern economy is interacting with globalization to generate a new wave of innovations. These innovations, alongside the prevalence of Western consumer society and the commoditization of culture, are creating the rise of informational work of various descriptions. These relations rest on the ability of capital to be flexible, adaptable and responsive to the dynamics of the market. The underlying organizational form is that of the network, which enables the configuration and reconfiguration of people and resources for project-based production. These relations require an infrastructure suitable for the networked production and distribution patterns of the informational economy. The Internet provides the technological capability for the form and relations of this mode of production. Moreover, the human and organizational aspects of the Internet as a social form give the relations of production its cultural sensitivity to changing markets – the Internet then goes beyond a socio-technical form to become a socio-cultural form.

One aspect of capital accumulation is a reserve army of labour and this is emerging in contemporary society in situations of exclusion that cut across socio-economic strata. The multidimensionality of situations of exclusion is interacting with changes in welfare provision. The relations of production involve the organization of welfare, and the classic welfare state is being reconstructed as workfare whilst maintaining a minimal level of service provision – however, key institutions in society are still significant. For example, education is adapting, albeit unevenly, across society to produce labour with the relevant skills and aptitude for the entrepreneurial culture of the current economy. Other institutions adapting to this new economy are the family, work, cultural industries and the media. The cultural mores of these institutions are restricting any unfettered change driven by technology on the one hand, while, and on the other hand, the knowledge of institutions is also important in shaping the economy and its cultural forms.

Narratives of the Form

This brings the discussion to the narratives of the Internet as a socio-cultural form. Narratives are a key aspect of the innovation process, shaping the visions, articulating envisaged forms and informing the ongoing development and shaping of Internet-related forms. A central and almost iconic theme is the narrative of freedom, which is realized in open and free communication and underpinned by an ideal of interactive, flexible and networked communication technology. The design of the Internet was based on these ideas – the WWW in particular being based on free and open communication. The vision that Berners Lee had for the WWW was that anything could be connected to anything else and that the connections between people, ideas, data and resource would be discernable. This would, he felt, provide new freedoms for people to grow faster than previously when they were constrained by hierarchical classifications that they had in fact constructed. During the Internet's innovation process these ideals were interpreted and shaped by different actors and communities. For instance, counter cultural movements picked up on the ideal of freedom and appropriated the Internet in attempts to create communities based on their particular utopian visions and aspirations.

This search for freedom is adapted, inverted or popularized in some of the narratives of cyber culture. Cyberpunk, for instance, inverts the ideal of freedom in virtual anarchic scenarios, whereas cyber feminists adapt the vision to counter gendered categorizations and play with boundaries to free women from their ascribed identity. However, popular cyber cultures found in online gaming and in virtual reality sites (such as Second Life) show that the concept of freedom through popular emancipation is largely illusionary and achieved mainly within the field of entertainment. The liberal narrative of the Internet dovetails with the neoliberal rhetoric of socio-economic and political culture. In this context, freedom is associated with maximizing the freedom of the capitalist market with attendant de-regulation. This idea of freedom involves the break-up of worker organizations such as unions and is undermining notions of public service broadcasting. In practice, this freedom is narrated in the form of a flexible workforce, which is adaptable in becoming labour entrepreneurs building portfolios of skills and which is mobile enough to follow market flows. Those who do not have the resources to demonstrate flexibility and mobility are left in ghettos of low paid, unprotected generic labour with varying periods of unemployment. The flexibility of the Internet as it was first envisioned for military use has therefore been rewritten as flexibility for capitalist markets. In addition, Berners Lee's ideal of freedom has largely been interpreted and developed into late modern narratives of choice and freedom with popular participation.

Modes of Participation in the Form

There are several key themes of the forms of participation in Internet-related socio-cultural forms, which are linked with the narratives of the form as well as its relations of production. The initial promise of the Internet and the WWW was one of participation within a democratic and egalitarian ethos, including open access to information and the exchange of information within networks of individuals and communities. The history of the Internet shows that participatory communication was shaped by the culture of research, hacker culture and countercultural communities. The early forms of participation were characterized by an ethos of collaborative research in which researchers – from senior to graduate level – were given the space and resource to experiment with ideas regarding communication. Their passion for developing interactive technologies that could 'get computers to talk to each other' encompassed the spirit in which the WWW was developed and refined. This spirit of innovation carried over into hacker culture in which its members refined the technology within a gift economy and into the countercultural movements and users who shaped the technology for community based use.

The commercialization of the Internet and WWW exploited the culture of open, interactive and networked communication. It introduced commercial principles into the WWW and cyberspace and, thus, freedom – in and of communication – became a commodity. This commoditization, however, moved the Internet from use by pockets of elite groups to the mass market, but that process of commercialization and popularization generated a new dynamic in the forms of participation in Internet-related communication. In the same way that the spirit of innovation and the early developers' and users' gift economy shaped the characteristics of Internet participation, wider society is also shaping the Internet through the market-based exchange of consumption. The character of participation in Internet communication maintains its interactive and flexible aspects and continues to provide access to a world wide web of information. However, within the various domains of social life, participation in Internet communication is individualized as well networked. This characteristic informs the reworking of social and cultural forms as well as social institutions in contemporary cultural change. The fragmentation of contemporary culture alongside the increase of mobility within patterns of everyday life means that individuals are creating senses of 'connectiveness' through the use of ICT.

There is diversity in the ways these forms of participation are being created to generate feelings of being connected. Participation varies depending on the situation and cultural context, thus for instance, a teleworker will develop networks across his/her world of work to coordinate and connect with co-workers as well as integrating everyday life and domestic responsibilities into his/her daily routine. Within political culture, social movements utilize the Internet to mobilize collective action on a global stage of protest, whereas the use of the Internet within parliamentary politics is not fostering engaged political participation. Within cyber culture, teens and students use social networking sites to generate feelings of belonging and 'connectedness' where they develop communication rituals to organize both on and off-line life. Fan cultures may also use ICT as well as main-stream media as a way of forming an identity to participate in popular culture. These popular forms of participation give semblances of emanci-pation from the constraints of social and cultural life through informaliza-tion. However, despite its flexibility and interactivity, this participation has not generally resulted in progressive freedoms of communication to proffer an alternative socio-cultural life, gender, sexual or ethnic emancipation, or to improve social conditions, or to use culture as a platform of critique. In many ways, certain aspects of participation may be illusionary – it may connect people across networks but the meaningfulness of those networks depends on the culture of the institutions they are embedded in.

Technological change is about institutional change and the interdepend-ency of the relations of production, its narratives and forms of participation bring the Internet into the centre of social and cultural life. The Internet as a socio-cultural form of contemporary society is providing people, organ-izations and institutions with an interactive and flexible form of commu-nication. Broad social and cultural change is shaping the way in which that communication is used and this, in turn, is producing new forms of organizations and sensibilities, which are networked and rooted in social institutions. This suggests that changes in the ways in which people can communicate are creating spaces and an openness in which some institu-tions are being challenged – some in positive ways but others in negative ways. It is therefore important that people are aware of the social, economic, political and cultural dynamics of the Internet so that they can shape its future usage and its relationship to broader social life.

Internet as a Socio-Cultural Form in Contemporary Society

Contemporary cultural changes such as the fragmentation of everyday life, the consumerism of the public sphere and the individualization of private life all form contexts in which the Internet is shaped. The Internet is being used to develop new patterns of association, to manage new working prac-tices, to negotiate the dynamics of inclusion and exclusion and as a commu-nication medium in which individuals and social groups can understand their social and cultural identities and organize their everyday public and private lives. These practices are resulting in new socio-cultural forms such as remote mothering, chat-rooms, blogs, SNS, interactive digital television and so on. These processes of production and use are not straightforward though, and the contradiction of the Internet, that is between 'commercial' and 'open and free' communication, along with its decentralizing and centralizing dynamics, generate further tensions. They are seen in the blurring between public, semi-public and private spheres of life, in flexible work practices that, paradoxically, also become more controlling, and in the development of formal and informal practices of political participation other than class/locality-based politics, such as protest movements.

Contradictions also manifest themselves in new forms of exclusion and in the pervasiveness of surveillance. Nonetheless, social actors are using the Internet in innovative ways to negotiate their mediated and lived worlds, gender and ethnic identities and in rethinking the local and the global in their respective senses of community. Through these evolving uses of the Internet, social actors are, to a degree, shaping the Internet within the dynamics of contemporary culture. The contested ways in which social actors are using the Internet in relation to the contradictions and complexity of contemporary culture means that the Internet can only be understood in the ways in which it is embedded in the various dimensions of social life. The analysis of the Internet as a technology shaped through its social relations thus moves beyond many current binary accounts of the Internet as either a utopian or dystopian force in society – rather, the Internet is understood through its social dynamics and cultural meanings, and this understanding produces a more rounded and valid interpretation of society and its forms of communication.

In conclusion, the book shows how there have been some changes in late capitalist society towards an informational and intermediated society, but there is also continuity in our social practices and cultural sensibilities which are shaping the Internet and militating against a narrow technocratic society. Ultimately, the focus is on communication, with the evolvement of a highly communicative society in which the ability to connect is of paramount importance. Communication is cultural and the forms it takes both create and challenge institutions. The current communicative turn is both social and cultural and shapes the technologies which humans create. Given the contradictions of the Internet and of society, there is a need to secure culturally, the ethos and capacity for everyone to be able to shape and participate in the forms of communication that the Internet allows. In Berners Lee's words, the Internet and WWW have given us all the potential 'to enquire' and seek knowledge about the world in which we live – the question that remains is how we do that, culturally and socially.

Notes

1 Addressing the Internet as Socio-Cultural Forms

1. For full referencing, the Internet is part of the broader category 'Information and Communication Technology' (ICT). Dutton defines ICT as 'all kinds of electronic systems used for broadcasting, telecommunications and computer-mediated communication' (2001, p. 7). He also gives examples such as 'personal computers, video games, interactive TV, cell phones, the Internet [and] electronic payments systems' (p. 3). The way in which the WWW is developing can be seen through: 'Web 1.0' applications that connect documents and collect intelligence; through 'Web 2.0' services that connect people within the Social Web; and through the semantic 'Web 3.0' that connects information and creates data commons. Those working in Web development are looking ahead to 'Web 4.0', which moves beyond the semantic Web towards conceptions of intelligent personal agents.
2. See Chaney, 1983 and 1990.
3. The term 'people' has been adopted following Lievrouw and Livingstone's (2006) discussion. They argue that the term 'people' is an advance to the term user. Using the term people rather than users in social science and engineering evokes human interests, concerns, knowledge and rights. They argue that it seems odd to talk about the civic potential of audiences, the rights of users or the creativity of consumers. However, using the term people captures their individuality and collectivity; the word is neutral about their abilities and interests but advances their needs and rights and takes plurality and diversity for granted. The word can be used by any academic discipline and includes us, the observers, in the frame of analysis. The word also puts agency and action at the centre of new media studies (p. 8).

2 The Cultural History of the Internet

1. Linux is one of the most prominent examples of free software and open source development, with which, typically, all underlying source code can be freely modified, used and redistributed by anyone. Linux is a Unix-like computer operating system and its name comes from the Linux kernel, originally written in 1991 by Linus Torvalds. The system's utilities and libraries usually come from the GNU operating system, announced in 1983 by Richard Stallman. Mainly known for its use in servers, Linux is supported by corporations such as Dell, Hewlett-Packard, IBM, Novell, Oracle Corporation, Red Hat and Sun Microsystems. It is used as an operating system for a wide variety of computer hardware, including desktop computers, supercomputers, video game systems such as the PlayStation 2 and PlayStation 3, several arcade games and embedded devices such as mobile phones, routers and stage lighting systems.
2. Many of these countercultural computer scientists were, in fact, relieved to leave the military research environment due to the Vietnam War. They sought to democratize the power of computing as a tool in the fight for social justice and to foster a spiritual ethos, which would aid the dismantling of the technocratic state (Bell, 2001).
3. A gift economy refers to the way in which goods and services are given without any explicit agreement for immediate or future *quid pro quo*. Typically, a gift economy occurs in a culture or subculture that emphasizes social or intangible rewards for solidarity

and generosity: karma, honour, loyalty or other forms of gratitude. In some cases, simultaneous or recurring giving serves to circulate and redistribute valuables within a community, which can be considered a form of reciprocal altruism. Sometimes there is an implicit expectation of the return of comparable goods or services, political support, or the gift later being passed on to a third party. However, in what is considered to be the true spirit of gift economics, giving is frequently done without any expectation of reciprocity. The concept of a gift economy stands in contrast to a planned, market or barter economy. In a planned economy, goods and services are distributed by explicit command and control rather than informal custom whereas, in barter or market economies, an explicit *quid pro quo* – an exchange of money or some other commodity – is established before the transaction takes place. In practice, most human societies blend elements of all of these, in varying degrees.

4. Gift in this context refers to Mauss's (1990) classic work *The Gift*, in which Mauss argues that gifts are never 'free'. Instead, human history is full of examples that gifts give rise to reciprocal exchange. In his anthropology, he asked 'What power resides in the object given that causes its recipient to pay it back?' (p. 3). He argues that the gift is a total prestation, imbued with 'spiritual mechanisms', engaging the honour of both giver and receiver. Such transactions transcend divisions between the spiritual and the material in a way that, according to Mauss, is almost 'magical'. The giver does not merely give an object but also part of himself/herself, because the object is indissolubly tied to the giver: 'the objects are never completely separated from the men who exchange them' (p. 31). Because of this bond between giver and the gift, the act of giving creates a social bond with an obligation for the recipient to reciprocate. Not reciprocating means losing honour and status, but the spiritual implications can be even worse: in Polynesia, failure to reciprocate means losing *mana*, one's spiritual source of authority and wealth. Mauss distinguished between three obligations: giving – the necessary initial step for the creation and maintenance of social relationships; receiving – since refusing to receive means rejecting the social bond; and reciprocating –to demonstrate one's own liberality, honour and wealth.

5. Also known as the European Particle Physics Laboratory.

6. The Whole Earth 'Lectronic Link – often simply known as WELL – is an online community generating from the Bay Area in San Francisco. It is one of the best known online communities and is the focus of Rheingold's 1993 book *The Virtual Community*. It grew from the countercultural movement in the Bay Area and has strong links with the Electronic Frontier Foundation (EFF).

7. Deadheads are fans of the American jam band, the Grateful Dead. In the 1970s, a number of fans began travelling to see the band at as many concerts as they could, from which a community developed. During the early 1980s, the number of Deadheads taping shows grew, and the band created a section for fans who wished to record the show. Deadheads share and circulate these tapes without any money changing hands. The practice of taping has continued into the digital age and, by the 2000s, Deadheads were circulating digital recordings of shows.

8. A podcast is a series of digital-media files which are distributed over the Internet using syndication feeds for playback on portable media players and computers. The term podcast, like broadcast, can refer either to the series of content itself or to the method by which it is syndicated; the latter is also called podcasting. The host or author of a podcast is often called a podcaster.

9. A blog (a contraction of the term weblog) is a website, usually maintained by an individual, with regular entries of commentary, descriptions of events or other materials such as graphics or video. Entries are commonly displayed in reverse chronological order. The word blog can also be used as a verb, meaning to maintain or add content to a blog. Many blogs provide commentary or news on a particular subject; others function as more personal online diaries. A typical blog combines text, images and links to other blogs, web pages and other media related to its topic. The ability for readers to leave comments in an interactive format is an important part of many blogs. Most blogs are

primarily textual, although some focus on art (artlog), photographs (photoblog), sketches (sketchblog), videos (vlog), music (MP3 blog), audio (podcasting) – all of which form part of a wider network of social media. Micro-blogging is another type of blogging, which consists of blogs with very short posts.

10. Vlogs, video blogging or vlogging is a form of blogging for which the medium is video. Entries are made regularly and often combine embedded video or a video link with supporting text, images and other metadata.

11. Web 2.0 is a term describing the trend in the use of World Wide Web technology and Web design that aims to enhance creativity, information sharing and, most notably, collaboration among users. These concepts have led to the development and evolution of Web-based communities and hosted services, such as social-networking sites, wikis and blogs. A wiki is a collection of web pages designed to enable anyone who accesses it to contribute or modify content, using a simplified mark-up language. Wikis are often used to create collaborative websites and to power community websites.

3 Cultural Forms and Socio-Technical Change

1. The reference to post-modernism is only given in relation to placing Poster's position within his idea of the 'influences' of technologies on social relations. Key elements of post-modernism as an intellectual and social phenomenon can be summarized as being the rejection of modernist thought, values and practices; the rejection of claims to identify 'truth' on grounds that there are only versions of 'truth'; the rejection of the search for authenticity since everything is inauthentic; the rejection of quests to identify meaning because there are an infinity of meanings; and the celebration of differences, an emphasis on pleasure, a delight in the superficial, in appearances, in diversity, in parody, irony and pastiche (Webster, 1995, p. 175).

2. By this he means that, as actors can no longer believe in a 'reality' beyond signs, the self is left fragmented, unfocused and incapable of discerning an objective reality (Poster, 1990, p. 14).

3. Also see Callon et al. 1986; Fyfe and Law, 1988; Callon, 1996; Latour, 1987; and Woolgar, 1988.

4. Further examples include Atkinson and Drew, 1979; Bittner, 1967; Sudnow, 1978; and Heritage, 1984.

5. She argues that previous conceptualizations of technology have focused selectively on agency or structure, resulting in ambiguous knowledge of technology in organizations. See Attewell and Rule, 1984; Davis and Taylor, 1986; Hartmann et al., 1986; and Scott, 1981. Working within philosophical positions in social sciences (Bernstein, 1978), she identifies structural approaches in her 'Technical Imperative' model. See Aldrich, 1972; Blau et al., 1996; Hickson et al., 1969; and Perrow 1967. She identifies agency-based approaches in her 'Strategic Choice' model – see Bijker, 1987; Bijker et al., 1987; Boland and Day, 1982; Bostrom and Heinen, 1977; Child, 1972; Collins, 1987; Cooley, 1980; Davis and Taylor, 1986; Edwards, 1979; Hirschheim et al., 1987; Markus, 1983; Mumford, 1981; Newman and Rosenberg, 1985; Noble, 1984; Perrow 1983; Pinch and Bijker, 1984; Powell 1987; Sabel 1982; Shaiken 1985; Trist et al., 1963; Woolgar, 1985; Wynne, 1988; and Zuboff, 1988. She identifies economic deterministic Marxist accounts of technology – see Braverman, 1974; Cooley, 1980; Edwards, 1979; and Noble, 1984. Her model of 'technology as a trigger of structural change', focuses on soft, deterministic approaches – see Barley, 1986 and 1990.

6. Structuration theory is an approach adopted by Giddens (1976) in which social relations are seen as structured in time and space as the outcome of the 'duality of structure'. He argues that, through the regular action of knowledgeable and reflexive actors, patterns of interactions become established as standardized practices in organizations. Over time, habitual use of such practices eventually becomes institutionalized, forming

organizations' structural properties. These structural or institutionalized properties (structure) are drawn on by humans in their ongoing interactions (agency) even as such use, in turn, reinforces the institutional properties (Giddens, 1976).

7. There are several approaches to action and agency. These approaches stem from Weber who stresses that action is defined in the terms of 'meaningfulness' and that sociological analysis must proceed by identifying the meanings that actions have for actors (1922, 1949). They can broadly be defined as 'hermeneutic' and 'positivist' approaches. 'Hermeneutic' action theories make 'meaningfulness' an absolute theoretical priority (Schutz, 1971). 'Positivist' approaches (Parsons, 1937 and 1951) tend to be more interested in social structure and how it sets the goals and means available to actors.

8. Social structure refers to the enduring, orderly and patterned relationships between elements of a society, although there is debate about what should count as an 'element'. Social structures as relationships of a general and regular kind between people (Radcliffe-Brown); roles as the elements (Nadel); and social institutions as organized patterns of behaviour – all of which are proposed as the elements of social structures by a wide range of sociologists, particularly functionalists, who then define societies in terms of functional relations between institutions. Sociologists typically wish to use concepts of social structure to explain something; usually the explanation is a causal one.

9. Other theorists who have addressed this reformulation include Berger and Luckmann, 1967; Berger and Pullberg, 1966; and Bhaskar, 1979.

10. There are a large number of types of functionalist arguments, three of which are as follows: that a social activity or institution may have latent functions for some other activity; that a social activity may contribute to the maintenance of the stability of a social system; and that a social activity may contribute to satisfying basic social needs or functional prerequisites. Theorists in this tradition include Parsons, Merton and Durkheim.

11. They situate their work in the 'moral economy', which they define in terms of '... households are conceived as part of a transactional system of economic and social relations within the formal or more objective economy and society of the public sphere' (Silverstone and Hirsch, 1992, p. 16). The technology is shaped through a system of relations that consists of four non-discrete elements or phases: appropriation, objectification, incorporation and conversion. They also pointed to the 'double articulation' of ICTs which exist as a means in that they are the media though which public and private meanings are mutually negotiated, as well as being products themselves, through consumption, such as negotiations of meaning; for example, the television is both an object and a medium, one which can provide a basis for 'education' as a competence in all aspects of culture (Silverstone and Hirsch, 1992, p. 21).

12. For Turner, social dramas typically have four main phases of public action: 1. *Breach* of regular norm-governed social relations; 2. *Crisis* – during which there is a tendency for the breach to widen. Each public crisis has liminal characteristics, since it is a threshold (*limen*) between more or less stable phases of the social process; 3. *Redressive action* – ranging from personal advice and informal mediation or arbitration to formal juridical process, or in the metaphorical and symbolic idiom of a ritual process; 4. Either the *reintegration* of the distributed social group, or the social recognition and legitimation of a schism between parties (Turner, 1988, pp. 74–75).

13. This approach has also been used in studying institutions. Edelman (1964, 1971), for instance, has interpreted much governmental action and labour-management relations as performances by government and management to persuade members of the public and workers of 'realities' that are often belied by the 'backstage' practices.

14. Burke (1989) argues that any sociologist who examines the symbolic order of a social group is inquiring into the concepts and ideas used to produce understanding in that group. These are the visions and versions of reality through which perceptions of physical and social life are expressed and experienced.

15. For example, Willis, 1978 and Williams, 1974.
16. Chaney defines it as 'the ways in which we might assess the dignity and value of different forms of life' (1994, p. 11).
17. See Turner, 1990.
18. These approaches argue that the media, for example, exist to meet certain needs or requirements of society and that a function refers to the meeting of such a need. Thus, it can be argued that a taxonomy of 'social functions of the media' could include a 'dysfunction' – the 'narcotising function', which renders 'large masses of the population politically apathetic and inert' (Lazarsfeld and Merton, 1948). Also, see McQuail, 1983 for discussion of media effects. Hall criticized media effects research for not addressing the reception of media texts, and developed a model of three moments of production: ('encoding'), text (meaningful discourse) and reception (decoding). Each may be viewed as 'relatively autonomous' but each is also part of a wider process (Hall, 1973). This work resulted in an array of audiences studies, see Hobson, 1982; Ang, 1985; Radway, 1987; Scannell et al., 1992; Morley, 1980 and 1986; Silverstone, 1990; and Silverstone et al., 1989.
19. Critical theory derives from traditions of Kantian critical philosophy and from a Marxian critique of ideology.
20. Leading members of the school include: Adorno, 1947; Adorno and Horkheimer, 1973; Benjamin, 1970; and Marcuse, 1964. Habermas adapted this tradition in 1973 and 1989; and the most recent work is Steinert, 2002.
21. Hall is given as the representative of the Birmingham Centre for Contemporary Cultural Studies method, as he was the key figure of this approach.
22. This is a term used by Gramsci (1971) to describe how the domination of one class over others is achieved by a combination of political and ideological means. He asserts that, although political force – coercion – is always important, the role of ideology in winning the consent of dominated classes may be even more significant. The Birmingham School also embodied an idea of determination and denied that the 'ways of making meaningful [are graspable] in their own terms, in their forms of appearance in the world' (Johnson, 1979, p. 65), and instead argued that culture makes the world meaningful as an articulation of ideology (Grossberg, 1986).
23. McGuigan (amongst others) argues that, although lip service is still paid to the notion of hegemony, the theory has been exhausted by its attempt to straddle two stools: 'Hegemony theory bracketed off the economics of cultural production in such a way that an exclusively consumptionist perspective could emerge from its internal contradictions' (McGuigan, 1992, p. 76).

4   The Socio-Cultural Environment of the Internet

1. In the social sciences the concept of 'community' is a highly debated. However, in general terms community connotes: some sense of 'geographical expression' – namely a fixed and bounded locality; a 'local social system' referring to social relationships that take place mostly in a specific locality; and types of relationships that provide individuals with a sense of identity at the level of both the individual and the collective (Lee and Newby, 1983, p. 57). Often there are elements of all three aspects in the development and experience of a sense of community for social actors. Some sociologists, however, such as Barnes (1954) and Bott (1957) use the term 'social network' to depict relationships as being like a set of points joined by lines, the lines indicating which individuals, groups and/or institutions interact with each other. This conceptualization seeks to avoid romantic connotations of community (Wessels, 2007a, pp. 175–186; Wessels, 2007 in Steinert and Pilgram, 2007).

2. Also see 1996 paper by Marshall van Alstyne and Erik Brynjolfsson.
3. Also see Chapters 8, 9 and 10 for more details.
4. Fuchs argues from a Marxist view that the class relation is based on an exploiting class and an exploited class or classes. The exploiting class excludes other classes from ownership and appropriates the resources they produce, using hierarchies and unequal distributions of power and skills.
5. These dimensions are covered in the remaining chapters of the book.
6. For further discussion and expansion of these themes see Chapters 5, 6, 8 and 9.

5   Work and the Internet

1. Taylorism or 'scientific management' is a theory of management that analyzes and synthesizes workflow processes, improving labour productivity. Taylor (1903, 1911) believed that decisions based upon tradition and rules of thumb should be replaced by precise procedures developed after careful study of an individual at work. Taylorism pushes the division of labour to its logical extreme, with a consequent deskilling of the worker and dehumanisation of the workplace.
2. Gramsci (trans. 1971) used the term Fordism to describe a form of production characterized by an assembly line (conveyor belt factory system) and standardized outputs linked to the stimulation of demand brought about by low prices, advertising, and credit. Fordism, exemplified by the mass-production systems based on the principles of Taylorism used by the car maker, Henry Ford (1863–1947), gave workers high wages in return for intensive work.
3. The development of portfolios in the work place and in career strategies is also part of a broader trend of a 'dossier society' (Laudon, 1986).
4. There is a further business dimension to marginalizing women, which is that firms will fail to tap into potential new markets by not understanding women as consumers and therefore not intelligently targeting products and services to them (Dutton, 2001; Cunningham and Roberts, 2006). Cunningham and Roberts (2006) point out that women make 80% of purchasing decisions in Western economies.

6   Public Policy and the Internet

1. Baggulay (1994) modifies Esping Andersen's (1990) three models of welfare (liberal, conservative and social democratic) in order to identify a restructured welfare regime – one which is comprised of layers of welfare forms: past, present and in the process of formation. Both Baggulay and Williams's points add the dimension of human agency and non-class-based collective action to a post-Fordist account that posits a 'dual society' driven by technology and the processes of recommodification.
2. The countries include Finland, the Netherlands, Slovenia, the Czech Republic, the United Kingdom, Ireland, Hungary, Portugal, Italy, France and Luxembourg, Australia, Malaysia, India, Indonesia, Japan, South Korea, Philippines, Thailand, Taiwan and Sri Lanka.
3. Cost reductions were often predicated on shifting services from higher cost channels (e.g. face-to-face) to lower cost channels (such as telephone call centres or the web). However, the need to maintain established channels, while simultaneously developing new channels, has increased overall costs. At the same time, the opportunities to make savings on established, high cost, face-to-face channels have been limited as this is widely seen as potentially unpopular with many local authority client groups who, for various reasons, prefer a face-to-face assisted service.

4. This section of the chapter is based on three research projects: 1) the EU ATTACH project (1995–1998), a project that addressed the innovation of Telematics in seven sites across Europe including the East End of London. 2) The 'Learning School' project, which was part of the European Schoolnet Multimedia project (1998–2000), funded by the EU and 20 ministries of education that focused on the integration of ICT in education. 3) The EU project 'Webatclassroom' (1998–2001). The three research projects are international multi-site case studies. The methodology for each was surveys, qualitative interviews, observations, focus group and evaluation of the developments.

5. One way in which the differences between the two can be delineated is a choice between a good that is voluntary (Internet) and one where there is a degree of coercion to join (NHSnet). A case for the Internet is that NHSE doesn't need to be the network regulator, which would enable GPs to create their own space and select the services they want to access. The case against the Internet involves the fact that it would be voluntary, which means there will be a co-ordination problem because a critical mass of GP users will be needed before it is worthwhile to participate. It is difficult to say which is better, but the Internet will affect the debate by offering a 'real' alternative (Keene et al., 1998).

6. Note: the term 'community' is here used as shorthand for care in home-based neighbourhood environments. The term 'community' has been borrowed from policy rhetoric, with an awareness of the sociological debates about community.

7. In the context of services for disabled children, one of the key themes of the National Service Framework (NSF) External Working Group on Disabled Children is participation. The NSF document states that disabled children and their parents need to be involved as active partners in making decisions about treatment and care. The involvement of parents and children extends to the actual shaping of all aspects of services, which includes the use of ICT in the delivery of services and provision of information. See www.dh.gov.uk/PolicyAndGuidance/HealthAndSocialCareTopics/ChildrenServices/fs/en

8. Currently there are still debates about defining key working and key workers – see Mukherjee et al. (1999). However, here key workers are defined as welfare professionals with health and social care backgrounds who are working in multi-agency services.

9. This is an approach to designing technology which includes the technology's users as participants in the design of new systems and appliances. Participant Design has strong roots in Scandinavian research – see Dittrich et al. (2002).

7   Exclusion, Inclusion and the Internet

1. Madanipour argues that the spatial aspect of social exclusion (SE) is societal in that wider changes in society are worked through to form what *living in place* contributes to human flourishing (1998, p. 17). He characterizes five themes that contribute to the experience of what *living in a place* means: 1. the role of social partners in different systems; 2. the role of non-state agencies; 3. the division between central and local responsibilities; 4. the social construction of reciprocity and deviance; and 5. the role of residence. National welfare systems play a role in transmitting and shaping the impact of wider changes on those people who find themselves excluded.

2. Senker (2000) argues that the development, application and use of ICT have stimulated economic growth in numerous countries. In advanced countries, the ICT industry has fostered growth in employment of highly-skilled workers. This trend, however, is leaving less qualified people vulnerable to the steady erosion of demand for lower-skilled workers as quality thresholds rise. As noted previously in this book, ICT has played a major role in the globalization of financial markets (they have reduced the costs of communication and increased its speed). The low costs of transport and communication make it economic for companies to relocate some aspects of ICT production to developing countries. Demand for skills is rapidly growing in East Asia where ICT is an important

element in generating competitiveness and growth (ILO, 1998, pp. 33–41). Software markets are attractive prospects for developing countries including Chile, India, Singapore and Taiwan. These countries have entered the low-value segments of the international software market with the expectation that cheap labour will secure them competitive advantage (Millar, 1998). Although Senker (2002 in Wyatt et al., 2002) argues that ICT production in the 'tiger economies' of Singapore, Hong Kong, Taiwan and South Korea has significantly reduced poverty, this is not the case for all developing countries. He also argues that ICT is not the only technology that should be considered, since: 'information is only one of many needs. E-mail is no substitute for vaccines and satellites cannot produce clean water ' (UNDP, 1999 p. 59). Furthermore, international companies interested in large profitable markets often use technologies of agriculture, genetic engineering and pharmaceuticals which benefit the wealthy first world but exploit the third world and rarely addresses those nations' needs in terms of agricultural necessities and health care (Senker, 2000 in Wyatt et al., 2000).

3. This approach is also extended to 'information' which, likewise, seeks to go beyond technical interpretations, to assert that it is also a social relation. It is therefore necessary to consider how the new cyber culture relates to prevailing power relations (Robins and Webster, 1999, p. 2).

4. Chris Freeman addresses the relationship between technology, economic development and social policy using ideas from Schumpeter (1939), who drew on Kondratieff to identify waves of innovation and cycles of economic growth. For example, the industrial revolution using mechanization processes with resources such as cotton and water power; the Victorian Boom with steam engine railways and cheap coal and iron; the Belle Epoque of heavy engineering (civil, chemical, electrical) using cheap steel; the Keynesian Boom based on mass production involving automobiles and durable goods; production of weapons and petrochemicals with the key resource of cheap petroleum; and a question of the next boom based, perhaps, on flexible production, information technology for equipment, goods and services founded on cheap microelectronics (Freeman in Wyatt et al., 2000, p. 158).

5. The groups are: 1. elite category which covers omnivores, connecters, lacklustre veterans and productivity enhancers; 2. middle-of-the-road category which covers mobile centrics and connected but hassled; 3. the few assets category which covers inexperienced experimenters, light but satisfied, indifferents and off the networks (Horrigan, 2006, p. ii).

6. Omnivores are active participants in shaping cyberspace, particularly by taking, sharing and downloading video content (Horrigan, 2007).

7. Connectors surround themselves with technology and use it to connect with people and digital content. They value their mobile devices highly and participate actively online (p. 12).

8. Mobile centrics are strongly attached to their cell phones and take advantage of a range of mobile applications (p. 21).

9. Early developments towards an information society were detailed in the 1993 EU White Paper 'Growth, Competitiveness, Employment: the Challenges and Ways Forward in the 21st Century'. This White Paper set an agenda for using ICT as a tool to foster economic growth and improve levels of employment. However, the 1994 Report of the Members of the High Level Group on the Information Society: 'Europe and the Global Information Society: Recommendations to the European Council' set a broader strategy for the development and use of ICT. The report stated that the widespread use of ICT had the potential to 'build a more equal and balanced society', 'reinforce social cohesion' and provide a 'wider choice of services and entertainment' (1994, p. 6), (Wessels, 2009).

10. Signed on 11 June 2006 by 34 European countries.

11. For example, historically, the rise of Nazi Germany's regressive inclusion (based on perceptions of race) is an example of extreme exclusionary politics. Inclusion, therefore, needs to be framed in an open society (Steinert, 2007, in Steinert and Pilgram 2007).

12. Participation in cyberspace is, by its very character, semi-public and privacy is therefore threatened (Bromseth, 2007; Bakardjieva and Feenberg, 2004).
13. A further dimension is the control of public space via CCTV (Lyon, 2001b), which has the potential to create differentiated spaces of inclusion and exclusion, leading to fragmented cities (Graham, 2004).

8   Culture, Everyday Life and the Internet

1. To recap, the Internet is part of the broader category 'Information and Communication Technology' (ICT). Dutton defines ICT as: 'all kinds of electronic systems used for broadcasting, telecommunications and computer-mediated communication' (2001, p. 7). He also gives examples such as: 'personal computers, video games, interactive TV, cell phones, the Internet [and] electronic payments systems (p. 3).
2. As Haddon (2004, p. 1) notes the concept of everyday life has an intellectual heritage stemming from the work of Lukacs, Lefebrve and de Certeau in Europe and also in the work of the Chicago School, Goffman and Garfinkel in the US.
3. The way in which the Internet is shaped through the activities of everyday life means building on the discussions in Chapter 3 of culture and meaning in the development of technology and communication and Chapter 4 of the social environment of the Internet and the debates surrounding the concept of an information society. As discussed in Chapter 3, there are a various perspectives on culture. In general terms, determinist approaches to culture in which the material and social aspects of life determine culture leaves little room for creativity and for the ways change is contested. Interpretive approaches to culture allow more scope for human agency in modes of institutionalized knowledge, material practices and forms creativity that constitute social experience and cultural life.
4. Forms of life, which become meaningful through culture, are often imbued with moral force, seen mainly in traditions as well as being constitutive of group identity.
5. Creative industries refers to a set of interlocking industry sectors, and are often cited as being a growing part of the global economy. The creative industries focus on creating and exploiting intellectual property products such as music, books, film, and games, or providing business-to-business creative services such as advertising, public relations and direct marketing. Aesthetic live performance experiences are also generally included, contributing to an overlap with definitions of art and culture, and sometimes extending to include aspects of tourism and sport. Cultural industries are an adjunct-sector of the creative industries, including activities such as cultural tourism and heritage, museums and libraries, and sports and outdoor activities, through a variety of 'way of life' activities that arguably range from local pet shows to a host of hobbyist concerns. The difference between the cultural industries and creative industries is that the cultural industries are more concerned with delivering other kinds of value to society than simply monetary value, such as cultural wealth or social wealth.
6. The first age of the Internet dates from its inception to its commercialization around 1995. The ethos of this time was one of excitement about its 'newness', which was seen in both positive and negative terms.
7. The danger of the taken-for-granted aspect of current Internet use is that it might be ignored as a focus of research. This, however, should be guarded against, as its very boringness and routine-ness makes the Internet important – because this shows that it is being pervasively incorporated into people's lives.
8. This marks a move away from a determinist position looking at the use of the Internet in the ways it impacts on existing behaviours. Rather, Wellman and Haythornthwaite (2002) and their contributors start to explore the way in which the use of the Internet is integrated with behaviour. They develop this position from research in Computer

Mediated Communication (CMC) and on-line behaviour that identifies differences between computer-mediated and face-to-face communication. They argue that the research done within this approach is important, the focus on CMC versus face-to-face, on-line versus off-line, virtual versus real has perpetuated a dichotomized view of human behaviour, which needed to be questioned. Furthermore, such either/or dichotomies pit one form of CMC against another – for example, synchronous versus asynchronous communication (e.g. chat versus email), text versus graphics, as well as one category of human endeavour against another, such as computer use at work versus at home, on-line content for adults versus children and computer and Internet users versus non-users.

9. In 2002, people in the US were spending the following time on-line: 19–55 yrs 9hrs a week; 25–35 yrs 11hrs; 12–15 yrs 6hrs; and over 65 yrs 7hrs. In the UK, time on-line was lower by 1–3 hrs across all age groups (Wellman and Haythornthwaite, 2002).

10. Internet users spend approximately 4.6 hours watching television per week (ibid.).

11. Managing the Internet at home requires defining boundaries – both temporal and spatial – so that users and their work or learning activities can be cordoned off from the activities and presence of others. Learners and workers at home actively construct a barrier to social interaction because it is not so obvious to others that the individual is 'at work' (ibid.).

12. To recap: Silverstone and Hirsh (1994) define the 'moral economy' as '... households are conceived as part of a transactional system of economic and social relations within the formal or more objective economy and society of the public sphere' (p. 16). The technology is shaped through a system of relations that consists of four non-discrete elements or phases – appropriation, objectification, incorporation, and conversion. Silverstone and Hirsh (ibid.) also point to the 'double articulation' of ICT, which means seeing the media on the one hand as a medium through which public and private meanings are mutually negotiated; and, on the other hand, the media are products themselves through consumption, for example, the television is both an object and a medium, one which can provide a basis for 'education' as a competence in all aspects of culture (p. 21).

13. Domestication also involves decisions about where to put televisions, telephones and PCs, which influences how and when they are used. The television can be a centrepiece that the family gathers around to watch or a bedroom fixture. Another example is the way the single telephone in the hallway has given way to multiple fixed and cordless phones that permit calls from anywhere around the household (ibid.).

14. The use of ICT is shaping the design of homes. The use of CAD packages in home design is another example of the way in which ICT can change the relationship between consumers and designers.

15. For example, the negotiation between children, teens and adults for TV access, often seen in the aptly-named 'politics of the remote control' has resulted in the notion of 'two TVs' per household, then VCRs and then multiple televisions. Families negotiate when and where TV is watched, as well as what programming is suitable for children, using devices such as cable lock-boxes and V-chips to control viewing.

16. First generation Internet use and users is understood in the context of the emergence of the Internet. As discussed in Chapters 2 and 4, the discourse in those early times addressed the ideas of how the Internet would transcend existing social and cultural mores (Baym, 1998; McRae, 1996; Watson, 1997; Jones, 1995a). Some commentators were optimistic, arguing that the Internet would draw in a new emancipated and participatory society (Plant, 1995, 1997). A range of writers address the virtual in this context such as Featherstone and Burrows (1995), Shields (1996), Porter (1997), Heim (1998), and Young (1994) – see Chapter 9. However, writers such as Hine (2000), Dodge and Kitchin (2002) and Slevin (2000), alongside Castells (2001) and Silverstone (1992) argue that the use of the Internet is integrated into ongoing social life, hence positing a 'second generation' and 'second age' focus on the Internet.

9   Cyber Cultures and the Internet

1. Building on Giddens' work on time-space distantiation (1984).
2. See Chapter 2 for Barlow's role in the history of the Internet.
3. In fact, the term cyberpunk was first used in a short story by Bruce Bethke called 'Cyberpunk' published in *Amazing Stories* (November 1983).
4. Moral panics often emerge around immersive virtual reality, such as the media's fascination with cybersex and 'dirty tech'.
5. Jordan (1999) goes as far as to argue that: 'cyberpunk fiction has become a self-fulfilling prophecy in which we understand cyberspace through its fantasies but then we find that cyberspace is in fact like cyberpunk'.
6. Cyberpunk stories are a subgenre of science fiction and are sometimes seen as a distinctly 'postmodern' take on science fiction. Popular authors include Bruce Sterling, Pat Cadigan, Samuel Delany, Neal Stepfenson, and William Gibson.
7. The video games culture has promoted moral panics in which the immersive gets rewritten as 'addictive' and interactive as 'anti-social'. However, Haddon's 1993 study disputes this, while Miller and Slater show the sociality of games culture and cybercafés, arguing that there are 'dense relationships around a computer'. Wakeford too uses her empirical studies to assert that users are located in real life while they are in cyberspace.
8. The virtual pet emerged from Japanese company and was invented by a Japanese mother who didn't have enough room for a pet for her daughter.
9. As discussed in Chapter 4, debates about virtual community tend to centre around a split between those who argue that cyberspace re-enchants community, which is perceived to have been eroded in 'real life' on the one hand, whilst arguing that, on the other hand, on-line community is damaging real-life community by encouraging people to withdraw from 'real life' (Wellman and Gulia, 2001).
10. A bund is an elective grouping, bonded by affective and emotional solidarity inherent in the sharing of a strong sense of belonging.
11. See Chapter 4 regarding virtual or on-line communities comprising communities based on shared interests.
12. This means a good that can potentially benefit everyone and is openly given, regardless of who has contributed to its production.
13. See Chapter 2 regarding the role of the gift economy in the history of the Internet.
14. Cheung (2000) draws on Goffman's (1959) development of a dramaturgical analysis of the presentation of self.
15. See Chapter 3 for a discussion on performance.
16. Another key theorist on this issue is Sadie Plant, who develops a psychoanalytic approach that seeks to rewire and liberate women by celebrating, in a Freudian sense, the weaving work of women.
17. LambdaMOO is an on-line community of the variety called a MOO – a multi-user system where programs are contributed by any number of connected users. The MOO programming language supports the MOO system. LambdaMOO was the first MOO and one of the most active, with just under 3,000 regular members. Typically, around 100–200 members are connected at any given time. LambdaMOO was founded in 1990 by Pavel Curtis and hosted in the state of Washington, it is operated and administered entirely on a volunteer basis. Guests are allowed, and membership is free to anyone with a paid or institutional email address.
18. The genders are male, female, spivak, neuter, splat, egotistical, royal, second, either and plural (Bell, 2001, p. 124). When going online, users post 'desc' before choosing a gender.
19. Compu-sex is defined as a blend of phone sex, computer dating and high-tech voyeurism (Branwyn in Bell, 2001).
20. Although there is less published research in this area – see Kolko et al. (2000).

21. This site takes Leonardo's 'Kanon' – a classical image of a human body – and allows users to use the picture to make their own ideal body by computer. People can reconstruct the body in any kind of way, for example, to tattoo the body, to wear the body, to manipulate any parts of the body, and so on. There are nine worlds of classification: Wonderland Hero; Monster; Hero; Cult Image; God Alien; Something; Fantastical Image; and Mythological Hero. See http://digbody.atlant.ru/undina/!undina.htm

22. Bodies INCorporated addresses such issues as the legitimacy of cultural institutions being the only socially sanctioned site for displaying art, and the ways in which structures of physical and ephemeral spaces effect collectively embodied behaviour. From within computer networks, its participants constantly project their senses of themselves, and play complicated identity survival games. Participants are invited to construct a virtual body out of predefined body-parts, textures, and sounds, and gain membership to the larger body-owner community. The main elements of the on-line site are three constructed environments (subsidiaries of Bodies INCorporated), within which different sets of activities occur: 1. LIMBO INCorporated – a grey, rather nondescript zone, where information about inert bodies that have been put on hold – bodies whose owners have abandoned or neglected them – is accessed; 2. NECROPOLIS INCorporated – a richly textured, baroque atmosphere, where owners can either look at or choose how they wish their bodies to die; 3. and SHOWPLACE!!! INCorporated – where members can participate in discussion forums, view 'star' featured bodies of the week, bet in the deadpools, and enter 'dead' or 'alive' chat sessions. See http://www.bodiesinc.ucla.edu/

23. The term 'subculture' is open to debate and to a variety of definitions. Its history started in sociology and criminology in the 1950s and it was adapted to sociology of deviance and cultural studies in the 1960s. There is ambiguity surrounding the ways in which 'sub' is related to culture and what the characteristics are of 'sub' activity. See Wessels, 2007a; Bell, 2001; and Chaney, 2002.

24. Irony is part of fan culture tradition.

10 The Communications Environment and the Internet

1. Ubiquity refers to the fact that, although not every individual may use new media technologies directly, still the pervasive and, at times, invisible reach means that the information and communication technologies underpin much of public and everyday life, as an infrastructure, a communication medium and as media. In this sense, they are ubiquitous because they affect everyone in the societies where they are employed. The reach of ICT extends far beyond the obvious arenas of entertainment and workplace. Banking systems, utilities, education, law-enforcement, military and the defense industry, health care and politics, for example, are all dependent on ICT for recording, monitoring and transmitting information, which affects everyone. (Lievrouw and Livingstone, 2006).

2. This section of the chapter is based on their article and Wessels' own research.

3. Verhulst (2005, p. 9) in Lievrouw and Livingstone (2006) argues for a new mediation ecology because the promise that ICT will decrease mediation has not happened. Rather than disintermediation, we are seeing reintermediation which is marked by new actors and methods of disseminating information and framing reality. Silverstone's understanding of mediation is defined in the previous chapter and he extends Verhulst's point by arguing that mediation is both 'literal and metaphorical' because 'technologies, institutions, messages and meanings all interact and influence each other recursively' (2006, p. 30).

4. See Harrison and Woods (2001) for a discussion of complaints made to the Commission relating to state aid.
5. See section 2 of http://europa.eu.int/Comm/av policy/legis/key_doc/legispdf files/staid_en.pdf
6. Profiles are unique pages that allow individuals to express themselves within the system. A profile is generated using whatever content the individual provides. Common fields that users fill out include: age, sex, location, interests, and an open 'about me' section. Most profiles allow users to upload a photo to represent themselves. Some allow users to enhance their profiles by adding other multimedia content or modifying their profile's look and feel. The visibility of a profile varies by site and by user discretion. Sites like MySpace allow users to choose whether or not they want their profile to be public or 'Friends only'. Facebook takes a different tactic to privacy – any Facebook user who is part of the same 'network' as the profile owner can view the individual's profile, unless that user has decided to deny permission to those in their network (Boyd and Ellison, 2007).
7. For example, Asian Avenue, MiGente, and Black Planet were popular community sites that added social network site features six to eight years after their initial inception. QQ began as a Chinese instant messaging service, Cyworld was originally a Korean forum tool, and SkyBlog was a French blogging tool before adding social network site features. Beyond profiles, friends, comments, and private messaging, social network sites vary tremendously in what they do or do not support (Boyd and Ellison, 2007).
8. Ning (launched in 2005) is an online platform for users to create their own social websites and social networks. Ning seeks to compete with large social sites like MySpace and Facebook by appealing to users who want to create networks around specific interests or have limited technical skills. The unique feature of Ning is that anyone can create their own customised social network for a particular topic or need, catering to specific audiences. It offers a single customizable template aimed at allowing non-developers to more easily customize their copy of the social website but it stills allows developers to have some source level control of their social networks, enabling them to change features and underlying logic.
9. To set the scene in terms of devices, mobile phones are widespread: 94% of the Internet users had them; 18% of Internet users (in the UK survey sample) had hand-held devices and, of those that had them; 46% visited websites and 62% accessed email every day (others did both but less frequently). It is interesting that a further 18% of people with these devices never used email and 25% never visited websites – implying that, even with the capacity to access the Internet and, arguably, a slightly more useful user-interface than the mobile phone, a substantial minority still do not use these devices to go on-line (Haddon, 2008).
10. One influence on this age group is being a student and SNS, especially Facebook, was designed by students for students to help keep students connected.
11. Silverstone (2007) recognizes that Derrida's notion of ethics-as-hospitality is important because hospitality as an obligation rather than a right is a primary ethic in a cosmopolitan world. The capacity, indeed the expectation, of welcoming the other into one's space, with or without any expectation of reciprocity, is a particular and irreducible component of what it means to be human. Hospitality is a mark of the interface we have with strangers. It speaks of the long relationship between the sedentary and the nomad. It is inscribed into the cultures of most of the world's religions as an ethic beyond the political, an ethic of humility and generosity, which bypasses differences of power and inequalities of wealth and status (p. 139).

Bibliography

Abbate, J. (2000), *Inventing the Internet* (Cambridge, MA: MIT Press).

Abrams, P. (1982), *Historical Sociology* (Ithaca: Cornell University Press).

Alcoff, R. (1969), 'Management Misinformation Systems', *Management Science*, 14(4), pp. B147–B156.

Ackroyd, S., R. Harper, J.A. Hughes, D. Shapiro and K. Soothill (1992), *New Technology and Practical Police Work: The Social Context of Technical Innovation* (Buckingham, Philadelphia: Open University Press).

Adams, J. (2000), 'Hypermobility' in *Prospect*; March, http://www.prospect-magazine. co.uk/highlights/hypermobility/index.html.

Adorno, T. (1947), 'Culture Industry Reconsidered', in J.M. Bernstein (ed.) (1991) *The Culture Industry: Selected Essays on Mass Culture* (London: Routledge), pp. 85–92.

Adorno, T. and Horkheimer, M. (1973), *Dialectic of Enlightenment* (London: The Penguin Press).

Aldrich, H.E. (1972), 'Technology and Organisation Structure: A Re-examination of the Findings of the Aston Group', *Administrative Science Quarterly* 17, pp. 26–43.

Allen, I.E. and Seaman, J. (2003), *Sizing the Opportunity: The Quality and Extent of Online Education in the United States, 2002 and 2003*. The Sloan Consortium. http://www.sloan-c. org/resources/sizing_opportunity.pdf.

Anderson, J.Q. (2005), *Imagining the Internet: Personalities, Predictions, Perspectives* (New York: Rowman & Littlefield).

Anderson, J.Q. and Tracey, K. (2002), 'Digital Living: The Impact (or otherwise) of the Internet on Everyday British Life', in C. Haythornthwaite and B. Wellamn (eds) *The Internet and Everyday Life* (Malden, MA: Blackwell Publishing).

Ang, I. (1985), *Watching 'Dallas': Soap Operas and the Melodramatic Imagination* (London: Methuen).

Archer, M. (1992), 'Morphogensis versus Structure and Action', *British Journal of Sociology* 33: 4, pp. 56–78.

Arrow, K. (1962). 'The Economic Implications of Learning by Doing', *Review of Economic Studies*, 29, pp. 155–173.

Association of London Government (2002), *The Digital Divide in a World City* (London: Greater London Authority).

Atkinson, J.M. and Drew, P. (1979), *Order in Court: The Organisation of Verbal Interaction in Judicial Settings* (London: Macmillan).

Attewell, P. (1987), 'Big Brother and the Sweatshop: Computer Surveillance in the Automated Office', *Sociological Theory* 5, pp. 87–100.

Attewell, P. and Rule, J. (1984), 'Computing and Organisations: What We Know and What We Don't Know', *Communications of the ACM*, 27: 12, pp. 1184–1191.

Baggulay, P. (1994), 'Prisoners of the Beveridge Dream? The Political Mobilisation of the Poor Against Contemporary Welfare Regimes', in R. Burrows and B. Loader (eds), *Towards a Post-Fordist Welfare State?* (London: Routledge).

Bakardjieva, M. and Feenberg, A. (2004), *Virtual Community: No 'Killer Implication'*. (London: Sage Publications).

Bangemann, M. (1994), *Recommendations to the European Council: Europe and the Global Information Society* (Brussels: European Commission).

Baran, Paul (1964), *On Distributed Communications* (Santa Monica, USA: RAND Publications).

Barker, J. and Downing, H. (1985), 'Word Processing and the Transformation of Patriarchal Relations of Control in the Office', in D. MacKenzie and J. Wajcman (eds) *The Social Shaping of Technology* (Milton Keynes: Open University Press), pp. 147–165.

Barley, S. (1986), 'Technology as an Occasion for Structuring: Evidence from Observation of CT Scanners and the Social Order of Radiology Departments', *Administrative Science Quarterly* 31, pp. 78–108.

Barley, S. (1990), 'The Alignment of Technology and Structure through Roles and Networks', *Administrative Science Quarterly* 35, pp. 61–103.

Barnes, J.A. (1954), *Class and Committees in a Norwegian Island Parish* (London School of Economics: University of London).

Barney, D. (2004), *The Network Society* (Cambridge: Polity Press).

Bassett, C. (1997), 'Virtually Gendered: Life in an On-line World', in K. Gelder and S. Thornton (eds) *The Subcultures Reader* (London: Routledge).

Baudrillard, J. (1983), *Simulations* (New York: Semiotext(e)).

Baudrillard, J. and Glaser, S.F. (1994), *Simulacra and Simulation* (Ann Arbor: University of Michigan Press).

Bauman, R. (1977), *Verbal Art as Performance* (Massachusetts: Newbury House Publishers).

Bauman, Z. (1998), *Globalization: The Human Consequences* (Cambridge: Polity Press).

Baym, N. (1998), 'The Emergence of an On-line Community', in S. Jones (ed.) *Cybersociety 2.0: Revisiting Computer-mediated Communication and Community* (London: Sage), pp. 35–68.

Beck, U. (1992), *Risk Society: Towards New Modernity* (London: Sage).

Beechey, V. (1982), 'The Sexual Division of Labour and the Labour Process: a Critical Assessment of Braverman', in Wood, S. (ed.) *The Degradation of Work* (London: Hutchinson).

Bell, D. (1973), *The Coming of the Post-Industrial Society* (New York: Basic Books).

Bell, D. (1974), *The Coming of Post- industrial Society* (London: Heinemann).

Bell, D. (2001), *An Introduction to Cybercultures* (London: Routledge).

Bell, D. and Kennedy, B.M. (2000), *The Cybercultures Reader* (London: Routledge).

Bellamy, C. and Taylor, J.A. (1997), *Governing in the Information Age* (Buckingham: Open University Press).

Benjamin, W. (1970), *Illuminations* (London: Cape).

Benson, D. (1990), 'Science, Science Policy and Ethics', in A. Elzinga (ed.) *In Science We Trust?* (Lund: Lund University Press).

Berger, P.L. and Luckmann, T. (1967), *The Social Construction of Reality* (London: The Penguin Press).

Berger, P.L. and Pullberg, S. (1966), 'Reification and the Sociological Critique of Consciousness', *New Left Review* 35: 2, pp. 56–73.

Berker, T., Hartmann, M., Punie, Y. and Ward, K. (eds) (2005), *Domestication of Media and Technologies* (Maidenhead: Open University Press).

Berker, T., Hartmann, M., Punie, Y. and Ward, K.J. (eds) (2006), *Domestication of Media and Technology* (Berkshire: Open University Press).

Berman, M. (1982), *All That Is Solid Melts into Air: The Experience of Modernity* (New York: Penguin Books).

Berners-Lee, T. (1999), *Weaving the Web: The Past, Present and Future of the World Wide Web by Its Inventor* (San Francisco: Harper Collins).

Bernstein, R.J. (1978), *The Restructuring of Social and Political Theory* (Philadelphia: University of Pennsylvania).

Bhaskar, R. (1979), *The Possibility of Naturalism* (Brighton: Harvester Press).

Bijker, W.E. (1987), 'The Social Construction of Bakelite: Toward a Theory of Invention', in W.E. Bijker, T.P. Hughes and T. Pinch (eds) (1987), *The Social Construction of Technology Systems* (Cambridge, MA: MIT Press), pp. 159–187.

Bijker, W.E., Hughes, T.P. and Pinch, T. (eds) (1987), *The Social Construction of Technology Systems* (Cambridge, MA: MIT Press).

Bittner, E. (1967), 'Police Discretion in the Emergency Apprehension of Mentally-ill Persons', *Social Problems* 14, pp. 699–715.

Blau, P., McHugh-Falbe, W. and Phelps, T. (1996), 'Technology and Organisation in Manufacturing', *Administrative Science Quarterly* 21, pp. 20–40.

Blumler, J.G. and Gurevitch, M. (1995), *The Crisis of Public Communication* (London: Routledge).

Boland, R.J. and Day, W. (1982), 'The Phenomenology of System Design', *Proceedings of the Third International Conference on Information Systems* (Ann Arbor, MI), Dec. pp. 31–45.

Bolter, J.D. and Grusin, R. (1999), *Remediation: Understanding New Media* (Cambridge, MA: MIT Press).

Bostrom, R.P. and Heinen, J.S. (1977), 'MIS Problems and Failures: A Socio-technical Perspective', *MIS Quarterly* 1: 4, pp. 11–28.

Bott, E. (1957), *Family and Social Network: Role Norms and External Relationships in Ordinary Urban Families* (London: Tavistock).

Bourdieu, P. (1977), *Outline of a Theory of Practice* (trans. R. Nice) (Cambridge: Cambridge University Press).

Boyd, D. and Ellison, N. (2007), 'Social Network Sites: Definition, History and Scholarship', *Journal of Computer-Mediated Communication* 13: 1, article 18 http://jcmc.indiana.edu/vol13/issue1/boyd.ellison.html.

Braithwaite, J. and Drahos, P. (2000), *Global Business Regulation* (Cambridge: Cambridge University Press).

Branwyn, G. (2000), 'Compu-Sex: Erotica for Cybernauts', in D. Bell and B.M. Kennedy (eds) *The Cybercultures Reader* (London: Routledge).

Braverman, H. (1974), *Labor and Monopoly Capital: The Degradation of Work in the Twentieth Century* (New York: Monthly Review Press).

Bromberg, H. (1996), 'Are MUDs Communities? Identity, Belonging and Consciousness in Virtual Worlds', in R. Shields (ed.) *Cultures of the Internet* (London: Sage).

Bromley, R. (2000), 'The Theme that Dare Not Speak its Name: Class in Recent British Film', in S. Munt (ed.) *Cultural Studies and the Working Class* (London: Cassell).

Bromseth, C.H.J. (2007), 'Nordic Feminism in a Cyberlight?' in M. Svenningson and J. Sunden (eds), *Cyberfeminism in Northern Lights: Digital Media and Gender in a Nordic Context* (Newcastle Upon Tyne: Cambridge Scholars Publishing).

Brown, R.H. (1977), *A Poetic For Sociology* (London: Cambridge University Press).

Bryant, C. and Jary, D. (eds) (1991), *Giddens' Theory of Structuration: A Critical Appreciation* (London: Routledge).

Büchner, P. (1990), 'Das Telefon im Alltag von Kindern', Forschungsgruppe Telefonkommunikation, in U. Lange, K. Beck and A. Zerdick (eds) *Telefon und Gesellschaft*, vol. 2 (Berlin: Volker Spiess).

Burgess, R. (1991), *In the Field: An Introduction to Field Research* (London: Routledge).

Burke, K. (1945), *A Grammar of Motive* (New York: Prentice Hall).

Burke, K. (1950), *A Rhetoric of Motives* (New York: Prentice Hall).

Burke, K. (1957), *The Philosophy of Literary Form: Studies in Symbolic Action* (New York: Vintage Books).

Burke, K. (1977), 'Bodies that Learn Language', Lecture at University of California, San Diego.

Burke, K. (1984), *Attitudes toward History* (Berkeley and Los Angeles: University of California Press).

Burke, K. (1989), *On Symbols and Society* (Chicago, IL: University of Chicago Press).

Burrell, G. and Morgan, G. (1979), *Sociological Paradigms and Organisational Analysis* (London: Heinemann).

Burrows, R. (1997a), 'Cyberpunk as Social Theory: William Gibson and the Sociological Imagination', in S. Westwood and J. Williams (eds) *Imagining Cities: Scripts, Signs, Memory* (London: Routledge).

Burrows, R. (1997b), 'Virtual Culture, Urban Social Polarisation and Social Science Fiction', in B. Loader (ed.) *The Governance of Cyberspace: Politics, Technology and Global Restructuring* (London: Routledge).

Burrows, R. and Loader, B. (eds) (1994), *Towards a Post-Fordist Welfare State?* (London: Routledge).

Butler, J. (1990), *Gender Trouble: Feminism and the Subversion of Identity* (New York: Routledge).

Byrne, D. (1999), *Social Exclusion* (Buckingham, Philadelphia: Open University Press).

Button, G. (ed.) (1996), *Technology in Working Order. Studies of Work, Interaction, and Technology* (London and New York: Routledge).

Byrne, D. (1999), *Social Exclusion* (Buckingham, Philadelphia: Open University Press).

Callon, M. (1996), 'Some Elements of a Sociology of Translation', in J. Law (ed.) *Power, Action and Belief* (London: Routledge & Kegan Paul), pp. 196–233.

Callon, M., Law, J. and Rip, A. (eds) (1986), *Qualitative Scientometrics: Studies in the Dynamic of Science* (London: Routledge).

Carey, J. (1993), 'Everything that Rises Must Diverge: Notes on Communications, Technology and the Symbolic Construction of the Social', in P. Gaunt (ed.) *Beyond Agendas Westport* (CT: Greenwood), pp. 171–181.

Carnoy, M. (2000), 'Sustaining the New Economy: Work, Family and Community in the Information Age', in M. Castells (ed.) *The Internet Galaxy* (Cambridge: Harvard University Press).

Castells, M. (1996), *The Rise of the Network Society* (Malden, MA: Blackwell Publishing).

Castells, M. (2001), *The Internet Galaxy: Reflections on the Internet, Business and Society* (Oxford: Oxford University Press).

Cavallaro, D. (2000), *Cyberpunk and Cyberculture: Science Fiction and the Work of William Gibson* (London: Athlone).

Chaney, D. (1983), 'The Department Store as Cultural Form', *Theory, Culture and Society* 1: 3 (Sage Publications), pp. 64–87.

Chaney, D. (1990), 'Subtopia in Gateshead: The MetroCentre as Cultural Form', *Theory, Culture and Society* 7: 4 (Sage Publications), pp. 49–68.

Chaney, D. (1993), *Fictions of Collective Life: Public Drama in Late Modern Culture* (London: Routledge).

Chaney, D. (1994), *The Cultural Turn* (London: Routledge).

Chaney, D. (1996), *Lifestyles* (London: Routledge).

Chaney, D. (2002), *Cultural Change and Everyday Life* (Basingstoke: Palgrave).

Chapple, E.D. (1953), 'Applied Anthropology in Industry', in A.L. Kroeber (ed.), *Anthropology Today* (Chicago, IL: Chicago University Press), pp. 69–94.

Cheung, C. (2000), 'A Home on the Web: Presentations of Self on Personal Home-pages', in D. Gauntlett (ed.) *Web. Studies: Rewiring Media Studies for the Digital Age* (London: Arnold).

Child, J. (1972), 'Organisational Structure, Environment and Performance: The Role of Strategic Choice', *Sociology* 6: 1, pp. 1–22.

Clerc, S. (2000), 'Estrogen Brigades and "Big Tits" Threads: Media Fandom On-Line and Off', in D. Bell and B.M. Kennedy (eds) *The Cybercultures Reader* (London: Routledge).

Clifford, J. (1984), *The Predicament of Culture* (Cambridge: Harvard University Press).

Clifford, J. and Marcus, G. (1986), *Writing Culture, the Poetics of Ethnography* (Berkeley: University of California Press).

Cockburn, C. (1983), *Brothers: Male Dominance and Technological Change* (London: Pluto).

Cockburn, C. (1985), 'Caught in the Wheels: The Higher Cost of Being a Female Cog in the Male Machinery of Engineering', in D. MacKenzie and J. Wajcman (eds), *The Social Shaping of Technology* (Milton Keynes: Open University Press), pp. 55–65.

Cohen, C. and Rai, S. (2000), *Global Social Movements* (London: Athlone Press).

Cohen, R. and Rai, S. (2004), *Global Social Movements* (London: Continuum International Publishing Group).

Coleman, S.J., Taylor, J. and Van der Dunk, W. (eds) (1999), *Parliament in the Age of the Internet* (Oxford: Oxford University Press).

Collins, H.M. (1987), 'Expert Systems and the Science of Knowledge', in W.E. Bijker, T.P. Hughes and T. Pinch (eds), *The Social Construction of Technical Systems* (Cambridge, MA: MIT Press), pp. 329–348.

Cooley, M. (1980), 'Computerization: Taylor's Latest Disguise', *Economic and Industrial Democracy* 1, pp. 523–539.

Cornford, J. and Pollock, N. (2003), *Putting the University Online: Information, Technology and Organizational Change* (Buckingham, Philadelphia: Open University Press).

Cornford, J., Wessels, B., Richardson, R., Gillespie, A., McLoughlin, I., Belt, V., Martin, M. and Kohannejad, J. (2004), *Local e-Government: Process Evaluation of Electronic Local Government in England* (London: ODPM).

Corrigan, P. (1996), *No More Big Brother* (London: Fabian Society).

Corrigan, P. and Joyce, P. (1997), 'Reconstructing Public Management: A New Responsibility for the Public and a Case Study of Local Government', *International Journal of Public Sector Management*, 10: 6 (London: MCB UP Ltd), pp. 417–432.

Cowan, R.S. (1983), 'More Work for Mothers: The Ironies of Household Technologies', *Open Hearth to the Microwave* (New York: Basic Books).

Crompton, R. (1993), *Class and Stratification: An Introduction to Current Debates* (Cambridge: Polity Press).

Crook, C. (1994), *Computers and the Collaborative Experience of Learning* (London: Routledge).

Cunningham, J. and Roberts, P. (2006), *Inside Her Pretty Little Head: A New Theory of Female Motivation and What It Means for Marketing* (London: Marshall Cavendish).

Danet, B. and Herring, S.C. (eds) (2007), *The Multilingual Internet: Language, Culture, and Communication Online* (Oxford: Oxford University Press).

Davis, L.E. and Taylor, J.C. (1986), 'Technology, Organisation and Job Structure', in R. Dubin (ed.), *Handbook of Work, Organisation, and Society* (Chicago, IL: Rand McNally), pp. 379–419.

Davis, M. (1990), *City of Quartz: Excavating the Future in Los Angeles* (London: Verso).

Deakin, R. (1984), *Women and Computing: The Golden Opportunity* (London: Macmillan Publishing).

De Certeau, M. (1984), *The Practice of Everyday Life* (London: University of California Press).

Derrida, J. (2003), cited in Borradori, G. (2003), *Philosophy in the Time of Terror: Dialogues with Jurgen Habermas and Jacques Derrida* (Chicago, IL: University of Chicago Press) p. 128.

Dery, M. (1996), 'An Extremely Complicated Phenomenon of a Very Brief Duration Ending in the Destruction: The 20th Century as a Slow Motion Car Crash', in V2_Organisation (eds) *Techomorphica* (Rotterdam: V2_Organisation).

Dewey, J. (1939), *Intelligence and the Modern World* (New York: Modern Library).

Dilthey, W. (1914–1936), *Gesammelte Schriften*, vols 1–12 (Stuugart: Teubner).

Dilthey, W. (1957), *Dilthey's Philosophy of Existence* (trans. W. Kluback) (New York: Bookman).

Dittrich, Y., Floyd, C. and Klischewski, R. (2002), *Social Thinking, Software Practice* (Cambridge, MA: MIT Press).

Dochartaigh, N. (2002), *The Internet Research Handbook: A Practical Guide for Students and Researchers in the Social Sciences* (London: SAGE).

Dodge, M. and Kitchin, R. (2002), *Mapping Cyberspace* (London: Routledge).

Dunkel, P. (1991), 'The Effectiveness Research on Computer-assisted Instruction and Computer-assisted Language Learning', in Dunkel, P. (ed.), *Computer-Assisted Language Learning and Testing: Research Issues and Practices* (New York: Newbury House), pp. 5–36.

Dutton, W.H. (2001), *Society on the Line: Information Politics in the Digital Age* (Oxford: Oxford University Press).

Dutton, W.H. and Guthrie, K. (1991). An Ecology of Games: The Political Construction of Santa Monica's Public Electronic Network. Informatization in the Public Sector, 1, 279–301, in *Policy Studies Journal*, 20: 4, pp. 574–597 (Policy Studies Organisation) Published online 9th September 2009.

Edelman, M. (1964), *The Symbolic Uses of Politics* (Urbana: University of Illinois Press).

Edelman, M. (1971), *Politics as Symbolic Action* (Chicago, IL: Markham Publishing Co).

Edwards, P. (1996), *The Closed World: Computers and the Politics of Discourse in Cold War America* (Cambridge, MA: MIT Press).

Edwards, R. (1979), *Contested Terrain: The Transformation of the Workplace in the Twentieth Century* (New York: Basic Books).

Ellison, N. (1997), 'Towards a New Social Politics: Citizenship and Reflexivity on Late Modernity', *Sociology* 31: 4, pp. 697–717.

Entrikin, N. (1992), 'The Geographical Moment', *Contemporary Sociology* 21: 3, pp. 23–46.

Esping Andersen, G. (1990), *The Three Worlds of Welfare Capitalism* (Cambridge: Polity Press).

European Commission Office (1994), Europe and the Global Information Society: Recommendations to the European Council. (Also known as the Bangemann Report). ISPO. Brussels, Belgium (May 26), www.ispo.cec.be/infosoc/backg/bangeman.html.

Featherstone, M. and Burrows, R. (eds) (1995), *Cyberspace, Cyberbodies, Cyberpunk: Cultures of Technological Embodiment* (London: Sage).

Fellner, W. (1951), 'The Influence of Market Structure Upon Technical Progress', *Quarterly Journal of Economics* 65, pp. 556–577.

Finsinger, J. and Pauly, M.V. (eds) (1986), *The Economics of Insurance Regulation: A Cross-National Study* (New York: St Martin's Press).

Flew, T. (2002), *New Media – An Introduction* (Oxford: Oxford University Press).

Foot, K. and Schneider, S.M. (2006), *Web Campaigning (Acting with Technology)* (Massachusetts: MIT Press).

Foucault, M. (1977), *Discipline and Punish: The Birth of the Prison* (London: Allen Lane).

Fox, S. (2005), *Digital Divisions: There are Clear Differences among Those with Broadband Connections, Dial-up Connections, and No Connections at all to the Internet* (Pew Internet & American Life Project).

Frank, A.G. (1966) 'The Underdevelopment of Development,' in S. Chew and R. Denemark, (eds) *The Underdevelopment of Development: Essays in Honor of Andre Gunder Frank* (Thousand Oaks, CA: Sage Publishers), pp. 17–56 and 363–404.

Frank, A. and Hanani, U. (1966), 'Intelligent Information Harvesting Architecture: An Application to a High School Environment', *Online Information 96. Proceedings of the International Online Information Meeting* (20th Olympia 2, London, England, United Kingdom, December 3–5, 1996); see IR 056 631.

Freeman, C. (1992a), 'The Human Use of Human Beings and Technical Change', in C. Freeman (ed.), *The Economics of Hope: Essays on Technical Change, Economic Growth and the Environment* (London: Pinter), pp. 175–89.

Freeman, C. (1992b), 'Technology, Progress and the Quality of Life', in C. Freeman (ed.) *The Economics of Hope: Essays on Technical Change, Economic Growth and the Environment* (London: Pinter), pp. 212–30.

Freeman, C. (1994), 'The Economics of Technical Change, Critical Survey', *Cambridge Journal of Economics* 18, pp. 463–514.

Freeman, C. (1997), *The Economics of Industrial Innovation* (London: Routledge Publishing).

Freeman, C. (2000), 'Social Inequality, Technology and Economic Growth' in Wyatt, S. and Henwood, F. (eds) *Technology and In/equality: Questioning the Information Society* (London: Routledge Publishing) pp. 149–171.

Freeman, C. and Soete, L. (1997), *The Economics of Industrial Innovation* (London: Routledge Publishing).

Freire, P. (2000), *Pedagogy of the Oppressed*, 30th anniversary edition (Portland: Book News Inc.).

Frenier, C. (1997), *Business and the Feminine Principle: The Untapped Resource* (Massachusetts: Newton).

Friedland, R. (1992), 'Space, Place and Modernity', *Contemporary Sociology* 21: 3, pp. 74–89.

Friedman, A. and Cornford, D.S. (1989), *Computer Systems Development* (New York: Wiley).

Frissen, V. (2008), Towards a User Generated State? The Impact of Web 2.0 for Government and the Public Sector', Conference Paper at LSE Media and Humanity Conference 22–23 September 2008.

Fuchs, C. (2007a), *Internet and Society: Social Theory in the Information Age* (New York: Routledge).

Fuchs, C. (2007b), 'The Notions of Class and Knowledge Labor in Informational Capitalism', Paper presented at the annual meeting of the American Sociological Association, TBA, New York, New York City Online.

Fuentes, A. and Ehrenreich, B. (1983), *Women in a Global Factory* (Institute for Global Communications: South End Press).

Fyfe, G. and Law, J. (eds) (1988), *Picturing Power: Visual Depictions and Social Relations* (London: Routledge).

Galpin, S. and Sims, D. (1999), 'Narrative and Identity in Flexible Working and Teleworking', in Jackson, P. (ed.) *Virtual Working* (London: Routledge Publishing).

Garfinkel, H. (1984), *Studies in Ethnomethodology* (New York: Prentice-Hall).

Garfinkel, H. (1991), 'Evidence for Locally Produces, Naturally Accountable Phenomena of Order, Logic, Reason, Meaning, Method, etc. in and as of the Essential Haecceity of Immortal Ordinary Society (I) – an Announcement of studies', in G. Button (ed.) *Ethnomethodology and the Human Sciences* (Cambridge: Cambridge University Press), pp. 10–19.

Garfinkel, H. (ed.) (1986), *Ethnomethodological Studies of Work* (London: Routledge).

Garfinkel, H. and Wiley, N. (1980), Transcribed Tape-recording of a Discussion of Agnes and Social Construction (transcriber unknown), cited in G. Button (ed.), *Technology in Working Order. Studies of Work, Interaction, and Technology* (London: Routledge).

Garnham, N. (1990), 'The Media and the Public Sphere', in Garnham, N. and Inglis, F. (eds) *Capitalism and Communication* (London: Sage), pp. 104–114.

Garnham, N. (1998), *Information Society Theory as Ideology* (Loisir et Société) 21: 1, pp. 97–120.

Garnham, N. (2005), *Political Economy of the Information Society* (London: Taylor and Francis).

Gauntlett, D. (ed.) (2000), *Web. Studies: Rewiring Media Studies for the Digital Age* (London: Arnold).

Gauntlett, D. (2004), 'Web Studies: What's New?' in Gauntlett, D., Horsley, R. (eds) *Web Studies*, 2nd edition (Arnold: London).

Gay, G., Stephanie, M., Grace-Martin, M. and Hembrooke, H. (2000) 'The Effects of Wireless Computing in Collaborative Learning Environments', *International Journal of Human-Computer Interaction*, 13: 2, pp. 257–276 (Cornell University).

Geertz, C. (1964), 'Ideology as a Cultural System', in D. Apter (ed.), *Ideology and Discontent* (Glencoe, IL: Free Press), pp. 34–51.

Geertz, C. (1965), *The Social History of an Indonesian Town* (Cambridge, MA: MIT Press).

Geertz, C. (1973), *The Interpretation of Cultures* (New York: Basic Books).

Geertz, C. (1975), *Kinship in Bali* (Chicago, IL and London: University of Chicago Press).

Geertz, C. (1976a), 'Art as a Cultural System', *MLN* 91, pp. 1473–1499.

Geertz, C. (1976b), 'From the Native's Point of View: On the Nature of Anthropological Understanding', in K. Basso (ed.), *Meaning of Anthropology* (Albuquerque: University of Mexico Press).

Gerth, H.H. and Wright Mills, C. (eds) (1948), *From Max Weber: Essays in Sociology* (London: Routledge).

Gibson, W. (1984), *Neuromancer* (London: Grafton).

Gibson, W. (1991), 'Academy Leader', in M. Benedikt (ed.) *Cyberspace: First Steps* (Cambridge, MA: MIT Press).

Gibson, J., Chapman, C. and Hardy, C. (2003), *ADR in Employment Law* (London: Cavendish).

Giddens, A. (1976), *New Rules of Sociological Method: A Positive Critique of Imperative Sociologies* (London: Hutchinson).

Giddens, A. (1979), *Central Problems in Social Theory, Action, Structure and Contradiction in Social Analysis* (Berkeley: University of California Press).

Giddens, A. (1984), *The Constitution of Society: Outline of the Theory of Structure* (Berkeley: University of California Press).

Giddens, A. (1991), *On Modernity and Self-Identity: Self and Society in the Late Modern Age* (Cambridge: Polity Press).

Gilbert, N., Burrows, R., and Pollert, A. (eds) (1992), *Fordism and Flexibility: Divisions and Change* (Basingstoke: MacMillan).

Gilfillan, S.C. (1935), *The Sociology of Invention: An Essay in the Social Causes of Technic Invention and some of its Social Results* (Chicago, IL: Follet).

Gillespie, M. (1995), *Television, Ethnicity and Cultural Change* (London: Routledge).

Georgiou, M. (2005), 'Mapping Diasporic Media Cultures: A Transnational Cultural Approach to Exclusion', in R. Silverstone (ed.) *Media, Technology and Everyday Life in Europe: From Information to Communication* (Ashgate: Aldershot).

Goddard, J.B. (1992), 'New Technology and the Geography of the UK Information Economy', in K. Robins, *Understanding Information Business, Technology and Geography* (Times Higher Education Supplement).

Goddard, J.B. (1994), 'ICTs, Space and Place: Theoretical and Policy Challenges', in R. Mansell (ed.), *Management of Information and Communications Technologies: Emerging Patterns of Control* (London: ASLIB).

Goddard, J. and Richardson, R. (1996), 'Why Geography Will Still Matter: What Jobs Go Where?', L. in Dutton, and M. Peltu (eds) *Information and Communication Technologies: Visions and Realities* (Oxford: Oxford University Press).

Goffman, E. (1959), *The Presentation of Self in Everyday Life* (Garden City, New York: Doubleday Anchor).

Goffman, E. (1974), *Frame Analysis: An Essay on the Organisation of Experience* (Cambridge, MA: Harvard University Press).

Gonzalez, J. (2000), 'The Appended Subject: Race and Identity as Digital Assemblage', in B. Kolko, L. Nakamura and G. Rodman (eds) *Race in Cyberspace* (London: Routledge).

Gould, A. (1993), *Capitalist Welfare Systems: A Comparison of Japan, Britain and Sweden* (London: Longman).

Gouldner, A.W. (1979), *The Future of Intellectuals and the Rise of the New Class: A Frame of Reference, Theses, Conjectures, Arguments, and an Historical Perspective on the Role of Intellectuals and Intelligentsia in the International Class Contest of the Modern Era* (London: Macmillan).

Graham, S. (ed.) (2004), *CyberCities Reader* (London: Routledge).

Graham, S. and Marvin, S. (1996), *Telecommunications and the City, Electronic Spaces, Urban Places* (London: Routledge).

Graham, S. and Marvin, S. (2001), *Splintering Urbanism, Networked Infrastructures, Technological Mobilities and the Urban Condition* (London: Routledge).

Gramsci, A. (1971), *Selections from the Prison Notebooks* (London and New York: Academic Press).

Griliches, Z. (1958), 'Hybrid Corn: An Exploration in the Economics of Technical Change', *Econometrica* 25, pp. 501–522.

Grossberg, L. (1986), 'On Postmodernism and Articulation: An Interview with Stuart Hall', *Journal of Communication Inquiry* 10: 2, pp. 37–60.

Grusky, D.B. (ed.) (1994), *Social Stratification: Class, Race, and Gender in Sociological Perspective* (Boulder, CO and Oxford: Westview).

Gurak, L.J. (2001), 'The Promise and the Peril of Social Action in Cyberspace: *Ethos*, Delivery and the Protests over MarketPlace and the Clipper Chip', in M.A. Smith and P. Kollock (eds) *Communities in Cyberspace* (London: Routledge), pp. 243–263.

Gusfield, J.R. (ed.) (1989), 'Introduction', in K. Burke, *On Symbols and Society* (Chicago, IL: University of Chicago Press), pp. 1–49.

Guthrie, K. and Dutton, L. (1991), *An Ecology of Games: The Political Construction of Santa Monica's Public Electronic Network: Informatization in the Public Sector* (Sage Publications).

Habermas, J. (1973), *Legitimation Crisis* (London: Heinemann Educational Books).

Habermas, J. (1989), *The Structural Transformation of the Public Sphere: An Inquiry into a Category of Bourgeois Society* (trans. T. Burger) (Cambridge: Polity Press).

Hacker, S. (1990), *Doing it the Hard Way: Investigations of Gender and Technology* (Winchester, MA: Unwin Hyman).

Haddon, L. (1993), 'Interactive Games', in P. Hayward and T. Wollen (eds) *Future Visions: New Technologies of the Screen* (London: BFI).

Haddon, L. (1998), 'The Experience of Teleworking: A View from the Home', in P. Jackson and J. Van de Wielen (eds) *Teleworking: International Perspectives* (Routledge, London).

Haddon, L. (2000), 'Social Exclusion and Information and Communication Technologies: Lessons from Studies of Single Parents and the Young Elderly', *New Media and Society* 2: 4, pp. 387–406 (London: Sage Publications).

Haddon, L. (2004), *Information and Communication Technologies and Everyday Life* (Oxford: Berg).

Haddon, L. (2008), 'Mobile Access to Social Networking Sites: A UK Survey', May, http://members.aol.com/leshaddon/Index.html.

Haddon, L. and Skinner, D. (1991), 'The Enigma of the Micro: Lessons from the British Home Computer Boom', *Social Science Computer Review, 9*, pp. 435–449 (Oxford: Berg).

Haddon, L. and Silverstone, R. (1992), Information and Communication Technologies in the Home: The Case of Teleworking, Working Paper 17 (Falmer, CICT, SPRU, University of Sussex).

Haddon, L. and Silverstone, R. (1993), *Teleworking in the 1990s: A View from the Home* SPRU/CICT Report Series, No. 10 (Falmer, University of Sussex).

Haddon, L. and Silverstone, R. (1994), 'The Careers of Information and Communication Technologies in the Home', in K. Bjerk and K. Borreby (eds) *Proceeding of the International Working Conference on Home Orientated Informatics, Telematics and Automation,* Copenhagen 27 June–1 July (Copenhagen: University of Copenhagen).

Hall, S. (1973), 'Encoding and Decoding in the Television Discourse', *CCCS Stencilled Paper No.7* (Birmingham Centre for Contemporary Cultural Studies).

Hampton, K.N. and Wellman, B. (2002), 'The Not So Global Village', in C. Haythornthwaite and B. Wellman (eds) *The Internet and Everyday Life* (Malden, MA: Blackwell Publishing).

Haraway, D. (1985), 'A Manifesto for Cyborgs: Science, Technology and Socialist Feminism in the 1980s', *Socialist Review,* 80, pp. 82–99.

Haraway, D. (1991), *Simians, Cyborgs and Women: The Reinvention of Nature* (London: Free Association Books).

Harrison, J. and Wessels, B. (2005), 'A New Public Service Communication Environment? Public Service Broadcasting Values in the Reconfiguring Media', *New Media and Society,* 7: 6, pp. 834–853.

Harrison, J. and Wessels, B. (eds) (2009), *Mediating Europe: New Media, Mass Communications and the European Public Sphere* (Berghahn: Oxford).

Harrison, J. and Woods, L.M. (2001), 'Defining European Public Service Broadcasting', *European Journal of Communications* 16: 4, pp. 477–504.

Hartmann, H.I., Kraut, E. and Tilly, L.A. (1986), *Computer Chips and Paper Clips: Effects of Technical Change* (Washington, DC: National Academy Press).

Hartmann, M. (2004), *Technologies and Utopias: The Cyberflaneur and the Experience of 'Being Online'* (Munchen: Verlag Reinhard Fischer).

Hartswood, M., Procter, R., Slack, R., Voss, A., Butcher, M., Rouncefield, M. and Rouchy, R. (2002), 'Co-realisation: Towards a Principled Synthesis of Ethnomethodology and Design', *Scandinavian Journal of Information Systems*, 14: 2, pp. 9–30.

Hayles, N.K. (1999), *How We Became Posthuman: Virtual Bodies in Cybernetics, Literature, and Informatics* (Chicago, IL: University of Chicago Press).

Heath, C. and Luff, P. (1991), 'Collaborative Activity and Technological Design: Task Coordination in London Underground Control Rooms', *Proceedings of the Second European Conference on Computer-supported Cooperative Work* (Amsterdam, The Netherlands: Springer), pp. 65–80.

Heim, M. (1998), *Virtual Realism* (New York: Oxford University press).

Heritage, J.C. (1984), *Garfinkel and Ethnomethodology* (Cambridge: Polity Press).

Hetherington, K. (1998), *Expressions of Identity: Space, Performance, Politics* (London: Sage).

Hickson, D., Pugh, S. and Pheysey, D. (1969), 'Operations Technology and Organisational Structure: An Empirical Reappraisal', *Administrative Science Quarterly* 14, pp. 378–397.

Hill, D. (1994), *Citizens and Cities: Urban Policy in the 1990s* (New York: Harvester Wheatsheaf).

Hills, M. (2001), 'Virtually Out There: Strategies, Tactics and Affective Spaces in on-line Fandom', in S. Munt (ed.) *Technospaces; Inside New Media* (London: Continuum) pp. 147–160.

Hine, C. (2000), *Virtual Ethnography* (London: Routledge).

Hirsch, E. and Silverstone, R. (1992), *Consuming Technologies: Media and Information in Domestic Spaces* (London: Routledge).

Hirsch, W.Z. (1952), 'Manufacturing Progress Functions', *Review of Economics and Statistics* 34: 2, pp. 143–155.

Hirschheim, R., Klein, H. and Newman, M. (1987), 'A Social Action Perspective of Information Systems Development', *Proceedings in the Eight International Conference on Information Systems* (Pittsburg, PA), pp. 45–56.

Hobson, D. (1982), *'Crossroads': The Drama of the Soap Opera* (London: Methuen).

Hochschild, A.R. (1983), *The Managed Heart: Communication of Human Feeling* (Berkeley: University of California Press).

Hoggett, P. (1987), 'A Farewell to Mass Production? Decentralisation as an Emergent Private and Public Sector Paradigm', in P. Hoggett and R. Hambleton (eds) *Decentralisation and Democracy*, Occasional Paper 28 (School of Advanced Urban Studies: University of Bristol).

Hoggett, P. (1990), 'Modernisation, Political Strategy and the Welfare State', *Studies in Decentralisation and Quasi-Markets* 2 (School for Advanced Urban Studies: University of Bristol).

Hoggett, P. (1991), 'Long Waves and Forms of Capitalism', *New Intervention*, 2, pp. 27–42.

Hoggett, P. (1994), 'The Politics of Modernisation of the UK Welfare State', in R. Burrows and B. Loader (eds) *Towards a Post-Fordist Welfare State?* (London: Routledge).

Horrigan, J.B. (2006), Home Broadband Adoption 2008: Home Broadband Adoption is Going Mainstream and that Means User-generated Content is Coming from All Kinds of Internet Users. *Pew Internet & American Life Project*, pp. 202–415 http://www.pewinternet.org/.

Horrigan, J. (2007), *Wireless Internet Access* (Pew Internet and American Life Project).

Hughes, G. (ed.) (1998), *Imagining Welfare Futures* (London: Routledge).

Hughes, J.A. (1990), *The Philosophy of Social Research* (London: Longman).

Hughes, J.P. (1985), 'Edison and the Electric Light', in D. MacKenzie, and J. Wajcman (eds) *The Social Shaping of Technology* (Milton Keynes: Open University Press), pp. 39–52.

Hutton, W. and Giddens, A. (2001), *On the Edge: Living with Global Capitalism* (London: Vintage).

Huws, U. (1982), *Your Job in the Eighties* (London: Pluto).

Huws, U., Korte, W.B. and Robinson, S. (1990), *Telework: Towards the Elsusive Office* (Chichester: John Wiley).

ILO (1998), Overview of Global Developments and Office Activities Concerning Codes of Conduct, Social Labelling and Other Private Sector Initiatives Addressing Labour Issues. Geneva.

Innis, Harold (1951), *The Bias of Communication* (Toronto: University of Toronto Press).

Innis, Harold (1952a), *Changing Concepts of Time* (Toronto: University of Toronto Press) (New Edition, 2004).

Innis, Harold (1952b), *The Strategy of Culture* (Toronto: University of Toronto Press).

Innis, Harold (2004) *Changing Concepts of Time* (London: Rowman and Littlefield).

Jackson, P. (ed.) (1999), *Virtual Working: Social and Organisational Dynamics* (London: Routledge).

Jankowski, N.W. and van Selm, M. (2000), 'The Promise and Practice of Public Debate in Cyberspace', in K. Hacker and J. van Dijk (eds) *Digital Democracy: Issues of Theory and Practice* (London: Sage) pp. 149–165.

Jewkes, J., Sawers, D. and Stillerman, R. (1958), *The Sources of Invention* (London: Macmillan).

Jessop, B. (1994), 'The Transition to Post-Fordism and the Schumpeterian Workfare State', in R. Burrows and B. Loader (eds), *Towards a Post-Fordist Welfare State?* (London: Routledge).

Johnson, R. (1979), cited in D. Chaney (1994), *The Cultural Turn* (London: Routledge).

Jones, S. (1995a), *CyberSociety: Computer-mediated Communication and Community* (Thousand Oaks: Sage).

Jones, S. (1995b), 'Understanding Community in the Information Age', in S. Jones (ed.) *Cybersociety: Computer-mediated Communication and Community* (London: Sage).

Jonscher, C. (1983), 'Information Resources and Economic Productivity', *Information Economics and Policy* 1, pp. 13–35 (Amsterdam: Elsevier).

Jordan, T. (1999), *Cyberpower: The Culture and Politics of Cyberspace and the Internet* (London: Routledge Publishing).

Kaloski, A. (1999), 'Bisexuals Making out with Cyborgs: Politics, Pleasure, Confusion', in M. Storr (ed.) *Bisexuality: A Critical Reader* (London: Routledge).

Kant, I. (1983), *Perpetual Peace and Other Essays* (trans. T. Humphreys) (Indianapolis: Hackett).

Karazman-Morawetz, I. and Ronneling, A. (2007), 'Legal Exclusion and Social Exclusion: "Legal" and "Illegal" Migrants', in H. Steinert and A. Pilgram (eds) *Welfare Policy From Below Struggles against Social Exclusion in Europe* (Aldershot: Ashgate).

Katz, J.E., Rice, R.E. and Aspden, P. (2001), 'The Internet, 1995–2000: Access, Civic Involvement, and Social Interaction', *American Behavioral Scientist* 45: 3, pp. 405–419.

Keane, J. (1991), *The Media and Democracy* (Cambridge: Polity Press).

Keene, J., Ferguson, B. and J. Mason (1998), 'The Internet, Other "nets" and healthcare', in Loader, B. (ed.) *Cyberspace Divide: Equality, Agency and Policy in the Information Society* (London: Routledge), pp. 217–235.

Kellner, D. (1995), *Media Culture: Cultural Studies, Identity and Politics between the Modern and Postmodern* (London: Routledge).

Kendall, L. (1996), 'MUDder? I hardly know 'er! Adventures of a Feminist MUDder', in L. Cherney and E. Reba Weise (eds) *Wired Women: Gender and New Realities in Cyberspace* (Seattle: Seal Press).

Kluver, R., Jankowski, N., Foot, K. and Schneider, S.M. (eds) (2007), *The Internet and National Elections: A Comparative Study of Web Campaigning* (London: Routledge).

Kneale, J. (1999), 'The Virtual Realities of Technology and Fiction: Reading William Gibson's Cyberspace', in M. Crang, P. Crang and J. May (eds) *Virtual Geographies: Bodies, Space and Relations* (London: Routledge).

Knights, D. and Wimott, H. (eds) (1988), *New Technology and the Labour Process* (London: Macmillan Press Ltd.).

Knights, D., Wimott, H. and Collinson, D. (1985), *Job Redesign: Critical Perspectives on the Labour Process* (Aldershot: Gower).

Knorr-Cetina, K.D. and Mulkay, M. (eds) (1983), *Science Observed: Perspectives on the Social Study of Science* (London: Sage).

Kolko, B.E., Nakamura, L. and Rodman, G.B. (eds) (2000), *Race in Cyberspace* (London: Routledge).

Kolko, B., Nakamura, L. and Rodman, G.B. (eds) (2000), 'Race in Cyberspace: An Introduction', in B. Kolko, L. Nakamura and G. Rodman (eds) *Race in Cyberspace* (London: Routledge).

Kolloch, P. (2001), 'The Economies of Online Cooperation: Gifts and Public Goods in Cyberspace', in M.A. Smith and P. Kollock (eds) *Communities in Cyberspace* (London: Routledge), pp. 220–242.

Kroker, A. and Kroker, M. (2000), 'Code Warriors: Bunkering In and Dumbing Down', in D. Bell and B. Kennedy (eds) *The Cybercultures Reader* (London: Routledge), pp. 350–359.

Kuhn, A. (ed.) (1990), *Alien Zone: Cultural Theory and Contemporary Science Fiction Cinema* (London: Verso).

Lakoff, G. and Johnson, M. (1980), *Metaphors We Live By* (Chicago, IL: University of Chicago Press).

Lange, P. (2007), 'Publicly Private and Privately Public: Social Networking on YouTube', *Journal of Computer-Mediated Communication* 13: 1, article 18 http://jcmc.indiana.edu/vol13/issue1/lange.html.

Langer, S. (1964), *Philosophical Sketches* (New York: Mentor Books).

Lash, S. and Urry, J. (1987), *The End of Organized Capitalism* (Cambridge: Polity Press).

Latour, B. (1987), *Science in Action* (Cambridge, MA: Harvard University Press).

Latour, B. (1987) *Science in Action: How to Follow Scientists and Engineers through Society.* (Milton Keynes, England: Open University Press).

Lauden, L. (1977), *Progress and its Problems* (Berkeley: University of California Press).

Laudon, K.C. (1986), *Dossier Society: Value Choices in the Design of National Information Systems* (New York: Columbia University Press).

Law, J. (1987), 'Technology and Heterogeneous Engineering: The Case of Portuguese Expansion', in W. Bijker, T.P. Hughes and T. Pinch (eds), *The Social Construction of Technical Systems* (Cambridge, MA: MIT Press), 113–134.

Layder, D. (1981), *Structure, Interaction and Social Theory* (London: Routledge and Kegan Paul).

Lazarsfeld, P.F. and Merton, R.K. (1948), 'Mass Communication, Popular Taste and Organised Social Action', in L. Bryson (ed.), *The Communication of Ideas* (New York: Harper & Bross), pp. 76–93.

Leach, E. (1976), *Culture and Communication* (Cambridge: Cambridge University Press).

Lee, D. and Newby, H. (1983), *The Problem of Sociology: An Introduction to the Discipline* (London: Routledge).

Levi-Strauss, C. (1966), *The Savage Mind* (Chicago, IL: University of Chicago Press).

Lievrouw, L. and Livingstone, S. (2006), *The Handbook of New Media* (student edition/2nd) (London: Sage).

Ling, R.S. (2004), *The Mobile Connection: The Cell Phone's Impact on Society* (San Francisco: Morgan Kaufmann).

Lipsig-Mummé, C. (1991), 'Future Conditional: Wars of Position in the Québec Labour Movement', *Studies in Political Economy*, 36: Fall.

Littlejohn, J. (1963), *Westrigg* (London: Routledge and Kegan Paul).

Livingstone, S. (2002), *Young People and New Media* (London: Sage).

Livingstone, S. (ed.) (2005), *Audiences and Publics: When Cultural Engagement Matters for the Public Sphere* (Bristol: Intellect).

Lukes, S. (2005), *Power: A Radical View*, 2nd edition (London: MacMillan).

Lyon, D. (1988), *The Information Society: Issue and Illusions* (Cambridge: Polity Press).

Lyon, D. (2001a), *The Information Society: Issues and Illusions* (Cambridge: Polity Press).

Lyon, D. (2001b), *Surveillance Society* (Buckingham, Philadelphia: Open University Press).

Machlup, F. (1962), *The Production and Distribution of Knowledge in the United States* (Princeton: Princeton University Press).

MacKenzie, D. and Wajcman, J. (eds) (1985), *The Social Shaping of Technology* (Milton Keynes: Open University Press).

MacKenzie, D. and Wajcman, J. (eds) (2002), *The Social Shaping of Technology*, 2nd edition (Maidenhead: Open University Press).

Madanipour, A. (1998), *Social Exclusion in European Cities* (London: Jessica Kingsley).

Manceron, V. (1997), 'Get Connected: Social Uses of the Telephone and Modes of Interaction in a Peer Group of Young Parisians', in *The Future European Telecommunications User, Home and Work Group: Blurring Boundaries: When are Information and Communication Technologies Coming Home?* COST248 Report (Farsta: Telia).

Manning, P.K. (1980), 'Crime and Technology: The Role of Scientific Research and Technology in Crime Control', in National Academy of Sciences (ed.) *Five Year Outlook for Science and Technology in the United States* (Washington, DC: National Science Foundation), 2, pp. 607–623.

Manning, P.K (1981), 'Technical Conceit', Draft Paper.

Manning, P.K. (1982), 'Organisational Work: Enstructuration of Environments', *British Journal of Sociology* 33: 1, pp. 118–134.

Manning, P.K. (1992), 'Technological Dramas and the Police: Statement and Counterstatement in Organisational Analysis', *Criminology* 30: 3, pp. 327–346.

Mansell, R. and Silverstone, R. (1996), *Communication by Design. The Politics of Information and Communication Technologies* (Oxford: Oxford University Press). Re-printed in 1997.

Mansell, R. and Steinmueller, W.E. (2000), *Mobilizing the Information Society: Strategies for Growth and Opportunity* (Oxford: Oxford University Press).

Mansfield, E. (1961), 'Technical Change and the Rate of Imitation', *Econometrica* 29, pp. 741–766.

Mansfield, E. (1963), 'Size of Firm, Market Structure, and Innovation', *Journal of Political Economy* 71, pp. 556–576.

Marcuse, H. (1964), *One Dimensional Man: Studies in the Ideology of Advanced Industrial Society* (London: Routledge and Kegan Paul).

Marks, D. (1999), *Disability: Controversial Debates and Psychosocial Perspectives* (London: Routledge).

Markus, M.L. (1983), 'Power, Politics and MIS Implementation', *Communications of ACM* 26, pp. 430–444.

Marshall, T.H. (1950), *Citizenship and Social Class and Other Essays* (Cambridge: Cambridge University Press).

Marshall, T.H. (1977), *Class, Citizenship and Social Development* (Chicago, IL: University of Chicago Press).

Marx, K. (1976), *Capital: A Critique of Political Economy, Vol. 1* (Harmondsworth: Penguin Books).

Matoo, A. and Payton, L. (eds) (2007) *Services, Trade and Development: The Experience of Zambia* (Washington: Palgrave Macmillan and the World Bank).

Maus, M. (1967), *The Gift: Forms and Functions of Exchange in Archaic Societies* (New York: Norton and Company).

Mauss, M. (1990), *The Gift: Forms and Functions of Exchange in Archaic Societies* (London: Routledge).

McGuigan, J. (1992), *Cultural Populism* (London: Routledge).

McLaughlin, J., Rosen, P., Skinner, D. and Webster, A. (1999), *Valuing Technology: Organizations, Culture and Change* (London: Routledge).

McLoughlin, I. (1999), *Creative Technological Change: The Shaping of Technologies and Organisations* (London: Routledge).

McQuail, D. (1983), *Mass Communication Theory: An Introduction* (London: Sage).

McRae, S. (1996), 'Coming Apart at the Scenes: Sex, Text and Virtual Body' in L. Cerney and E.B. Weise (eds) *Wired Women* (Washington: Seal).

Meikle, G. (Graham) (2002), *Future Active: Media Activism and the Internet* (London: Routledge).

Millar, J. (1998), *International Software Trade: Managing Knowledge Sharing between Developing Country Producers and Their Clients* (SPRU: University of Sussex Press).

Millard, J. (ed.) (2007), *European eGovernment 2005–2007: Taking Stock of Good Practice and Progress towards Implementation of the i2010 eGovernment Action Plan* (European Commission: European Communities).

Millar, J. and Jagger, N. (2001), *Women in ITEC: Courses and Careers* (London: DfES Publications).

Miller, D. and Slater, D. (2000), *The Internet: An Ethnographic Approach* (Oxford: Berg).

Mills, C. Wright (1959), *The Sociological Imagination* (Harmondsworth: Penguin Books).

Mitter, S. (1986), *Women in the Global Economy* (London: Pluto).

Molina, A.H. (1995), 'Sociotechnical Constituencies as Processes of Alignment: The Rise of a Large-scale European Information Initiative', *Technology in Society* 17: 4, pp. 385–412.

Moores, S. (2000), *Media and Everyday Life in Modern Society* (Edinburgh: Edinburgh University Press).

Moores, S. (2001), 'The Doubling of Place: Electronic Media, Time-Space Arrangements and Social Relationships', in N. Couldry and A. McCarthy (eds) *MediaSpace* (London: Routledge).

Morley, D. (1980), *The Nationwide Audience* (London: British Film Institute).

Morley, D. (1986), *Family Television: Cultural Power and Domestic Leisure* (London: Methuen).

Morton, D. (1999), 'Birth of Cyberqueer', in J. Wolmark (ed.) *Cybersexualities: A Reader on Feminist Theory, Cyborgs and Cyberspace* (Edinburgh: Edinburgh University Press).

Moss, M. (1987), 'Telecommunications, World Cities and Urban Policy', *Urban Studies*, 24, pp. 534–546.

Mukherjee, S., Beresford, B. and Sloper, P. (1999), *Unlocking Key Working: An Analysis and Evaluation of Key Worker Services for Families of Disabled Children* (Bristol: Policy Press).

Mumford, E. (1981), 'Participative Systems Design: Structure and Method', *Systems, Objectives, Solutions* 1, pp. 5–19.

Myerhoff, B. (1982), 'Life History among the Elderly: Performance, Visibility and Re-Membering', in J. Ruby (ed.) *A Crack in the Mirror: Reflexive Perspectives in Anthropology* (Philadelphia: University of Pennsylvania Press), pp. 99–120.

Naisbitt, J. (1984) *Megatrends* (New York: Warner Books).

Nakamura, L. (2000), 'Race in/for Cyberspace: Identity Tourism and Racial Passing in the Internet', in D. Bell and B.M. Kennedy (eds) *The Cybercultures Reader* (London: Routledge).

Naughton, J. (2000), *A Brief History of the Future: The Origins of the Internet* (London: Phoenix).

Negroponte, N. (1995), *Being Digital* (London: Hodder & Soughton).

Negroponte, N. (1998), 'Beyond Digital', *Wired* 6: 12, p. 288.

Newman, M. and Rosenberg, D. (1985), 'System Analysts and the Politics of Organisational Control', *International Journal of Management Science* 13: 5, pp. 393–406.

Nie, N. (2001), *Sociability, Interpersonal Relations and the Internet* (Stanford University Press).

Nie, N.H., Hillygus, D.S. and Erbring, L. (2002), 'The Internet and Other Uses of Time', in C. Haythornthwaite and B. Wellman (eds) *The Internet and Everyday Life* (Malden, MA: Blackwell Publishing).

Noble, D.F. (1984), *Forces of Production: A Social History of Office Automation* (New York: Oxford University Press).

Norris, P. (2000), *Digital Divide: Civic Engagement, Information Poverty, and the Internet Worldwide* (New York: Cambridge University Press).

Norris, P. (2001), *Digital Divide: Civic Engagement, Information Poverty and the Internet Worldwide* (Cambridge: Cambridge University Press).

O'Riordan, K. and Phillips, D.J. (2007), *Queer Online: Media, Technology & Sexuality* (Bern: Peter Lang Publishing).

Orlikowski, W.J. (1992), 'The Duality of Technology: Rethinking the Concept of Technology in Organisations', *Organisational Science* 3: 3, pp. 398–427.

Orlikowski, W.J. and Gash, D.C. (1994), 'Technological Frames: Making Sense of Information Technology in Organizations', *ACM Transactions on Information Systems (TOIS)* 12: 2, pp. 174–207 (ACM, New York).

Ow, J. (2000), 'The Revenge of the Yellowfaced Cyborg: The Rape of Digital Geishas and the Colonization of Cyber-coolies in 3D Realms' *Shadow Warrior*', in B. Kolko, L. Nakamura and G. Rodman (eds) *Race in Cyberspace* (London: Routledge).

Papacharissi, Z. (2002), 'The Virtual Public Sphere: The Internet as a Public Sphere', *New Media and Society*, 4: 1, pp. 9–27.

Parsons, T. (1937), *The Structure of Social Action* (New York: McGraw-Hill).

Parsons, T. (1951), *The Social System* (New York: Free Press).

Pelikan, C., Pilgram, A., Steinert, H., and Vobruba, G. (2007), 'Welfare Policies as Resource Management' in Steinert and Pilgram (2007).

Perkin, H.J. (1989), *The Rise of the Professional Society: England Since 1880* (London: Taylor and Francis).

Perrow, C. (1967), 'A Framework for the Comparative Analysis of Organisations', *American Sociological Review* 32, pp. 194–208.

Perrow, C. (1983), 'The Organizational Context of Human Factors Engineering', *Administrative Science Quarterly* 28, pp. 521–541.

Pfaffenberger, B. (1988), 'Fetishized Objects and Humanised Nature: Toward an Anthropology of Technology', *Man* 23, pp. 236–252.

Pfaffenberger, B. (1992), 'Technical Dramas', *Science, Technology & Human Values*, 17: 3, pp. 282–312.

Pinch, T. and Bijker, W. (1984), 'The Social Construction of Facts and Artefacts: Or how the Sociology of Science and the Sociology of Technology might Benefit each Other', *Social Studies of Science* 14, pp. 399–441.

Pinch, T. and Bijker, W. (1987), 'The Social Construction of Facts and Artefacts: Or how he Sociology of Science and the Sociology of Technology might Benefit each Other', in W. Bijker, T. P. Hughes and T. Pinch (eds), *The Social Construction of Technology Systems* (Cambridge, MA: MIT Press), pp. 399–442.

Piore, M.J. and Sabel, C. (1984), *The Second Industrial Divide: Possibilities for Prosperity* (New York: Basic Books).

Plant, S. (1995), 'The Future Looms: Weaving Women and Cybernetics in Featherstone', in M. Featherstone and Burrows, R. (eds) *Cyberspace/Cyberbodies/Cyberpunk* (London: Sage).

Plant, S. (1997), *Zeros and Ones: Digital Women and the New Technoculture* (London: Fourth Estate).

Plant, S. (1998), *Zeros +Ones: Digital Women and the New Technoculture* (London: Fourth Estate).

Porat, M.U. (1977), *The Information Economy: Definition and Measurement*, Vol. 1. (Washington DC. Department of Commerce/Office of Telecommunications).

Porter, D. (1997), *Internet Culture* (New York: Routledge).

Poster, M. (1990), *The Mode of Information: Post-structuralism and Social Context* (Cambridge: Polity Press).

Poster, M. (2006), 'Culture and New Media: A Historical View', in L. Lievrouw and S. Livingstone (eds) *The Handbook of New Media* (student edition) (London: Sage), pp. 134–141.

Powell, W.W. (1987), 'Review Essay: Explaining Technological Change', *American Journal of Sociology* 93: 1, pp. 185–197.

Prior, D., Stewart, J. and Walsh, K. (1995), *Citizenship: Rights, Community & Participation* (London: Pitman Publishing).

Pullen, K. (2000), 'I-love-Xena.com: Creating Online Fan Communities', in D. Gauntlett (ed.) *Web Studies: Rewiring Media Studies for the Digital Age* (London: Edward Arnold).

Putnam, R. (2000), *Bowling Alone: The Collapse and Revival of American Community* (New York: Simon and Schuster).

Radcliffe-Brown, A.R. (1952), *Structure and Function in Primitive Society* (London: Cohen and West).

Radway, J. (1987), *Reading the Romance: Women, Patriarchy and Popular Culture* (London: Verso).

Rakow, L.F. and Navarro, V. (1993), 'Remote Mothering and the Parallel Shift: Women meet the Cellular Telephone', *Critical Studies in Mass Communication 10* (Speech Communication Association).

Reich, R. (1997), *The Menace to Prosperity* (*Financial Times*, 3 March).

Rheingold, H. (1993), *The Virtual Community: Homesteading on the Electronic Frontier* (Cambridge, MA: Addison-Wesley).

Rheingold, H. (1995), *Which Part is Virtual? Which Part is Community?* Retrieved August 2008, from http://www.well.com/user/hlr/tomorrow/vcreal.html.

Richardson, R. and Belt, V. (2001), 'Saved by the Bell? Call Centres and Economic Development', *Less Favoured Regions: Economic and Industrial Democracy* 22: 1, pp. 67–98.

Richardson, R. and Gillespie, A. (2003), 'The Call of the Wild: Call Centers and Economic Development in Rural Areas', *Growth and Change* 39: 3, pp. 87–108 (Malden, MA: Blackwell Publishing).

Riga Dasboard (2007), Riga Dasboard: Measuring Progress in Einclusion, ec.europa.eu/.../einclusion/doc:2010-initiative/rigadashboard.pdf.

Robins, K. (1999), 'Against Virtual Community: For a Politics of Distance', *Angelaki: Journal of the Theoretical Humanities* 4, pp. 163–70 (London: Routledge).

Robins, K. and Webster, F. (1999), *Times of the Technoculture: From the Information Society to Virtual Life* (London: Routledge).

Robinson, J.P., Kestnbaum, M., Neustadtl, A. and Alvarez, A.S. (2002) 'The Internet and Other Uses of Time, in Wellman, B. and Haythornthwaite, C. (eds) *The Internet in Everyday Life* (Malden, MA: Blackwell Publishing).

Roche, M. (1992), *Rethinking Citizenship, Welfare, Ideology and Change in Modern Society* (Cambridge: Polity Press).

Roche, M. (2007), 'Cultural Europeanisation and the "Cosmopolitan Condition": EU Regulation and European Sport', in Rumford, C. (ed.) *Europe and Cosmopolitanism*, Chapter 8, (Liverpool: Liverpool University Press), pp. 126–141.

Roche, W.K. (1999), *The End of New Industrial Relations?* EUI Working Paper SPS; no.99/8 (Badia Fiesolana: European University Institute).

Roethlisberger, F.J. and Dickson, W.J. (1939), *Management and the Worker* (Cambridge: Harvard University Press).

Rogers, E.M. (1995), *The Diffusion of Innovations*, 4th edition (New York: Free Press).

Room, G. (ed.) (1995), *Beyond the Threshold: The Measurement and Analysis of Social Exclusion* (Bristol: Policy Press).

Rushkoff, D. (1997), *Children of Chaos: Surviving the End of the World As We Know It* (London: Harper Collins).

Sabel, C.F. (1982), *Work and Politics* (New York: Cambridge University Press).

Sacks, H., Schegloff, E.A. and Jefferson, G. (1974), 'A Simplest Systematics for the Organisation of Turn-taking in Conversation', *Language* 50, pp. 696–735.

Sackman, H. and Nie, N. (1970), *The Information Utility and Social Choice* (The American Federation of Information Processing Societies, United States: Afips Press).

Scannell, P. Schlesinger, P. and Sparks, C. (1992), *Culture and Power: A Media, Culture and Society Reader* (London: Sage).

Schechner, R. (1976), 'Towards the Poetics of Performance', *Alcheringa* 2: 2, pp. 46–86.

Schechner, R. (1977), *Essays on Performance Theory, 1970–1976* (New York: Drama Book Specialists).

Schechner, R. (1987), 'Preface', in V. Turner (ed.) *The Anthropology of Performance* (New York: PAJ Publications).

Schechner, R. and Appel, W. (1990), *By Means of Performance* (Cambridge: Cambridge University Press).

Schmookler, J. (1959), 'Technological Progress and the Modern American Corporation', in E.S. Mason (ed.), *The Corporation in Modern Society* (Cambridge, MA: Harvard University Press), pp. 141–165.

Schumpeter, J.A. (1934), 'The Theory of Economic Development: An Inquiry into Profits, Capital, Credit, Interest and the Business Cycle', *Harvard Economic Studies*, Vol. 46 (Cambridge, MA: Harvard University Press).

Schumpeter, J.A. (1939), *Business Cycles: A Theoretical Historical and Statistical Analysis of the Capitalist Process* (New York: McGraw Hill).

Schutz, A. (1962), *The Problem of Social Reality* (The Hague: Nijhoff).

Schutz, A. (1971), *Collected Papers*, Vols. 1 and 2 (The Hague: Nijhoff).

Schutz, A. and Luckmann, T. (1974), *The Structures of the Life-World* (London: Heinemann Educational Books).

Scott, W.R. (1981), *Organisations: Rational, Natural, and Open Systems* (Englewood Cliffs, NJ: Prentice-Hall).

Senker, P. (2000), 'A Dynamic Perspective on Technology, Economic Inequality and Development', in S. Wyatt, F. Henwood, N. Miller and P. Senker (eds), *Technology and Inequality: Questioning the Information Society* (London: Routledge), pp. 197–218.

Sennett, R. (1998), *The Corrosion of Character* (Cambridge: Polity Press).

Sennett, R. (2001), 'Street and Office: Two Sources of Identity', in W. Hutton and A. Giddens (eds) *On the Edge: Living with Global Capitalism* (London; Vintage).

Shaiken, H. (1985), *Work Transformed: Automation and Labor in the Computer Age* (New York: Holt, Rhinehart and Winston).

Shields, R. (ed.) (1996), *Cultures of the Internet: Virtual Spaces, Real Histories, Living Bodies* (London: Sage).

Silverstone, R. (1990), 'Television and Everyday Life: Towards an Anthropology of the Television Audience', in M. Ferguson (ed.), *Public Communication: The New Imperatives* (London: Sage), pp. 173–189.

Silverstone, R. (1994), *Television and Everyday Life* (Routledge).

Silverstone, R. (ed.) (2005a), *Media Technology and Everyday Life in Europe* (Aldershot: Ashgate).

Silverstone, R. (2005b), 'The Sociology of Mediation and Communication', in C. Calhoun, C. Rojek and B. S. Turner (eds) *The Sage Handbook of Sociology* (London: Sage), pp. 188–207.

Silverstone, R. (2006), 'Domesticating Domestication: Reflections on the Life of a Concept', in Berker, T., Hartmann, M., Punie, Y., Ward, K.J. (eds) *Domestication of Media and Technology* (Maidenhead: Open University Press).

Silverstone, R. (2007), *Media and Morality: On the Rise of the Mediapolis* (Cambridge: Polity Press).

Silverstone, R. and Hirsch, E. (1992), *Consuming Technologies: Media and Information in Domestic Spaces* (London: Routledge).

Silverstone, R. and Mansell, R. (1996), *Communication by Design: The Politics of Information and Communication Technologies* (Oxford: Oxford University Press).

Silverstone, R., Morley, D., Dahlberg, A. and Livingstone, S. (1989), 'Families, Technologies and Consumption: The Household and Information and Communication Technologies', *CRICT Discussion Paper* (Brunel University).

Simmel, G. (1950), *The Sociology of Georg Simmel* (New York: Free Press).

Simmel, G. (1955), *Conflict & The Web of Group Affiliations* (New York: Free Press).

Skolnick, J. (1966), *Justice Without Trail* (New York: Anchor).

Slater, D. (1998), 'Trading Sexpics on IRC: Embodiment and Authenticity on the Internet', *Body and Society* 4, pp. 91–117 (London: Sage Publications).

Slevin, J. (2000), *The Internet and Society* (Cambridge: Polity Press).

Smith, D. (1988), *The Everyday World as Problematic: A Feminist Sociology* (Milton Keynes: Open University Press).

Smith, M.A. and Kollock, P. (2000), *Communities in Cyberspace* (London: Routledge).

Smelser, N.J. (1959), *Social Change in the Industrial Revolution* (London: Routledge & Kegan Paul).

Squires, J. (2000), 'Fabulous Feminist Futures and the Lure of CyberCulture', in D. Bell and B.M. Kennedy (eds) *The Cybercultures Reader* (London: Routledge), pp. 360–373.

Sparks, M. (2007), *Switching to Digital Television: UK Public Policy and the Market* (Bristol: Intellect Books).

Stanislavski, K. (1946), *An Actor Prepares* (Harmondsworth: Penguin Books).

Steinert, H. (2002), *Culture Industry* (Cambridge: Basil Blackwell).

Steinert, H. (2007): 'Introduction: The Cultures of Welfare and Exclusion', in Steinert and Pilgram 2007.

Steinert, H. and Pilgram, A. (2007), *Welfare Policy from Below: Struggles against Social Exclusion in Europe* (Aldershot: Ashgate).

Sterling, B. (1990), 'Cyberspace™' in *Interzone: Science Fiction and Fantasy* 41 (Nov.), 54: 3.

Steuer, J. (1992), 'Defining Virtual Reality: Dimensions Determining Telepresence', *Journal of Communications* 42: 4, pp. 73–93.

Stoll, Clifford (1995), 'The Internet? Bah!', in *Hype Alert: Why Cyberspace isn't, and will Never be, Nirvana*. NEWSWEEK Magazine (Feb. 27).

Stonier, T. (1983), *The Wealth of Information: A Profile of the Post-Industrial Economy* (Thames: Methuen).

Sudnow D. (1978), *Ways of the Hand: The Organisation of Improvised Conduct* (Cambridge, MA: MITPress).

Synnott, A. (1993), *The Body Social: Symbolism, Self and Society* (London: Routledge).

Tannen, D. (1995), *Talking from 9 to 5* (London: HarperCollins Publishers).

Taylor, F.W. (1903), 'Shop management', *Transactions, American Society of Mechanical Engineers*, 24, pp. 1356–64.

Taylor, F.W. (1911), *The Principles of Scientific Management*, (Harper & Brothers, New York, NY).

Taylor, I., Evans, K. and Fraser, P. (1996), *The Tale of Two Cities: Global Change, Local Feeling and Everyday Life in the North of England* (London: Routledge).

Taylor, M.C. (1999), *About Religion: Economies of Faith in Virtual Culture* (London: University of Chicago Press).

Taylor, P. (2005), 'India Calling to the Far Away Towns: the Call Centre Labour Process and Globalization', *Work, Employment and Society* 19: 22, pp. 261–282.

Terkel, S. (1977), *Working: People Talk About What They Do All Day and How They Feel About What They Do* (Harmondsworth: Penguin Books).

Toffler, A. (1980), *The Third Wave* (London: Collins).

Thompson, J. (1985), *The Nature of Work*, 2nd edition (London: Macmillan).

Thompson, J. (1989), 'Theory of Structuration', in D. Held and J. Thompson (eds) *Social Theory and Modern Societies, Anthony Giddens and his Critics* (Cambridge: Cambridge University Press), pp. 56–76.

Thompson, J. (1995), *The Media and Modernity. A Social Theory of the Media* (Cambridge: Polity Press).

Thompson, J.B. (2000), *Political Scandal* (Cambridge: Polity Press).

Touraine, A. (1971), *The Post-industrial Society: Tomorrows Social History: Classes, Conflicts and Culture in the Programmed Society* (trans. L.F.X Mayhew) (New York: Random House).

Trist, E.L., Higgin, G.W., Murray, H. and Pollock, A.B. (1963), *Organisational Choice* (London: Tavistock).

Turkle, S. (1985), *The Second Self: Computers and the Human Spirit* (New York: Simon & Schuster).

Turkle, S. (1995), *Life on the Screen: Identity in the Age of the Internet* (London: Phoenix). Reprinted in 1997.

Turkle, S. (1997), 'Multiple Subjectivity and Virtual Community at the End of the Freudian Century', *Sociological Inquiry* 67: 1, pp. 72–84 (Alpha Kappa Delta).

Turner, B.S. (1988), *Status* (Milton Keynes: Open University Press).

Turner, B.S. (1990), 'Outline of a Theory of Citizenship', *Sociology* 24: 2, pp. 189–214.

Turner, B.S. (1993), *Citizenship and Social Theory* (London: Sage).

Turner, B.S. (2007), 'Enclave Society: Towards a Sociology of the Immobility Regime', *European Journal of Social Theory*, 10: 2, pp. 287–303.

Turner, G. (2003), *British Cultural Studies: An Introduction* (New York: Routledge).

Turner, V. (1974), *Dramas, Fields and Metaphors* (Ithaca, NY: Cornell University Press).

Turner, V. (1982), *From Ritual to Theatre* (New York: PAJ Publications).

Turner, V. (1987), *The Anthropology of Performance* (New York: PAJ Publications).

Uhlig, R.P., Farber, D.J. and Bair, J.H. (1979), *The Office of the Future: Communication and Computers* (Amsterdam: North Holland).

UNDP (1999), *Human Development Report 1999* (UNDP: Oxford: New York).

Urry, J. (2000), *Sociology beyond Societies: Mobilities for the Twenty-First Century* (London: Routledge).

Van Alstyne, M. and E. Brynjolfsson (1996), 'Could the Internet Balkanize Science?' *Science* 274: 5292, pp. 1479–1480.

Verhulst, S. (2005), 'Analysis into the Social Implication of Mediation by Emerging Technologies', Draft position paper for the MIT-OII Joint Workshop, *New Approaches to Research on the Social Implications of Emerging Technologies* (Oxford Internet Institute, University of Oxford), April 12–16, 2005. http://www.oii.ox.ac.uk.

Vickers, G. (1965), *The Art of Judgement: A Study of Policy Making* (London: Methuen).

Virilio, P. (1995), 'Red Alert in Cyberspace!', *Radical Philosophy* 74, pp. 2–4.

Virilio, P. (1997), *Open Sky* (London: Verso).

Virilio, P. (2000), *The Information Bomb* (London: Verso).

Wagner, G.G., Pischner, R. and Haisken-DeNew, J.P. (2002), 'The Changing Digital Divide in Germany', in C. Haythornswaite and B. Wellamn (eds) *The Internet and Everyday Life* (Malden, MA: Blackwell Publishing).

Wajcman, J. (1991), *Feminism Confronts Technology* (University Park: PA State University Press).

Wakeford, N. (1999), 'Gender and the Landscape of Computing in an Internet Café', in M. Crang, P. Crang and J. May (eds) *Virtual Geographies: Bodies, Space and Relations* (London: Routledge).

Wakeford, N. (2000), 'Networking Women and Girls with Information/Communication Technology: Surfing Tales of the World Wide Web', in D. Bell, and B. Kennedy (eds) *The Cybercultures Reader* (London: Routledge), pp. 350–359.

Ward, K. (2005) 'An Ethnographic Study of Domestic Internet Consumption in a Coastal Town, EMTEL2', in R. Silverstone (ed.) *Media Technology and Everyday Life* (Deliverable: Dublin).

Warner, W.L. and Lunt, P.S. (1941), *The Social Life of a Modern Community* (New Haven, Conn.: Yale University Press).

Warwick, D. and Littlejohn, G. (1992), *Coal, Capital and Culture: A Sociological Analysis of Mining Communities in West Yorkshire* (London: Routledge).

Watson, J. (1997), *A Dictionary of Communication and Media Studies*, 4th edition (London: Arnold).

Webb, J. (1991), 'The Mismanagement of Innovation? Organisational Factors', paper presented at ESRC/DTI New Technologies and the Firm Initiative, Technology Study Group Conference, University of Stirling, Stirling, 6–7 February.

Weber, M. (1922), *Economy and Society: An Outline of Interpretive Sociology* (New York: Bedminster Press).

Weber, M. (1930) (trans Parsons, T), *The Protestant Ethic and the Spirit of Capitalism* (London: Allen and Unwin).

Weber, M. (1949), ' "Objectivity" in *Social Science* and *Social* Policy', in *E. Shils and H. Finch* (eds) *The Methodology of the Social Sciences* (Glencoe: Free Press).

Webster, F. (1995), *Theories of the Information Society* (London: Routledge).

Webster, F.E. (2001), *The Changing Role of Marketing in the Corporation: Commentary* (Cambridge MA: Mass Science Institute).

Webster, F. (ed.) (2003), *The Information Society Reader* (London: Routledge).

Wellman, B. and Gulia, M. (2001), 'Virtual Communities as Communities: Net Surfers Don't Ride Alone', in M. Smith and P. Kollock (eds) *Communities in Cyberspace* (London: Routledge).

Wellman, B. and Haythornthwaite, C. (eds) (2002), *The Internet in Everyday Life* (Malden, MA: Blackwell Publishing).

Wessels, B. (2000a), *The Innovation of ICT in Police Service Environments* (Brighton: SPRU).

Wessels, B. (2000b), 'Telematics in the East End of London: New Media as a Cultural Form', *New Media and Society* 2: 4, pp. 427–444.

Wessels, B. (2007a), 'Community, Subculture, Secondary Association as a Resource: Patterns of Association to Counter Exclusion and Configured Networks to Manage Exclusion', in H. Steinert and A. Pilgram (eds) *Welfare Policy from Below: Struggles against Social Exclusion in Europe*, chapter 13 (Aldershot: Ashgate), pp. 175–186.

Wessels, B. (2007b), *Inside the Digital Revolution: Policing and Changing Communication with the Public* (Aldershot: Ashgate).

Wessels, B. (2008a), 'Exploring the Notion of the Europeanization of Public Spheres and Civil Society in Fostering a Culture of Dialogue through the Concept of "proper distance"', in *Sociology: Thought and Action* (Vilnius University Press).

Wessels, B. (2008b), 'Generating Agency within Regional Communities to Foster E-inclusion: The Case of South Yorkshire, UK', *European Journal of E-practice*, 3, pp. 1–11.

Wessels, B. (2009), 'The Public Sphere and the European Information Society', in J. Harrison and B. Wessels (eds), *Mediating Europe: New Media, Mass Communication, and the European Public Sphere* (Oxford: Berghan Publishers), 167–189.

Wessels, B. and Bagnall, V. (2002), *Information and Joining up Services: The Case of an Information Guide for Parents of Disabled Children* (Bristol: Policy Press).

Wessels, B. and Miedema, S. (2007), 'Towards Understanding Situations of Exclusion', in H. Steinert and A. Pilgram (eds), *Welfare Policy from Below: Struggles against Social Exclusion in Europe* (Aldershot: Ashgate), 61–76.

Wessels, B., Walsh, S. and Adam, E. (2008), 'Mediating Voices: Community Participation in the Design of E-Enabled Community Care Services', *The Information Society* 24: 1, pp. 30–39 (New York: Routledge).

White, L. Jr (1978), *Medical Technology and Social Change* (New York: Oxford University Press).

Wildavsky, A. (1975), *Budgeting: A Comparative Theory of Budgetary Processes* (London: Little Brown).

Wilkinson, B. (1983), *The Shopfloor Politics of New Technology* (London: Heineman).

Williams, F. (1993), 'Gender, Race and Class in British Welfare Policy', in A. Cochrane and J. Clarke (eds) *Comparing Welfare States: Britain in International Context* (London: Sage).

Williams, F. (1994), 'Social Relations, Welfare and the Post-Fordist Debate', in R. Burrows and B. Loader (eds) *Towards a Post-Fordist Welfare State?* (London: Routledge).

Williams, R. (1974), *Television: Technology and Cultural Form* (London: Fontana).

Williams, R. and Edge, D. (1992), 'Social Shaping Reviewed: Research Concepts and Findings in the UK', *Edinburgh PICT Working Paper No. 41*.

Williams, R., Stewart, J. and Slack, R. (2005), *Social Learning in Technological Innovation: Experimenting with Information and Communication Technologies*, (Cheltenham: Edward Elgar).

Willis, P. (1978), *Profane Culture* (London: Routledge and Kegan Paul).

Winner, L. (1985), 'Do Artefacts have Politics?', in D. MacKenzie and J. Wajcman (eds), *The Social Shaping of Technology* (Milton Keynes: Open University Press), pp. 26–38.

Wittengenstein, L. (1958), *Philosophical Investigations* (Oxford: Blackwell).

Woodfield, R. (2000), *Women: Work and Computing* (Cambridge: Cambridge University Press).

Woolgar, S. (1985), ' "Why Not a Sociology of Machines?" The Case of Sociology and Artificial Intelligence', *Sociology* 19, pp. 557–572.

Woolgar, S. (1988), *Knowledge and Reflexivity: New Frontiers in the Sociology of Knowledge* (London: Sage).

Woolgar, S. (1991), 'The Turn to Technology in Social Studies of Science', *Science, Technology and Human Values* 16: 1, pp. 20–50.

Woolgar, S. (1996), 'Science and Technology Studies and the Renewal of Social Theory', in S. Turner (ed.) *Social Theory and Sociology: The Classics and Beyond* (Oxford: Blackwell).

Woolgar, S (ed.) (2001), *Profile 2000 – Virtual Society: The Social Science of Electronic Technologies* (Said Business School, Oxford University, ESRC Programme).

Woolgar, S. and Coopmans, C. (2001), 'Virtual Witnessing in a Virtual Age: A Prospectus for Social Studies of E-Science', in C. Hine (ed.) *New Infrastructures for Knowledge Production* (Hershey, PA: Idea Group), pp. 1–25.

Wright, S. (ed.) (1994), *Anthropology of Organisations* (London: Routledge).

Wyatt, S., Henwood, F., Miller, N. and Senker, P. (eds) (2000), *Technology and In/equality: Questioning the Information Society* (London: Routledge).

Wynne, B. (1988), 'Unruly Technology: Practical Rules, Impractical Discourses and Public Understanding', *Social Studies of Science* 18, pp. 147–167.

Young, J. (2000), *The Exclusive Society* (London: Sage).

Young, P.H. (1994), *Electronic Communication Technology*, 3rd edition (Englewood Cliffs: Prentice Hall).

Zambia Information and Communication Technology Policy (2007), *Services, Trade and Development*, in A. Matoo and L. Payton (eds) (World Bank Publications).

Zook, M.A. (2001a), 'Internet Metrics: Using Hosts and Domain Counts to Map the Internet Globally', *Telecommunications Policy* 24, 6–7.

Zook, M.A. (2001b), 'The Web of Production: The Economic Geography of Commercial Internet Content Production in the United States', *Environment and Planning* A: 32 pp. 411–426.

Zuboff, S. (1988), 'In the Age of the Smart Machine', in D. Smith (ed.) *The Everyday World as Problematic: A Feminist Sociology* (Milton Keynes: Open University Press).

Technical Glossary

Blog: A website, usually personally maintained, with regular entries of commentaries and descriptions of events

Browser: A program, such as Netscape or Internet Explorer, which allows you to download and display Web documents

BBS: Bulletin Board Services

CMC: Computer Mediated Communication

HTML: HyperText Markup Language – the tool used to create Web documents

ICT: Information and Communication Technology

Internet: A co-operatively run global connection of computer networks with a common addressing scheme

Intranet: A non-public application of Internet protocols dedicated to one group of users

IP: Internet Protocol

ISDN: Integrated Services Digital Network. An international standard for digital communications over telephone lines which allows for the transmission of data at 64 or 128 kbps

ISP: Internet Service Provider

Modem: Modulator/Demodulator. A device for connecting computers through telephone lines to the Internet. The modem translates between digital and analogue signals

MOO: A multi-user system in which connected users contribute to programmes

MUDs: Multi user domains

Packet: A unit of data. In data transfer, information is broken into packets, which then travel independently through the Net. An Internet packet contains the source and destination addresses, an identifier, and the data segment

PSB: Public Service Broadcasting

Server: A networked computer on which applications and communication capabilities are resident

SNS: Social networking sites

TCP/IP: Transmission Control Protocol/Internet Protocol

URL: Universal Resource Identifier

Vlog: A form of blogging for which the medium is video

Web 2.0: A term to describe the use of WWW to enhance creativity, information sharing and collaboration amongst users. Examples include wikis and blogs

Wiki: A collection of web pages designed to enable anyone who accesses it to contribute or modify content

WWW: World wide web

Index

225